SPIN-FISHING

THE SYSTEM THAT

DOES IT ALL

Norman Strung and Milt Rosko

A SCARBOROUGH BOOK

STEIN AND DAY/*Publishers*/New York

SPIN-FISHING was originally published in hardcover
by Macmillan Publishing Co., Inc.,
and is reprinted by arrangement.

First Scarborough Books Edition 1977
First published in 1973
Copyright © 1973 by Norman Strung and Milton Rosko, Jr.
Library of Congress Catalog Card No. 72-90989
All rights reserved
Printed in the United States of America
Stein and Day/*Publishers*/Scarborough House
Briarcliff Manor, N. Y. 10510
ISBN 0-8128-2197-1

To Frank Johnson,
whose idea spawned this book

CONTENTS

ACKNOWLEDGMENTS

Quite honestly, it would be a virtual impossibility for both of us to sit down and in just a short page or two acknowledge the many people who have in some way contributed to the material that appears in this book on spin-fishing.

To begin with we both owe a great deal to parents who brought us up with a respect for the outdoors and an appreciation for everything that makes up fishing, particularly the aesthetics of this wonderful pastime.

Then there were editors who also should be acknowledged, for they helped us both develop as writers, so that while living thousands of miles apart we could collaborate and produce a work such as this. Those editors too, who helped us as fledgling authors in all the media. Without their patience we may never have come this far!

But most important are the many people whose expertise in spin-fishing added to our knowledge of this wide-ranging subject. You just don't become expert at anything on your own. You become proficient and knowledgeable by learning from others. What we have done in this book is to put together a lot of the information we've gleaned over many years of spin-fishing. It is by no means complete, for new techniques and improvements are indeed being developed as we write this book. But it was the people we met on a pack trip to high country in Montana that taught us how to coax cutthroats into striking just after ice-out, and a veteran jetty jockey who took the time to explain why it was important to speed up a retrieve after a wave had pushed your plug in towards the rocks; we could go on ad infinitum with people who helped make this book possible through contributions such as these.

Thus, we feel it fitting to here acknowledge the many friends, guides, chartermen, and good people whom we may never have formally met, for their contributions over the years. Their expertise has helped make this book what it is, and for this we are eternally grateful.

NORMAN STRUNG
MILT ROSKO

SPIN-FISHING

PREFACE

The history of angling is rich with milestones that began when man invented the first fish-hook. The artificial fly, the Kentucky or multiplying reel, and the use of glass for rod shafts are a few of the innovations that provided anglers with new and better ways to catch fish.

Today that history is capped by a fishing system known as spinning.

No other form of angling does so many jobs so well, nor lends itself to such a wide spectrum of species. Spinning rods and reels are capable of tempting half-pound grayling and whipping 50-pound striped bass. They can cast a wisp of a worm or a 6-ounce sinker. They're equally at home with bait or lures, and even flies. What's more, spinning is a simple sport to master.

Spin-Fishing: The System That Does It All is an incisive look at this form: the tackle, the methods, and the many tricks at the disposal of today's spin-fisherman. It's a how-to book, written for beginner and expert alike that covers all phases of spinning from basic tackle selection and casting to the delicate nuances of hair-lining for trout and stalking bonefish on sparkling tidal flats. It includes information for both the fresh- and salt-water fisherman—thorough explanations of the tackle and techniques best suited to spinning on streams and rivers, in lakes, on jetties, in the surf, and on the many bays along the seacoast, as well as the broad expanse of our oceans. The fish themselves aren't forgotten either. *Spin-Fishing* also includes a discussion of the nation's most popular fresh- and salt-water gamefish, and spinning techniques to which they're most susceptible.

In short, *Spin-Fishing* is a book about modern fishing, written for the modern fisherman; a book for all species, a book for all waters, a book for all seasons.

I

INTRODUCTION

"It borders on snobbishness!" Frank Johnson leveled a finger at me from across the living room of my cabin, careful not to upset the tacklebox that lay open in his lap.

I'd just presented Frank with an idea I hoped to turn into my next book; an exhaustive review of fly-fishing, including a chapter on the biology of aquatic insects.

"How many fishermen do you suppose there are in this country? 50 million? 80 million?"

I shrugged my shoulders. "Around there someplace, I guess."

"Well I'll bet that 90 percent of them could care less about flies. Kids, women, and a good portion of the men aren't interested in fly rods, and less yet in the life cycle of a bug. They're interested in the easiest, most uncomplicated way to catch a fish . . . and that's spinning." He grabbed a spin-caster from the bottom of the box and held it up to emphasize his point.

"I'm sure you're right," I agreed, "but how many good books on spinning have been done? There must be a pile of them."

Frank shook his head. "That's what I meant by being snobbish. Ever since Dame Juliana Berners published her *Treatise of Fishing with an Angle* in 1496, all you pristine outdoor writers have been tickled with feathers. Book after book about fly-fishing. But has anyone ever written anything substantial about a worm? Or the kinds of lures you can buy? Or the way to fish with a spinning outfit?"

I dredged up a few names and titles from memory.

"Antiquated . . . antediluvian . . . Why that one book you mentioned is fifteen years old, and the others only contain a chapter or two on spin-

fishing. By the way, most of them are concerned only with trout. More subtle snobbishness!"

I couldn't argue further. Frankly, I didn't know enough, so I again shrugged my shoulders and said feebly, "Maybe you're right."

"And I'll tell you something else. Salt water. Don't forget it. An awful lot of people would be happy to know the basics there, and that's another place where spinning is sadly overlooked."

I shook my head. "I'm stumped there. I haven't wet a line in salt since I was a kid."

"So get someone else to write about it."

"Any ideas?" I asked.

Frank nodded confidently. "Milt Rosko . . . he's the best."

The conversation ended there, and turned to our next day's plans, which incidently were to go trout fishing . . . with flies. But Frank's notion and reasoning stuck with me.

I checked his facts and figures; they were essentially right. I talked with other fishermen; they agreed there was a need.

The next week I called Milt. After a ten-minute conversation, we agreed on all points. *Spin-fishing* was born.

1

SELECTING
FRESH-WATER
SPINNING
TACKLE

There's an off chance that the day is still so clear because it was my tenth birthday, but I doubt it. Judging by what's happened since, the purchase of my first spinning outfit was the important thing.

Important enough at any rate for me to insist that I pick the outfit myself, in lieu of my parents' more traditional birthday surprises, and it was well that I did. I can still remember having to draw the salesman a crude, though complete, picture of exactly what kind of reel I wanted.

After several halfhearted attempts to suit me up with a conventional casting reel, he finally saw the light.

"Oh, you mean one of these things?" He reached far behind the counter, into a little corner well out of sight. "Son, we've had these around here for six months, and haven't sold a one. You sure you want to spend your money on this?"

I was polite but insistent, and left Mirskey's Tackle Shop the proud owner of an Airex Spinster, a 5½-foot solid-glass rod, braided linen line, some quarter-ounce sinkers, and a dozen number 8 snelled hooks.

That little rod did a lot for me; most important at that time, with the addition of a few doughballs, it helped me to become the Unqualified Carp King of Peak's Pond, Queens County, New York. Since then, its more modern equivalents have been my partners in memorable battles across the country: an 8-pound trout in Montana's Madison River, a 10-pound bass in Florida's Salt Springs Run, and in Minnesota and Canada, northern pike as long as your leg.

So I guess I owe an awful lot to that first spinning rod and reel, but before I wallow in too much nostalgia, I've got to admit that it could hardly be called an asset today.

The reel's primitive drag system would have exploded on the first run that husky brown made. My rod would have been as effective as a limp noodle when that bull bass headed for the bankbrush, and those northerns? They'd have chewed the linen line to shreds before looming into sight.

With all due respect to the past, spinning has changed radically in the past twenty years, and undeniably for the better. The selection of equipment has grown to a point of sophistication that performs tasks undreamed of in the days of straight-fly and bait casting. Techniques unheard of ten years ago are commonplace, new ones are evolving everyday, and applied, they catch more and bigger fish. The modern spin-fisherman is no longer just a guy with a newfangled reel, he's a dedicated sportsman with a head full of facts, figures, and a working knowledge of his equipment and quarry that comes close to a formal education.

Of course, chances are you know that. That's why you're reading this book. Since a carpenter must know his tools before he can build a house, and a student be aware of facts before he can theorize, let's then take a look first at tackle, the tools of a spin-fisherman's trade.

THE SPINNING REEL

Although the spinning reel was largely perfected in America, its roots go back to industrial England. Alfred Illingworth, owner of a textile mill, became enthralled with the idea of a reel that would release a cast line in much the same manner as thread was peeled off the stationary spindles in his factory. Peter Malloch, a Scotsman, already had a patent on a reel that cast like the modern spinner, but line was retrieved by revolving the spool— the principle still employed on conventional casting reels today.

Illingworth overcame the necessity for this clumsy changeover by mounting a revolving cup on the base of the spindle. A crude pickup arm wound the line around the nonmoving spool, and the basis for modern spinning was born.

The spinning reel has come a long way since Illingworth's first model, but automatic pickups and high-speed retrieves aside, the principles—and advantages—of the spinning system remain the same.

Spinning is based on the fixed-spool principle. A cast line spins off a spool that lies parallel to the shaft of a rod. During the process, there are no moving parts. Line is retrieved by winding it back around the spool. This is accomplished by a pickup arm that snares the line mounted on a revolving cup surrounding the base of the spool. Free the line from the pickup arm, and it's again ready to cast.

Simplicity is one big plus in spinning's favor. Conventional or multiplying reels—those with a revolving spool mounted at right angles to a rod shaft—require delicate mechanisms and a bucketful of parts to overcome friction and facilitate line release, retrieve, and tension. Spinning reels then, are cheaper to produce and buy and less subject to malfunction.

Spinning reels are also simpler to cast. In a conventional reel, there's inertia to be overcome and motive power to subdue. Although a full understanding of those factors requires a passing knowledge of basic physics, it doesn't take much of an education to learn what happens when you don't do it right. You get a nasty tangle of line called a backlash. The term is unheard of in spinning.

For that reason, and several others, a working knowledge of spin-fishing comes quickly to the greenest novice. But even the polished professional has many things to gain from spinning.

The fixed-spool principle lends itself to a wide range of lure and line weights, right down to gossamer wisps of 2-pound test, and sixteenth-ounce lures. Ultralight tackle like this is impossible to use with a conventional reel because of the inertia problem. Casting in a head or crosswind is easier with spinning too; a lure can be shot out like a bullet, reducing the wind resistance of your line to a minimum.

Alfred Illingworth developed this reel with its fixed spool; it's the forerunner of our modern spinning reels.

There are, of course, other, less general differences between spinning and conventional casting, but the best way to explore them is through a thorough knowledge of the modern spinning reel, its construction and function.

The Open-Face Spinning Reel

The open-face spinning reel is characterized by an exposed line spool, and direct fingertip control over the release of a cast line. This is as opposed to the closed face of spin-caster reels that we'll discuss a little later.

In terms of fresh-water use, open-face reels have a weight range of from 3 to 18 ounces, but both ends of the scale are extremes. A 3-ounce reel is the lightest of the ultralights, a classification of tackle suited only to small fish and/or extreme conditions. An 18-ounce reel finds little fresh-water application beyond the specialized sports of salmon, sturgeon, and musky fishing.

The midrange—the practical reel for the fresh-water angler—falls around 9 to 12 ounces. This size is usually capable of holding up to 200 yards of 8-pound test monofilament, and balances well with a 6½- to 7-foot rod. It's this reel that most anglers find suitable for most of their fresh-water fishing.

The Spool

The spool acts as a receptacle for your line. Above all else, it should oscillate—move in and out—as line is wound on. This ensures against a lump of line building in one spot, then sloughing off itself to lay line over line in a nonsequential tangle. When this happens, the resulting friction and resistance reduces the distance you can cast. It also will regularly foul your line.

Oscillating alone is not sufficient, however. The in-and-out movement should lap line over line rather than lay it down in a tight corkscrew pattern. This eliminates some line-to-line friction during a cast, and prevents a hard-fighting fish—and the pressure he exerts—from burying line deep in the spool.

The oscillating should also build up your spooled line in such a way that it either lies evenly on the spool or exhibits a gentle rise toward the body of the reel *at full-line capacity*. The best way to check for this feature is to load your spool while it's on the reel, rather than from sports-store machines.

If you find you have a reel that builds up line close to the lip, return it to the manufacturer. It will not cast efficiently, and your line will be extra-prone to develop slack loops and knotty snarls.

Easily interchangeable spools should come high on your list of re-

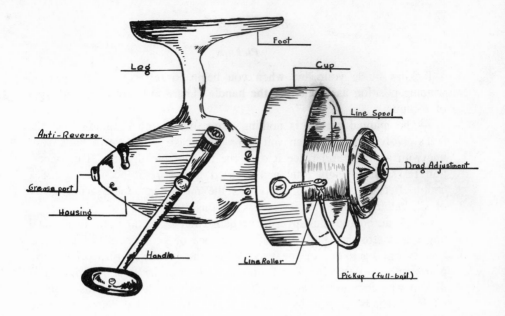

Foot

Leg

Cup

Line Spool

Anti-Reverse

Drag Adjustment

Grease port

Housing

Handle

Line Roller

Pickup (full-bail)

quirements too. My preference lies with those that pop out with the push of a button, since you don't have to keep fiddling with drag adjustments every time you change line.

A skirted spool is a pleasant advantage. These spools have an extra-long lip, or skirt, that extends over the edge of a reel's revolving cup. When fighting a heavy fish, this skirt functions as an instant, manual drag. Drop your index finger, apply pressure, and you check the run.

Unfortunately, I have something of an approach-avoidance reaction to skirted spools. At the writing of this book, I know of no manufacturer who offers both push-button changeover and skirted spools, and the push-button feature, the ability to quickly change lines, is one of spinning's many blessings.

The dimensions of the spool on a given reel should be another consideration. Generally, those with a large diameter and wide surface exposure will cast further than spools narrow in width and small in circumference. There are, of course, physical limits to just how large a spool can be. I'd call ¾ of an inch of line surface and 2 inches of diameter—with a full spool of line—comfortable in fresh-water reels.

Finally, a very pleasant feature to have on a spool is some sort of line clip—a spring or catch that will hold the tag end of your monofilament tight when not in use. Granted, a rubber band or plastic clip-on serves the same purpose, but like a cop, they never seem to be around when you need them most.

Pickups

Pickups guide your line when you begin to retrieve and keep it in winding position as you crank the handle. There are three popular types of pickups:

—The manual pickup is nothing more than a roller mounted on the reel's revolving head. When you complete a cast, you have to hook your line with a finger and place it onto the manual pickup arm. This operation takes surprisingly little getting used to before it becomes a reflex action. Because of its simplicity, it's the most dependable arrangement of all, but few contemporary reels offer this feature.

—The automatic pickup arm, or half-bail pickup amounts to a metal finger that stretches halfway across the face of your spool. To cast, the arm swings back out of the way. When the handle is turned, the arm pops back into the closed position and catches the line. Although this pickup was common when spinning was first introduced to this country, it's lost favor because of its undependability. By nature of its position and construction, the arm is easily bent. If the bend tightens its radius, the arm fouls the line and hits the spool. Should the arm be straightened, often it fails to engage the line immediately.

—The full-bail pickup is the most common device on today's reels. It curves in a complete hoop that rests in a socket on one side of the cup, and is attached to a spring-loaded release device on the other side. To free the line, the bail is pulled up, around, and down, cocked approximately 180 degrees from its original position. When the cast is completed, a crank of the handle releases the catch device, and the bail returns 180 degrees to its original position.

The advantages of this system are many. Because it's a complete hoop, there is no way the pickup can fail to engage the line once activated. That same hoop means that there are no protruding fingers to inadvertently snag a line on the move. This often occurs with a half-bail or manual pickup during a high wind or when executing specialized casts like the bow-and-arrow.

A full-bail's drawbacks all stem from the fact that it's a rather complex arrangement when compared with an arm or manual pickup. There's plenty of surface area that has to slide smoothly. Often it gets gummed up with dust and dirt. It's spring-loaded, and occasionally that spring breaks or weakens, which it does often enough for me to carry an extra spring in my tacklebox. Then too, the catch device that holds the cocked ball in place can get bent and put out of commission by a hard knock. So it pays to know something about a full-bail's operation, and how to fix them (see the section on reel maintenance).

But even with occasional malfunctions, the full-bail's performance is so reliable that it's the pickup system I prefer over all others.

The full-bail pickup automatic line-release mechanism deserves mention only because it's not the thing to buy. Several years ago reels appeared on the market whose bail not only picked up a cast line, but functioned in place of your index finger to release it.

In the closed position, the bail sprung to the open position with the touch of your finger, then closed again with a turn of the handle. I wouldn't go so far as to say it was purely a gimmick, but the complexities of manufacture and operation amounted to a too-delicate mechanism. It didn't hold up under normal use, and most anglers I've spoken to who have owned one were signally disappointed with its performance.

Rollers

Rollers are actually part of the pickup mechanism. Once the line is engaged, it comes to rest at the lowest point on the bail. As the line is drawn in, it slides across that point. Without special protection, the monofilament coupled with liberal sprinklings of sand, dust, and dirt would soon dig into the metal, leaving a groove that would cut any line to shreds. Rollers protect against that. They seldom "roll." Rollers that do usually don't after a while. If they roll, they gum up. But roll or not, they should be made of a very hard metal that is difficult to score. Most often this means a carbon alloy.

In addition, rollers should be replaceable. They're not indestructible, and will eventually score. When they do, you should be able to repair them with a fifty-cent part, not a complete seven-dollar bail. Another feature to look for are rollers that can be taken out, then turned around to an unscored side and used some more. It's not so much a matter of saving fifty cents as it is of saving a fishing trip. Parts are sometimes hard to get, and a little thing like a scored roller makes it virtually impossible to use your reel.

The Drag

The drag is an adjustable tension device that allows a taut line to pay out before it reaches the breaking point. Ninety-five percent of the fish you hook won't come close to bringing that drag into play, but anglers enjoy untold pleasure when big ones don't get away. Consequently that 5 percent—and your drag—amounts to an important consideration.

Drag adjustments are incorporated into either the line spool or the gear housing. When they're part of the line spool, the adjusting is most often done by turning a wing nut nestled in the front and center of the spool. Those located in the gear housing usually have a knob in the rear or side of the body of the reel.

I favor reels with these latter adjustments. They're a bit easier to get to

than front-mounted nuts, especially when you're fighting a fish. It's a com-
forting feature. Should you get a searing strike that peels off 50 yards in
the twinkling of an eye, you can slack up on your drag in a hurry.

However, the number of moving parts—rather than the location of the
tension device—is the measure of an acceptable drag.

Simple drags, incorporating an elementary spring and washer, are not
dependable. A piece of sand, or just the heat of friction, could freeze
them up at a critical point. Look for a drag that has several washers. New
wonder metals do not generate heat quickly; they should be placed between other washers made from asbestos, Teflon, felt or synthetics. Never
purchase the economical reels with all metal washers; metal against
metal generates heat during the run of a fish and, as the metal expands,
the drag in effect tightens and can result in a broken line.

Many fresh water species grow big; this
musky approached 50 pounds and was
landed from the St. Lawrence River.

When you're after heavyweights like this,
heavy fresh-water spinning tackle is a
must.

Drag construction is an indicator but not a final test. So try out a drag on a rod with your reel loaded with line. When you pull the line from the rod tip, does the drag operate smoothly and exert even pressure? Beware of choppiness—a tendency in the spool to turn and stop or chatter as you apply an even pull.

Still another indicator of quality and satisfactory performance is the control range of the adjustment. If a half-turn of the wing nut amounts to the full range of your drag—zero resistance up to frozen tight—chances are good the drag will prove unreliable. The adjustment is far too critical to be accurate.

Adjusting a drag should be done with your line fully threaded through the guides and tied to a weight. Just pulling on a line direct from the spool is an unreliable test; you're not taking the effect of roller and guide friction into account.

As a rule of thumb, I like to set my drag 25 percent lighter than the test of my line. I set for 6-pound test when I'm using 8, 3 when I'm using 4, and so forth.

Say you're setting for 6 and using 8; tie a 6-pound weight to the end of your line and lift, utilizing the flex of your rod. Back off on your drag mechanism until it starts to slip.

You'll also discover on a well-balanced rig that just tieing to a tree will turn the trick. You'll know almost intuitively, that point at which both rod and line are under heavy strain. Back off to what you judge to be a moderate strain. I'll bet you find it's roughly 25 percent less than the rated test of your line.

Internal Parts

Internal parts of a reel you plan to have around for a while should be metal and numerous. Plastic and/or nylon gears are sometimes used in reels. They're smooth as silk when they're new, but wear out in a hurry. They can also be stripped clean of their cogs by a big fish.

A good rule of thumb for many situations is simplicity, but a spinning reel is one exception. Plain and simple guts in a reel will soon wear down and start sounding like a coffee grinder. Look for lots of moving parts, preferably machined, not stamped, and roller bearings rather than surface-to-surface contact on moving parts other than gears.

Gear Ratios

Gear ratios in garden-variety spinning reels fall around 1 to 3. That means for every crank of the handle, the head turns three times, winding three turns of line onto your spool. So-called fast-retrieve spinning reels enjoy some popularity these days. Their gear ratio averages out around 1:5. The advantage of a fast retrieve amounts to less turns of a handle when you're hauling in a lure, and the ability to take up slack in a hurry, say, when a fish heads toward you rather than away.

Gear Housings

Gear housings, the "body" of your reel, should be made of noncorrosive metal, with colors bonded to, rather than painted on, the surface. In addition, a grease port should be incorporated into the body, either by way of a removable screw, or zirque. The leg and foot of the housing— your reel's connecting link to the rod handle—should cock the reel at a 3- to 5-degree angle. This allows escaping mono to align itself with your guides, thereby cutting down friction and increasing your casting distance.

Antireverse

Antireverse means just what the name implies. It's a catch that once activated allows your reel to move in only one direction—taking in line. All spinning reels should have an antireverse, and it should be in a place where it can quickly and easily be flicked on or off. The part providing this antireverse feature, usually a dog that jams in the cogs of a main gear, should be stout and solid rather than something stamped out of a sheet of tin. This light material wears out easily, and will bend out of shape under strain.

Reel Handles

Reel handles should fit your fingertips comfortably. It's not just a matter of comfort, but of grip. You'll need all the leverage you can get against a heavy fish. Handles should also be able to turn inward for storage and carrying. This not only saves space, it ensures against breakage.

Reel handles also provide the leverage for a test of quality in a product. When looking at a new reel, palm it in such a way that no part can turn. Attempt to turn the handle forward and backward; pull it away from, then push it toward, the body housing. If you feel play in any of those directions, chances are that reel won't stand up under heavy use.

Most reels are available in either left- or right-handed models. Some products incorporate a place for a handle on either side of their housing, so you can change over at will.

Although I'm a southpaw, I still prefer to use a right-handed model. I've used one all my life, so changing hands in midcast is a reflex action.

I also believe that manipulation of the handle is a more delicate operation in terms of line control than managing a rod. My left hand is more attuned to that kind of sensitivity.

The Spin-Casting Reel

The spin-casting reel is loosely billed as a cross between a conventional casting reel and an open-face spinning reel. It's the most automatic of all fishing reels, requiring the least amount of manual dexterity and savvy to operate. The line is cast by way of a button, usually located in the rear of the reel. Press the button down and you trigger the release mechanism. Wind up, snap your wrist, and the second you take pressure off the control your line is free to funnel through the guides. Pickup is just as simple; crank the handle and your line winds in.

The spin-caster is also known as a closed-face spinning reel, which is a bit more accurate, since the main difference between it and an open-faced spinning reel is that the spin-caster's spool is encased in a conical hood. The line from a spin-caster still spins off a fixed spool, but it is necked down as it passes through a hole in the center of the hood, rather than by contact with the rod's butt guide.

Line release and pickup is achieved by a mushroom-shaped interior cowl, centered over the spool. When you depress then release the casting button, the cowl is pushed forward, exposing the spool and freeing the line. Crank the handle, and the cowl falls back into its original position and begins to revolve. The line is snared by a projecting pin or a series of notches on the lip of the cowl. During operation, this action is hidden from view by the exterior hood.

All the advantages of a spin-caster stem from its simplicity of opera-

Many fresh water trollers prefer closed-face spinning reels. This fine walleye was landed from a Minnesota lake while trolling after dark with a live minnow.

tion. Used with the right combination of line, these reels are virtually foolproof, making them ideal for the beginning spin-fisherman, the night fisherman, and the angler who fishes in cool weather. Unlike an open-faced reel, spin-casters can be cast with gloves on.

As with all things in heaven and earth, however, the closed-face system is far from perfect. My biggest personal objection is its inherent insensitivity.

When using a spin-caster, your grip lies well behind the reel. This means your wrist and forearm are supporting a lot of forward weight. Under this strain, minor as it might seem, it's difficult to tell the difference between the bounce of a rocky bottom and the bobble of a nibbling fish.

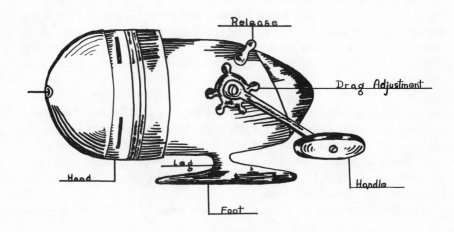

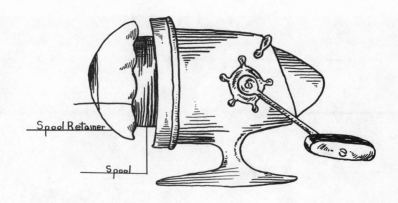

Casting accuracy suffers too. On a spin-caster, your hand never comes in contact with the line. You can't feel the momentum built up by your lure, and consequently, don't have that particular signal to tell you when your release will give you your greatest loft, distance, and accuracy.

Spin-casters can't handle extremely light lures or light line. Three-eighths to ⅝ths of an ounce are the best lure weights, and 6- to 15-pound test are the optimum line weights. Lines heavier or lighter than these tend to get fouled in the mechanism.

A few other limiting factors common to the spin-caster include:

—Below-freezing temperatures render them useless. Ice builds up inside the cowling and freezes line and release mechanism tight.

—Line condition, and the amount you have on your spool, can't be checked unless you remove the cowl. It's a simple operation, but being human, few anglers take the time to do it.

—Breaking down a closed-face rig requires some effort, especially if the tag end of your mono disappears inside the cowl. You'll have to remove the cowl, then will probably need a hairpin or toothpick to pry the line free before you can rig up again.

This might sound like I disapprove of spin-casters, but that's not quite the case. They have their value and their place, and I always carry one in my tacklebox for those times and situations when a closed-face system comes into its own. I'd recommend that every other angler with more than a passing interest in the sport do the same. And when you're choosing that supplementary spin-caster, here are a few things to look for:

—An oscillating spool. Your line will cast farther and freer, and foul less if it's fed onto the spool in evenly lapped coils. Remember, you won't be able to see this feature since it occurs under the hood. Remove the hood and check.

—Interchangeable spools. Many brands of spin-casters offer easy change of spools. This allows you the latitude of different line weights for different lure weights and fishing conditions.

—A reliable, accessible drag system. Check your reel's drag for smooth, regular release of line. Don't accept a product with a choppy, uneven drag-pressure. Your drag adjustment should be located in a place you can reach while you're fighting a fish. It should not have knobs or protuberances that might get snagged on a shirtsleeve or bank willow.

—Metal housings and gears. Some of the inexpensive spin-casters incorporate a lot of plastic or nylon inside and out. They won't stand up under heavy use, or the strain of a big, tackle-testing fish.

—A feathering feature. Often, there is need or reason to draw a cast up short. On an open-faced system, this is accomplished by applying gentle manual friction to the moving line. On a closed-face reel, applying manual control is awkward and difficult, so a means to feather a line mechanically should be built in. The most convenient arrangement is feathering control in the release mechanism.

SPINNING RODS

A good rod takes a back seat to no equipment. As a matter of fact, it deserves to be behind the wheel. Hooks and line are of course, important. But they're really no more than a connecting link between you and a fish. The keen machinery and smooth gears of a top-notch reel are a joy to hold and use, but when you get down to brass gears, even the best reel is nothing more than a receptacle for your line.

It's your rod that's the workhorse, functioning both as the spring that catapults a lure on its way and the backbone that stands behind any toe-to-toe battle with a lunker. Any piece of equipment holding that position of eminence should be selected with care and thoroughly understood.

Rod Weights

Rod weights are vital. The common range of weights for fresh-water spinning runs from 2 ounces to 10. A two-ounce rod is classified as an ultra-light, a 10-ouncer is capable of handling heavy fish like steelhead and northern pike.

In and of themselves, rod weights mean little. They don't begin to achieve significance until you consider them in relation to a rod's length and its action. A stiff- or heavy-action rod should weigh more than a light-action rod of the same length. There's more material in that rod providing backbone: a 7-foot medium-action rod is more rod than a 6½ footer.

Generally speaking, the lightest rod available in a given action and length will be the best quality and command the highest price. Don't go overboard on this though. Like cars that can do 160 miles physically but not legally, a 3-ounce spinning rod that can handle a half-ounce lure is a great conversation piece, but unless you go on fishing trips where you cast twenty-four hours a day for a week at a time, you'll never realize that rod's potential or fully appreciate its engineering.

Another consideration when evaluating rod weights is balance with your reel. A very light rod, even if it is capable of handling heavy fish, won't balance with the 14- to 16-ounce reels you'll need for line capacity and guts.

At the risk of oversimplification, here are a few middle-ground rod weights; these are intended only as a guide, not as final determination or absolute recommendation. They are only part of the picture. Action and taper play a big role in performance:

Ultralight: 4 to 5 feet, 1 to 3 ounces
Light-action: 5½ to 6½ feet, 3½ to 4½ ounces
Medium-action: 6 to 7½ feet, 4½ to 6 ounces
Heavy- or stiff-action: 6 to 7½ feet, 6 to 8 ounces

Rod Action

Rod action is puzzling to many anglers, but it needn't be. Begin by understanding that any rod is tapered: thick at the base, thin at the tip. These dimensions are achieved in a smooth progression for the most part, like a long, drawn-out cone. The wider the diameter of a given rod, the stiffer the action will be. In other words, assuming they're of equal length and material, a rod measuring a ½ inch at the butt and 3/16 of an inch at the tip will require more pressure to bend it to action than a rod measuring ⅜ of an inch at the butt and ⅛ of an inch at the tip. More material means more resistance.

The amount of resistance required to bend a rod to action then, is the determining factor in labeling a rod ultralight, light, medium, or stiff. Since a cast weight is one form of resistance, actions are often identified by the weights they can handle. Ultralight for example, is best suited for lures up to ¼ ounce. Light actions work best with ⅜ ounce of casting weight.

Norman Strung used a medium weight fresh-water spinning outfit to land this fine, brown trout while fishing Montana's famed Madison River.

Medium actions are designed for ⅜ to ½ ounce, and stiff up to ⅝ ounce. Lures of ⅝ ounce are generally accepted as the cutoff point between fresh- and salt-water classifications in spinning. A lure over this weight requires a two-handed cast for sufficient snap and carry.

Another form of resistance anglers occasionally meet is a fish. Consequently, some rods are labeled bass action, trout action, panfish action, and so forth. All this means is that the shafts are capable of handling the lures designed to attract these fish.

Rod Tapers

Rod tapers. The majority of the rods sold today incorporate a special taper. This amounts to an abrupt step-down in rod diameter, engineered somewhere along the shaft. This taper affords the fisherman both latitude and leverage.

A taper provides more drive, or *recoil power*, to a rod. How and why this occurs requires some knowledge of physics, but the net result in action is longer casts with less work.

Leverage is also provided when you hook a big fish. Essentially, a tapered rod has a light action above the point of taper. When a heavy fish puts it to the test, that part of the rod lying below the taper—toward the butt—springs into action, providing extra backbone.

Latitude enters the picture by way of the variety of lures a tapered rod can handle. When employing a light lure, just the limber forward-section of your rod springs to work. With heavier lures, the stress of action moves farther down the shaft into the stiffer portions of the rod.

Where that taper occurs is the determining factor in whether a rod is classified as fast or slow. A taper within six inches to a foot and a half of the tip is called a *fast taper*. When the taper moves back toward the mid-section of the rod, it becomes a *standard taper*. There are no set measurements or standards, but that limbo between location of a fast and standard taper is where manufacturers come up with a classification like *medium-fast* action.

When a rod incorporates no taper, when it necks down from butt to tip on a level plane, it's called a *slow*, or *worm*, action. Other monickers given to this shaft are *even taper, slow taper* or *parabolic rod*.

There is no best taper. Fast-tip rods are new, popular, and in the majority, but in at least half my fishing situations, I prefer the old, level-tapering parabolic rod. The key to picking the most useful taper lies in your fishing tastes and the number of rods you can afford.

Generally, the fast tip is the design for the lure fisherman. The action is crisp and clean, and the rod has plenty of backbone, making it also a good choice for those who like to troll.

As the point of abrupt taper moves back toward the butt, the snappy characteristics of a fast taper begin to disappear. When that taper occurs 30 to 40 percent down the shaft of the rod, you begin to approach the standard taper. This design amounts to a multipurpose rod. In fact, some manufacturers call them *omni*, or *universal* rods. They might not put the same drive behind a lure, but they won't crack a worm or minnow off during a cast. These standard tapers also exhibit the widest range of optimum lure-weights. A medium-action, standard taper will comfortably handle ⅜ to ⅝ ounce lures when matched with appropriate line.

Even taper or parabolic rods aren't snappy casters, but tend to bend in an even curve, imparting smooth power and motion to a weight. Where a fast taper shoots a lure forward, an even taper lobs it. As such, this rod is ideal for the live-bait fisherman whose offering just doesn't hold together as well as stamped steel on a long cast. Strangely enough, a rod that "bends into the corks" is also for fishing ultralight (lures under ¼ ounce). It provides more control and "feel" during a cast.

Testing Actions

Testing actions is a lot like kicking tires in a used-car lot. Salesmen and customers alike whip, vibrate, and bend rods—and often don't know why. Actually, putting a rod through a few paces in the showroom can give you a good idea of how it will deliver afield, and provide a cross-check on the manufacturer's accuracy in labeling.

What to look for and what it will tell you about your rod can best be conveyed by comparison. Let's place a parabolic rod and extra-fast taper side by side. Both rods are 6½ feet long and listed as medium-action.

With the butt of each rod held loosely in either hand, rest the tip-top guides on the floor. You should notice an abrupt curve along the last foot or so of the fast-taper tip. Beyond that point, the rod should have minimal bend, barely noticeable.

The even-taper rod should bend in a gentle arc, not a perfect circle (the thicker part of the rod is putting up more resistance than the tip) but a parabolalike curve that begins sharply, then flows smoothly to the butt.

Wrist-shake the rods side to side so the shaft seems to form two distinct curves. Your wrist will have to move faster to vibrate the fast-tip rod. The even-taper will feel slow and a little mushy. In addition, the nodal point— the point where the tip sections of those intersecting (vibrating) curves appear to meet—will be close to the tip on the fast-tip rod and closer to the midsection on the even-taper.

It follows then, that you can use these tests to determine more delicate differences of performance, say, between a rod the manufacturer claims to be fast-taper and a standard-taper or between a superfast and a fast.

Of course, differing rod weights and lengths will alter their physical responses, so characteristics won't be quite so easy to spot as with these examples. But under all circumstances, the fast-action will vibrate more rapidly and have its nodal point close to the tip. The slower a rod is, the slower its vibration and the closer the nodal point will be to you.

Shaft Materials

Shaft materials have reached a point now where only two are worth considering; glass and bamboo.

It's a false but common misconception that bamboo has been replaced by glass. It just isn't so. A fine bamboo rod is still a better tool than a fine glass rod. However, a fine glass rod costs between $40 and $50 and a fine bamboo is about $150. The quality and performance differential between the two is recognizable, but most anglers feel that it's not worth $100. I tend to agree.

Should you want to try that $100 worth of difference however, here are a few things to look for:

—Price and name are at the top of the list. Forget about bargains in a bamboo rod; you'll be buying a dog if you pay less than $75. A name you recognize isn't only an indication of quality, it means you can count on somebody to stand behind the product in case of malfunction.

—It's generally accepted that a six-sided shaft delivers the best performance. Each of those six sides should be an individual strip of bamboo.

—When bamboo grows, it forms rings 14 to 16 inches apart. These rings, once incorporated into a rod shaft, are the weakest part of the material. They should be staggered on all sides, with no ring opposite another anywhere on the rod. The rings aren't too apparent to the naked eye either. They usually look like a dark blemish in the material.

—The rod should not have a *set*. That is, when sighting down the shaft, it should develop only a slight, uniform arc, the result of gravity, that remains the same no matter which way the rod is turned.

—Don't overlook the possibilities provided by rod kits. Many manufacturers offer their bamboo rods in kit form—they supply you with the raw materials, you put them together. If you like to tinker around a workshop, building your own bamboo rod will result in substantial savings.

Glass rods have a price range from $5 to $50. Like bamboo, beware of bargains. Unless you're buying a rod in kit form, set your sights on $15 as a rock-bottom investment. Less expensive rods are bound to have had important features left out in manufacture.

Solid glass rods are unsatisfactory. They lack the resiliency and power of a hollow glass shaft and are soft and mushy in the extreme. This is often one of those corners cut to bring you a bargain, so check carefully if you're buying a less-known brand.

Hollow glass rods should be just that—hollow inside. Their exterior surface should not appear overly grainy, nor should layers of wrapped fiberglass be apparent. The best shafts are smooth and glassy to the eye and touch.

Like bamboo, the rod should have no set. Unlike bamboo, there should be no blemishes on the surface. Be particularly wary of a light discoloration-spot. It might be a sign of a fracture or material crystallization, virtually guaranteeing a break there as soon as the rod is put under strain.

When examining and testing a potential purchase don't try to put a mighty bend in the rod. Rods are designed to take a great deal of pressure, but only when it's exerted on a line, fed through and cushioned by the guides.

Glass rods are also sold in kit form by many manufacturers and mail-order houses. Again, you can put these together yourself for substantial savings.

Rod Length

Rod length should be determined by your fishing habits. If you frequent brushy shorelines, loaded boats, or do a lot of trolling, short rods, 5½ to 6½ feet, will perform best.

For most casting situations, however, I prefer to go the long route—7 to 7½ feet. These longer rods provide more power on a lobbed bait-cast. They also give you better control over a working lure. In addition, when you're fighting a big fish, they give you some extra elevation to get dragging line up and out of the water. This same elevation is extremely useful when you're trying to jiggle a snagged lure free.

Sectional Rods

Sectional rods are the most common design. While it's true that one-piece construction delivers the finest action, the convenience of a rod you can take down and carry comfortably is usually preferable.

What amounts to "comfortable carrying"? I'd call 3½ feet an optimum length. A longer rod-case seems to have trouble fitting into places where it would fare best; the corner of a car trunk, under the seat of an airplane, on the saddle of a pack horse, or in a small boat.

Sectional rods I've learned to avoid like the plague are those that break at the handle. These usually boast a butt section 1 foot long and a tip between 5 and 6 feet. When you've got something as unwieldy as a package 5 feet long, you might as well go the whole route and opt for one-piece construction. That extra foot won't make enough difference to count.

Rod Hardware

Rod hardware means any dressing above and beyond the shaft itself: guides, ferrules, corks, and reel seat. The quality of this hardware, and the way it's put together, will tell you a lot about the product you're buying.

The Tiptop

The tiptop is the common name given to the tip guide on a rod. Tiptops are subject to much wear and scoring—there's no getting away from it. Scored tiptops must be replaced, so look for rods that permit this changeover; a clinched tiptop won't (there will be an obvious pinch-mark in the metal), and neither will a tiptop secured with resin glue. The best form of adhesive on this part of your rod is heat cement. Warm the part, and the tiptop will slide off. A new one slides on just as easily, firming up tight when the metal cools.

Although any tiptop will eventually score, wear will at least be at a minimum if the eye is cast from carbon-alloy steel. The same holds true of guide eyes.

Guides

Guides are a particular bone of contention between me and manufacturers. In most cases, I find assembly-line products have guides that are too few, too small, too stiff, and too wrapped. I'm at the point now where I build virtually all my own rods, not just to save money, but because I end up rebuilding most of the brands I buy anyway. Here are my specific complaints and personal solutions—a catharsis for me, a catalog for you.

· Reel spools have a diameter of between 1½ and 2 inches. When you cast, the line spins off the spool in coils much larger than the spool. Yet virtually every rod on the market comes equipped with a butt guide the diameter of your thumb. In the sizing-down process, excessive friction occurs. This shortens your cast and alters accuracy. To correct this situation, I move the original butt guide to the number 2 position, and wrap a light salt-water guide, 1½ inches in diameter, in the butt position.

· A small butt-guide causes undue friction, and so do too few guides. Rather than holding the coils of a cast line to a minimum, widely spaced guides allow it to redevelop loops while it's on the move. These loops pass through one guide, slap against the rod shaft, then have to be necked down again to pass through the next guide. Experience has indicated that any spinning rod, to perform its best, should have one guide for every foot of length, including the tiptop as a guide.

· This large number of guides on a rod isn't without problems—at least not in contemporary rod manufacture. Six rigid-footed guides, with their accompanying 1½-inch windings take a lot of action from a glass shaft. So I use flex-type guides; the kind that are all one piece and bend like a spring. And when I wind them on, my wrappings never extend more than a ¼ inch beyond a guide foot. Granted, my rods don't sport fancy curlicues and gold trim, but when it comes to practical fishing situations, they will outperform 85 percent of the commercial rods sold in sports stores today.

Unfortunately, you won't find most of these features in guides unless you have a rod custom-built. So, using what's available, let's take a look at some features you can and should buy.

· Flex guides are sold on some shafts. They're far better than the rigid-foot type.

· Windings should be well varnished so they're glossy and smooth to the touch. It looks good, but more important, thick varnish protects the threads from bruises and breaks. Windings should be tied and finished separately on each foot of the guide, rather than in one continuous thread.

· The ends of guide feet should not peek through the winding; they should be ground down smooth and flush with the rod shaft.

· Choose a rod with the biggest butt-guide you can find. At present, that's about 1 inch in diameter.

Ferrules

Ferrules come in three varieties: glass, metal with a rubber lock ring, and all metal.

· Glass ferrules are the best. They provide flex in the joint, unlike un-yielding metal. They also up the price of a rod by $15 to $30. Make sure

Currituck Sound in North Carolina pro-duced this fine stringer of largemouth bass. A medium weight spinning outfit and subsurface swimming plug were the payoff combination.

any glass-to-glass ferrule has a good snug fit. The male part of the joint should seat fully into the female receptacle and unseat crisply. Glass ferrules can't be expanded or contracted to achieve a snug fit, so they must be fit right at the start.

The ferrule joint itself shouldn't be too bulbous, that is, it should not swell out far beyond the diameter of the shafts it joins. If it's too bulbous, chances are good the fiberglass walls of the ferrule are so thick that they won't flex much more than solid metal.

· Metal ferrules with a rubber lock-ring on the male joint come next on the list of preference. The rubber lock-ring holds the joined ferrule firmly in place and also ensures against jamming. They add only slightly to the cost of a rod and greatly improve its dependability.

· Metal-to-metal ferrules are the hardware most commonly found on commercial rods. They should be made of corrosion-resistant material, join smoothly, and come apart with a little pop. This pop is the result of a vacuum, and is a reliable indication of close tolerances. That close tolerance is necessary to keep your guides aligned, and sections together after repeated casts.

Grips

Grips on rods are occasionally synthetics or a covering of pressed cork. Neither material performs as well as the old standard cork rings.

These grips are constructed by forcing a series of cork rings onto a rod butt and gluing them in place. The grip is then turned and shaped to the proper diameter. Real cork has give—in your hand, and on the rod. The result is a nonslippery surface that gives you something to hang on to and a rod that has play all the way down the shaft.

Signs of quality in a cork grip include a one-piece appearance. Although the grip is in fact, constructed of many rings, they should appear as one solid mass. The grip should also appear to be of even texture. Rough, brown bruises are weak spots in the cork. Under heavy use, these will either flake away, leaving a depression, or shear through, leaving you minus one ring somewhere in the grip.

Reel Seats

Reel seats affix the foot of your reel to the rod. They come in three designs: sliding rings, the sliding reel-seat, and the fixed reel-seat.

· Sliding rings simply slip over each end of a reel foot. Forced into place, the reflex action of resilient cork holds rings and foot firmly in position. The rings do tend to work loose after repeated casting, however, and frequently have to be forced back into place. So-called tapered rings minimize this problem.

Sliding rings are the least expensive of the reel mounts. They also offer the advantage of positioning a reel anywhere along the grip, allowing an angler to achieve proper balance with virtually any reel and lure-weight combination.

· Sliding reel-seats offer this same advantage, and don't exhibit the rings' tendency to loosen up. A sliding seat amounts to a metal sleeve with a notch for the reel foot, and a screw-type ring that cinches down tight on the reel. It's this design that finds a happy home with me.

· Fixed reel-seats are part and parcel of the rod. They're locked in place and hold a reel in secure position by a screw-type ring. I favor them on my heavy fresh-water rods, since they'll never work loose from the pressure of a big fish. But because you're stuck with that one reel position, you're largely held to a narrow reel and lure-weight range to achieve balance.

Any reel seat should be made of noncorrosive metal. Steer clear of plastics; they don't stand up. Delrin is an exception, however.

Rod and Reel Balance

Rod and reel balance means that your wrist won't tire after a full day's casting and that you stand the best chance of achieving accuracy.

To test for balance, rig the rod, reel, and line with whatever weight lure is recommended. Use your finger as a fulcrum. The point of balance should fall within an inch of the end of your cork grip.

Realize that your outfit is acting somewhat like a scale and that you can change weights and their position—as with a scale—to maintain balance. Let's say the rod you hold on your finger sports a ⅜-ounce lure. Put a ⅝-ounce lure on, and you won't balance out. You will regain balance, however, if you move your reel back an inch or so. That's the advantage of a sliding reel-seat.

SPINNING LINE

There are two types of lines suitable for spinning; braided line and mono-filament.

Braided lines are made from synthetic fiber—usually nylon or Dacron. They incorporate several threads of fiber, braided or twisted, to make up the single strand of line.

Because of its lack of elasticity and resistance to abrasion and sun damage, Dacron is preferred. However, braided lines of any kind fall considerably short of monofilament for all-round use.

Their most practical application is in trolling. Being a heavier, more absorbent line than mono, they reach greater depths at shorter lengths. This factor, plus their lack of stretch, makes them quite sensitive to a strike and quick to set a hook.

Monofilament is just what the name implies: a single thread of line. The name is generic rather than scientific, since several synthetics, most notably Perlon, are used in its manufacture. But all monofilaments have several characteristics in common.

Their translucent properties are perhaps most important. Light passes through the pale strand, making it largely invisible to fish. Then too, it's extremely tough, abrasion-resistant stuff, with a smooth, hard surface that slips easily through guides. Finally, mono doesn't absorb water. Its casting characteristics don't change from the first cast to the last. This lack of absorption also accounts for several other features important to the angler. Mono sinks very slowly, facilitating more precise control over surface lures and still-fished bait. Its lightness makes for low water-resistance. Lures or bait fished in a current are less affected by line drag.

Choosing the Best Mono

Choosing the best mono is largely a matter of understanding how it will perform best for you. The thinner and more supple a given pound-test of line, the easier it will cast. Look for line that's soft to the touch, that lays down when it's loosely coiled (rather than falling into a bristling bird's-nest), and that boasts the smallest diameter in the store for that pound test. Line diameters are usually listed on the line spool.

Visibility is another factor. While you don't want the fish to see your line, it's a lot easier to work a lure or bait when you can. Test a line for below-water visibility by submerging it while you've got a pair of polarized glasses on. Above water, a strand of mono should stand out in plain sight with the sun coming over your shoulder and in all conditions of shade short of twilight.

Matching Mono to Your Tackle

Matching mono to your tackle is an important facet of all-round balance. Four-pound test simply isn't capable of handling the lures—or the fish—that bend a heavy-duty rod to peak performance. The same goes for fifteen-pound test on an ultralight rig.

A few rules of thumb might be in order before we get into specifics. First, the type of rod you're using has a lot to do with the range of line weights it works best with. For instance, let's say a 5-ounce rod delivers optimum performance with line weights from 6- to 10-pound test. If that rod has a soft action, if it bends to the corks, choose line in the lighter range. If it's got a fast tip, choose the heavier line. By virtue of their snap and drive, a fast tip works a line harder and is more prone to pressure a fish or cast a lure hard. Line in the lighter range might break.

The weight range of fish you're after should also influence line choice (and thereby choice of reel and rod choice as well). For example, when I lived near New York City, I loved to fish for sea-run trout on Long Island. The biggest I ever caught was 4 pounds, and that was my most frequently used line weight.

Occasionally, I'd fish for crappie in the little ponds near my home. Two-pound test on an ultralight rig was the rule then, and I might also point out that these light lines were perfect for casting panfish-sized lures.

On the other side of the coin, since coming to Montana, my favorite line is 8-pound test for trout. Other standards include 10-pound test for bass and eighteen-pound for northern pike. Although it seems apparent, these standards weren't determined solely by the biggest fish I caught. I arrived at them well before catching that 8-pound trout and the 10-pound bass. But those are the standards that have developed, and I'm now considering a 50-pound test for brown trout—just to see what happens.

Some specifics then, on just what weight of line balances with what tackle and what fish:

Pound test	Rod/reel type	Lure weight (oz.)	Fish
2	ultralight	1/16-¼	panfish, small trout, wary large trout
4	light	¼-⅜	trout (eastern), large panfish, small bass and pickerel
6	medium-light	⅜-⅝	trout (East and West), shad, pickerel, bass (average size, non-snaggy habitat)
8	medium	⅜-⅝	trout (western rivers), shad, small pike, bass (large, non-snaggy habitat), walleye
10	medium-heavy	½-1	bass (snaggy, weedy habitat), pike, dolly varden trout
15	heavy	1-2	bull bass in brush, big pike, steelhead, musky

I might mention one other thing. Using these rough guidelines, I've *never* had a fish break my line. That doesn't mean I didn't loose a few big ones, but in every one of those situations, I traced my break to a weak knot, worn line, or a cut by rock, brush, or toothy mouth.

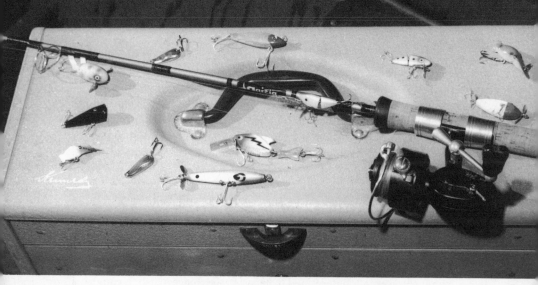

Where a delicate presentation and small
lures are required, you just can't beat an
ultra-light spinning outfit like this one.

Line Life

Line life is a subject that seldom gets the coverage it deserves.

On a winter trip down South for bass, I once ran into an angler who,
upon learning I was a sportswriter, started berating a line manufacturer.
"Damned company oughta be blamed with false advertising," he said.
"They claim their line was the best, but not six months after I filled my
spool it started to break and wear. . . ."

Well, if the company did advertise such a long life-span, perhaps they
should be prosecuted, but I find it hard to believe any manufacturer making
such a claim. No line is indestructible. No matter how expensive or "good"
it is, sun, guide wear, and just plain age will take its toll.

The life of a spoolful of mono is directly proportional to the amount
of use. A guy who fishes once a month and keeps his line stored in a cool,
shady spot, might get a year out of it, but I'd say six months is a better bet.
At the height of the fishing season, I find myself respooling my 8-pound
test once every two weeks, and my other spools about once a month.

It's quite easy to tell when you need new line; your mono will have a
chalky, rough appearance. It will feel rough and quite brittle to the touch.
Frequent, unreasonable breaks are another, less agreeable symptom. You
can even *hear* bad line. It rattles, rather than sings, through the guides.

If you do a lot of fishing and thereby a lot of line replacing, here's
another tip. You can buy bulk line from manufacturers in lengths up to
5,000 yards at a quarter the price you'd pay for individual 100-yard spools.

Bass boats are the rage throughout the country. The anglers fishing from this one are working the desert shores of Lake Mead in Nevada where spinning tackle and spinnerbaits take a heavy toll of largemouth bass from the shoreline.

Spooling New Line

Spooling new line should find the fresh line coming off its receptacle the same way it's going onto your reel. In other words, it should spin over the spool lip and not revolve on a pencil. This transfers coil to coil. Any other method will kink your line.

The best way to do this is with a partner. With reel on your rod, and line threaded through at least the butt guide, have the partner palm the spool with his fingers resting lightly on the line.

Reel at a normal speed, but keep tension on the line by exerting pressure between thumb and index finger. This keeps loose coils from forming and later interfering with casting.

Add enough fresh mono so the surface of the line comes to within 1/16 of an inch of your reel's spool lip. If you add more than this, you're bound to get a bird's nest. When your line gets much below this level, the friction of line on lip will cut short your casts.

TERMINAL TACKLE

The assorted gear—hooks, leaders, lures, and sinkers, that decorate the business end of a rod and reel is known as *terminal tackle*.

The term truly covers a multitude of sins. When you investigate lures, for example, you'll find four basic designs—spoon, spinner, plug, and jig. Spoons can be divided into lightweights for close-to-the-surface work, and heavies for deep running. Spinners have wide blades for slow-moving water, willow blades for fast streams. Plugs include deep divers, shallow divers, floaters, and poppers, while jigs are especially designed for mooching, ice-fishing, trolling, and casting.

Multiply all those styles by brand names, colors, and subtle but important variations in design, and you come very close to owning a tackleshop. Add the variations inherent in the areas of hooks, bait, sinkers, leaders, and snapswivels, and you might as well open for business.

My point is this: an incisive discussion of every variety of terminal tackle is a practical impossibility. So let's examine the subject here in the broadest terms and more specifically later on in the sections on technique and spinning for species.

Leaders

Leaders should kick off this topic since they fall into line before other types of terminal addenda. Their place is between the end of your line and your bait ("bait" here means anything a fish will try to eat); the purpose of leaders is to prevent the end of your line from being cut, either by rocks or sharp teeth.

Leader material is usually heavy monofilament or twisted steel wire covered with clear, soft plastic.

Even though steel won't cut and mono will, I prefer mono. Though they try to disguise it, manufacturers still haven't figured out how to make steel invisible and nonshiny. It stands out quite distinctly on a sunny day, while mono—even stout stuff—is relatively hard to spot. This counts in terms of the number of fish that will be enticed to strike a lure. Then too, abrasions on thick-leader mono are easy to spot, and when they occur, the material can be quickly replaced.

Of course, leaders aren't necessary for most fresh-water fishing. The sharp teeth of the genus *Esox* (pike) do make them necessary. So do the sharp rocks commonly found in the bottom of some steelhead rivers and walleye holes. But unless you're after these species or encounter these conditions, tie the tag end of your line directly to a *snapswivel*—an inexpensive little gadget that performs two admirable services: its safety-pinlike clasp means quick lure changeover without retying your terminal knot and its swivel helps keep a twisting, whirling lure from kinking your line.

Snapswivels shouldn't be prominent; the smaller the swivel the better. Even the smallest available tests out to 8 pounds, which is plenty for most situations. I also favor black swivels over shiny silver and gold.

One other feature that deserves close attention is the construction of the swivel. Those that incorporate ball bearings are the most effective.

Snapswivels should be employed in conjunction with any device that spins; however, some action is lost when you use them with hyperactive plugs that dart from side to side. Banana-type plugs like the Lazy Ike and jointed minnows like the L & S Brokenback are examples of these. Tie directly onto these lures.

Sinkers

Sinkers for the spin-fisherman fall into four categories: pinch-on or rubber-cored, tie-on, slip, and twist-on.

· Pinch-on sinkers, characterized by split-shot and those elongated sinkers with tabs on each end, are the least desirable. While they sink as effectively as any chunk of lead, when your line gets caught in their pinch, it's often damaged and weakened considerably. Rubber-cored sinkers with rubber cores in lieu of lead tabs are far superior.

· Tie-on sinkers have two subdivisions: those used for trolling and those used for bottom fishing.

In the trolling category, keel sinkers with a design like the keel on a sailboat are the most effective. They put up little forward water resistance, thereby keeping your line down, and plenty of side-to-side resistance, thereby keeping your line straight. They're best when used in conjunction with a keychainlike series of swivels.

Bottom-bouncing sinkers come in a variety of designs. They're all effective at keeping your hook down, but many of the bulbous designs are extremely prone to snag by getting wedged between rocks. If you have this problem, try a pencil lead. They're made of extra-soft lead, long and thin.

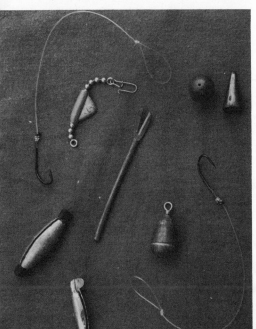

You should always carry a supply of sinkers with you. Included here are those in most popular use by spin-fishermen such as split shot, clinch-on, rubber-cored, keel trolling, egg with hole, cone-shaped and bass casting or dipsey with swivel. Snelled hooks and pencil lead, a type of sinker, are shown for size comparison.

This design is the least likely to snag in the first place, and gentle pressure bends them easily, so they're simple to pop free.

· Slip or "egg" sinkers have a hole through the middle of them, through which your line passes. When a fish picks up a bait, he then drags only line, not a heavy chunk of lead. The best slip sinker is in the shape of a tall, narrow-based cone, since it's the most snag-free and weedless.

· A twist-on (or rubber-core) sinker is a piece of elongated lead with a rubber insert running up the middle. Lay your line parallel to the rubber, take a few twists of both rubber and line, and the sinker is held firmly in place. Absence of line damage and easy removal make this design far more desirable than the pinch-on type.

Hooks

Hooks are one of those areas with a multiplicity of sizes, designs, and characteristics. However, there are some features to look for that will suit you up with the right hook for any situation.

· Hook material is the most important consideration. They should be made from high-quality steel and tempered for further strength. A hook should never break. When excessive pressure is applied, it should bend before snapping. Notice that I said *excessive* pressure; hooks shouldn't bend like soft wire either.

· Hook design is where we really get into a grab bag of terminology. Rather than identifying these designs by name, let's take a look at the results of variations in hook construction.

The point of a hook is that part which includes the sharpened end, and the barb, that sharp sliver of raised steel which holds a hook in a fish's mouth. (A low barb and short point are best for hard-mouthed fish like pike and trout.) The hook can be set more easily because less energy is needed for penetration.

Conversely, a soft-mouthed fish deserves a long point and high barb. Penetration is a simple matter, and the consideration now is to keep the fish from working the hook free.

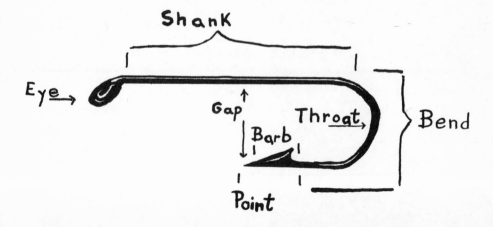

The bend of a hook is the curve that extends from immediately behind the barb up to the straight shank. A straight hook finds the point in alignment with the shank. An offset hook (called *kirbed* and *reversed*) has a twist at the bend that sets the point slightly off to the right or left. An offset hook is best for bait fishing. When you strike, you're virtually guaranteed that at some point, the hook point will come into contact with the fish's mouth. An offset hook is not for trolling or casting however. Its out-of-balance design causes the hook to spin, and the offset frequently hangs up on snags and weeds.

The shank of a hook is the straight shaft between bend and eye. Short shanks are handy when you want to bury a hook in your bait. They're frequently used for steelhead in conjunction with salmon eggs and for panfishing with grubs through the ice. Long-shanked hooks are the best choice for fish with toothy and abrasive mouths (pike and bass, for example) and for fish with small mouths that tend to ingest a hook deeply. In this case, they're just easier to remove.

The eye of the hook is the part that joins with the line. Eyes can be either straight (in perfect line with the shank) or turned down. A turned-down eye aligns a strike more perfectly with the point, providing more reliable penetration. However, like an offset hook, turned-down eyes don't ride well when trolled or retrieved. Turned-down eyes are best then, for bait fishing and straight eyes for artificial work.

A few more variations in hooks are worthy of note. The turned-in point—a slight bend at the very tip of a hook's sharpened end—like a turned-down eye makes penetration easier, but it doesn't alter the hook's performance while it's on the move. For this reason, I favor turned-in points on all my hooks—including trebles.

The bait-holder (or claw) hook has a series of barbs cut into the shank. The sharp points help keep a bait in place—a big plus for the bait fisherman.

Weedless hooks incorporate some sort of guard, usually thin, stiff wire that protects the point and bend from snagging in heavy brush, but that will pop out of the way when a fish chomps down. They're effective and efficient and belong in any tacklebox. In a pinch, you can make your own weedless hook by stretching a rubber band from hook-eye to barb—if you're in the habit of carrying rubber bands while you're fishing.

Snelled hooks come with a monofilament leader attached. They're not needed for most spinning situations since you'll be using mono anyway, and can tie directly to the hook, eliminating a weak point at the line-snell knot. They are handy, used in conjunction with a snapswivel, when you have to change leaders often; bottom-bouncing for walleye or steelhead or bait fishing for pike.

Treble hooks—or even single hooks used on an artificial lure—deserve special consideration. When you're bait fishing and get a strike, you've got plenty of time to wind up, sock it to 'em, and set the hook. When you're casting or trolling however, a strike always comes as a surprise, and the delay in reaction time often has you missing a fish.

To increase the probability of a fish hooking himself, use thin-wired hooks with short points and low barbs. With three hooks working for you, even jumpers like rainbow trout have a hard time disgorging these things.

Needle hooks come in single, double, and treble. What sets them apart from other hooks is their shank. Rather than ending in an eye, a needle hook forms a sharp, flat point with a tiny hole in it. The hook is designed to be threaded through a bait: a dead minnow, frog, or what have you. Once the hook is threaded and in place, a ringed eye is added by slipping a snap-clip, with eye, through the tiny hole.

This hook design is also known as a *bullhead hook* in the West and a *mullet rig* around salt water.

A variation on the theme is the hook harness—a device designed to hold a live fish in its grasp without piercing him with a hook point. Harnesses are also available for frogs and salamanders.

Lures

Lures fall into four major categories: spoons, spinners, jigs, and plugs. While flies are eminently fishable with a spinning rod, so much of their effectiveness depends upon technique that they're better discussed in the following section (see *Spinning With a Fly*, p. 93).

Generally, the smaller the lure, the more fish you'll catch. It's a matter of simple logic. An 8-inch trout isn't going to tackle a 6-inch plug. Conversely, an 8-pound trout finds a tiny inch-long minnow, perhaps not an epicurean feast, but certainly a tempting snack.

In matters of color, it's been my experience that colors imitative of nature consistently work best. A froglike plug catches more bass if it's green-and-black-spotted rather than electric blue. A silver-hammered brass spoon gets more strikes from trout than a red-and-white-striped one. There are of course, exceptions, but natural colors have proven to be a reliable rule of thumb. ·

The relative weights of lures are important too, not only because they must balance with the rest of your tackle, but because their ratio of bulk to weight determines both casting performance and action. A light, bulky plug like the Flatfish for example, is a poor caster. But its lightness in part accounts for its frenzied action in the water. The same thing can be said about light, stamped-metal spoons. On the other hand, a heavy, narrow spoon like the Crocodile, or a plug like the sinking Rapala, casts like a bullet but has relatively muted action underwater. This isn't to say that one type of action or lure is better than another. An understanding on your part of how a lure will perform above and underwater should be basic to terminal-tackle selection. That way you can carry a full spectrum of presentation and appeal.

Called spoons in some areas and wobblers in others, these spoon-shaped lures have an enticing action that brings strikes from many fresh-water species, and are a must in the tackle kit of the serious spin-fisherman.

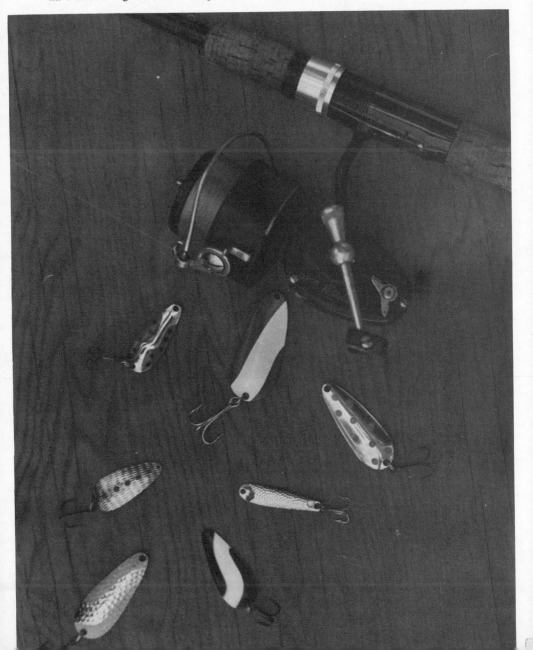

Beyond those generalizations, there are some specific properties of lure types that deserve mention:

· Spoons are generally solid, one-piece metal affairs with one treble hook. Although they sometimes sport little tabs that flutter and flap like a tail, spoon action is primarily a side-to-side swing, much like a swimming fish.

Broad-beamed, light spoons will have the most action at a given rate of retrieve. They'll also work close to the surface. Loosely translated into practical fishing situations, this means light spoons are most effective in lakes and sluggish streams. Heavy spoons work best when you want to get down deep or are fishing in fast-moving rivers.

· Spinners are basically a shaft around which revolves a flashing blade. They too, usually sport one treble hook, to which may be attached further persuasion in the form of feathers, hair, or a piece of bait. There are some performance parallels between spoons and spinners: the lighter the blade, the more action and less depth you can expect. However, one other factor enters the picture: blade width. Wide blades deliver a lot of action at very slow speeds, a combination that proves irresistible to many species of lake dwellers. Lures that fall into this category are characterized by the Mepps and Panther Martin. However, in fast water, these wide blades don't seem to be able to keep up with themselves, and ride either just under the surface or skip across the top.

Wisconsin anglers catch many fine walleyes while using spinning tackle in their abundant lakes. A slow moving bottom feeder, the walleye will readily strike a spinner and worm combination.

There are literally hundreds of different models of spinners available to the spincaster. Tiny models are often used with either a minnow or worm. The larger ones, dressed with either squirrel hair, feathers, or bucktail, are used alone.

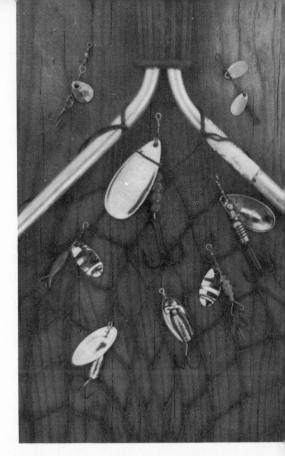

Daybreak is an excellent time to fish, and you can well appreciate that these Arizona anglers rose early to be on the water just as the sun came over the mountains. Bass and many other species are especially active at this time.

The solution to this problem is the narrow *willow-blade spinner*, characterized by brands like the Doty Raider. These narrow blades require quite a bit of water pressure to set them in motion, and even when they're whirling, don't set up much resistance, so they run deep. This also makes them an effective choice for the lake fisherman who wants to troll a spinner close to bottom.

· Plugs are solid-bodied lures incorporating several treble hooks. They're designed to imitate a host of aquatic-oriented fish foods that run the gamut from simple fare like minnows, crawdads, and frogs to exotic meals of mice and baby ducklings.

Floating plugs imitate land creatures that have fallen into the water or aquatic creatures that live near the surface—usually frogs or wounded minnows. They slurp, burble, and pop their way along, attracting notice as much by sound and surface disturbance as movement. I've found that the most agitated, irritating, noisy malcontents work the best.

Swimming plugs work under water. Their action, and the depth at which they work, is largely determined by a lip that digs into the water, rather than by their inherent weight.

The more action a swimming plug has, the better it will produce. A particularly pleasant variety is the swimming plug that will float to the surface. Not only will it be able to double as a surface lure, but it is also less prone to snag on the bottom, and it sells on the average for about two dollars. That's something of a consideration.

Some plugs boast offbeat appeal: steel balls inside them that rattle, designs that set off strange sounds underwater, even hollow insides that can be filled with Alka-Seltzer or fish meal for added attraction. I've found that while these gimmicks do add to a lure's appeal, the ultimate test should be action and lots of it. When you establish that action first, any further persuaders in a plug will be like frosting on a cake.

· Jigs are usually a single-hook lure with a heavy, lead head and a bushy tail made of feathers, bucktail, or synthetic fiber. Their success all stems from the rate at which they sink; when jigging, you impart an up-down, up-down action to the lure. You'll feel more hits and set more hooks if that jig falls quickly. The fall is a time of slack line; when a fish hits, you seldom know it, as he quickly drops the lure. By minimizing the period of fall through a fast-sinking jig, you'll maximize your success.

Another feature to look for are jigs with needle-point hooks. The sharper your hook, the easier it is to set. Since you're working with just one hook, and often will feel a strike when it's inconvenient or awkward to set (at the top end of an upstroke, for instance), an extra-keen point will help correct the disadvantage.

One variety of jig deserves special mention: rather than being a fanciful combination of lead and hair, this one looks just like a fish. It's

Plugs are a favored lure of spin-fishermen everywhere. Pictured here is a typical assortment that you should always include in your kit, including poppers, surface swimmers, deep divers, wobble plugs and intermediate runners.

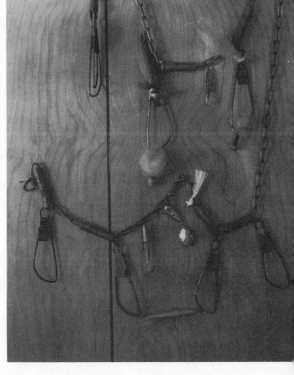

Tiny jigs aren't impressive-looking lures, but they give spin-fishermen many hours of action with crappie, yellow and white perch, white bass, and the many members of the sunfish clan.

designed so the point of line attachment occurs on the top-center of the pluglike lure and the hooks bristle out fore and aft, with a treble dangling from the bottom center. It's worked just like a jig, and is extremely effective.

· Rubber worms are a bit tricky: you just don't know what to do with them. Technically, they're a lure, but they're fished like bait, and bass chew on them like bait.

Lure, bait or whatever, bass certainly are suckers for them, and they come in some of the wildest colors this side of a psychedelic experience.

Sedate black is something of a standby, but purple—with white polka-dots yet—runs a close second in popularity. Sickly green has also caught its share of big fish. As a matter of fact, about the only color I've never had any luck on is natural worm pink!

Sizing runs from 6 inches to a foot long. I lean toward the little ones since they'll interest small as well as big fish.

The texture of the rubber seems to have something to do with it too. Rubber that feels wet or at least unpleasantly sticky to the touch, and is soft when squeezed, seems to work best. This material usually has a fairly shiny surface.

Design features to look for are a flat underside, and slim, wiggly tail. Broad flip-tails are popular when you plan to be jigging the worm.

Bait

Bait and the ability to present it naturally is one area where spinning really shines. Conventional reels need lots of weight to cast a bait, des-troying much of its appeal. The false-casting required of a fly rod will pop off most naturals, and even if it doesn't, it will never achieve the distance a spinning rig can.

But baits present something of a problem all their own. The kinds are myriad, but except for worms and occasionally minnows, you can't drop down to the local tackleshop and pluck a fish-tempting selection of the stuff from a card. For that reason, the rundown on baits you can use in-cludes ways you can come by them in the first place.

· Worms are easily the most commonly used of all the naturals. They come in two sizes: nightcrawlers and angleworms.

Nightcrawlers are inhabitants of the northern half of the country. They're big, up to 8 inches long, and logically enough, like to crawl around the grass at night. To catch nightcrawlers, use a flashlight on a well-cropped lawn on a rainy night. Be quick; once they have a hint you're nearby, they'll slip into their holes like greased lightning.

Angleworms are common nationwide. They grow up to six inches long, but generally are more slender than night crawlers. You'll have to dig for this bait. Look for them in moist spots of rich soil; compost heaps and barnyard dung piles are also productive.

When you get a mess of worms, they'll die quickly if they're not kept cool in a loose, moist bedding. Cut grass is good, so are coffee grounds, and commercial worm-bedding is tops. Don't keep them in pure dirt; they'll suffocate.

· Minnows rate as the second most popular bait. If it's legal in your state, the easiest way to come by them is seine netting. Minnow traps

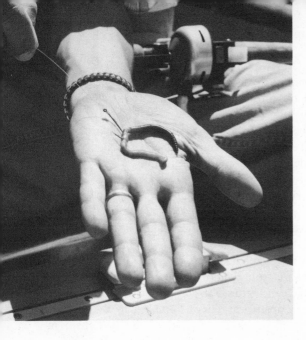

The common earthworm at one time or another will account for any fish that swims in fresh water. It's easily obtained in all our states and certainly rates as our most popular fresh water bait. Hook it so that it will drift along naturally, as pictured here.

Shirley McDowell landed this fine walleye from an Ontario lake while slowly trolling a live minnow along the bottom with spinning tackle. Walleyes will often ignore lures and the only way you can score is via natural baits.

are second choice. They amount to a thin-screened box with a conical entry-way. Bait them with bread or cornmeal. They'll find their way in but won't get out.

In a pinch minnows can be caught on a hook: bait a number 16 with a doughball. Some slow-movers like the sculpin can be scooped out on the run with a three-foot wide chunk of window screening.

To keep them alive, minnows must be kept cool, and their water must be well-aerated. Small battery-powered pumps are available to get this job done.

· Aquatic insects like mayfly nymphs, stonefly nymphs, and dobson fly nymphs are great bait for trout and smallmouth bass. Although they live in lakes, they're easiest to catch in a stream.

Build a small net 3 feet square from window screening. Attach a 4-foot handle on each side of the screen. Stretch it across a current and have a fishing partner dislodge rocks upstream. They'll tumble into the net.

Aquatics can be kept alive if you keep them cool and bed them in river moss.

· Terrestrial insects like grasshoppers and crickets can be caught by hand if you can find them on a cool morning. Cool temperatures make them sluggish. If you're chasing them down during midday, make a net out of old nylon stockings. Their sharp spines hang up in the nylon, and they're held prisoner.

Terrestrials can be kept in a jar. Stick a few leaves in with them to make them feel at home.

· Frogs of any size are suckers for a tiny fly. Just dangle one in front of their nose, and that swordlike tongue will dart out and gobble it down every time. It's almost more fun than fishing! Frogs need no more than to be wet to stay alive.

· Fish-flesh baits; pike-belly, perch-belly and sucker meat obviously require that you catch their owner first. They're usually prepared in one of two ways: cut in a long triangle, or rectangle. The rectangle has a notch cut in one end to impart a double-tail effect.

Action seems to be as important to a fish striking a piece of his neighbor as taste, so make sure the strip you cut is thin in depth. This will allow it more flutter and flash.

· Dough baits are popular with carp and catfishermen. To make the basic dough bait, just add enough water to flour to make a dough roughly the consistency of soft putty. Then let creativity take over. The thinking here is that these fish find their food by smell more than anything else, so some pretty smelly additives are frequently employed. Speaking from my own past experience, I can remember raiding my dad's blackberry brandy, my mom's cooking vanilla, and the local butcher shop for blood. Less pleasant but supposedly supereffective additives I've run across are

When trolling a minnow, hook it lightly through the lips, so that it may continue to swim naturally as you troll. You can add to its appeal by using, ahead of the minnow, one or two small spinners that will flash enticingly in the depths.

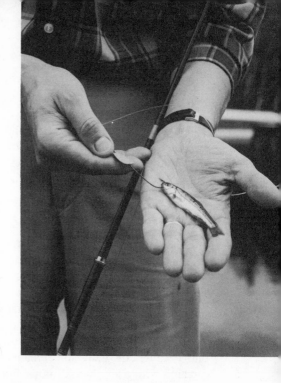

Frogs are a favorite bait of largemouth bass fishermen. They may be fished on a harness or hooked through the lips. Moments after this photo was taken this frog was taken by a 3-pound largemouth in Florida's Kissimmee River.

rotten chicken entrails; cheeses that smell bad enough to begin with, having been aged for a month in the hot sun; and well-cured chunks of liver.

Remember, at least in terms of the natural baits, that if the creature in question isn't present in and around the water you're fishing, chances are he won't amount to a very good bait. For example, I've never had much luck fishing dried grasshoppers in January, or on a more subtle level, worms during a long, dry hot spell.

Floats

Floats come in three varieties: snap-on, thread-on, and tie-on. The snap-on—round, bright, and with a plunger that releases a line lock—is the most convenient to use, due to its quick-change feature.

Line goes through the center of a thread-on float and is locked in place by a wedge. With some adaptive rigging, this float works great for fishing from top when you want your bait to go deep.

Floats you have to tie into fore and aft are a pain in the neck to rig, but because of their bullet-shaped design, they work better in conjunction with a fly than all other floats.

All these floats are available with a plugged port that allows the addition of water for casting weight, and for achieving near-neutral buoyancy. Both features are an asset to the spin-fisherman.

And all these floats do their individual jobs so well that I keep one of each kind in my tacklebox.

A good rig for youngsters is a float rig to suspend their bait at a desired level. The float keeps the bait just above weeds, rocks, or other debris where cruising fish can readily spot it.

SUPPLEMENTAL EQUIPMENT

A rod, reel, hook, and line is all you need to catch a fish, but you can make the job easier and become a more effective fisherman by employing some of the many aids available to the modern angler.

Boots

Boots of the wading variety lead off the list. They give you the freedom to step from shore and literally get in the middle of the action. With them, you can reach pools, pockets, and shorelines off-limits to the bank-bound angler and approach a feeding fish from the most effective position.

Wading boots come in two types: hip waders that reach close to your beltline and chest waders that come close to your armpits. Hip boots are lighter and cooler—a bit more bearable if you do a lot of walking in warm weather. They are limited in range; everytime I don them I regularly run into a situation where two more paces would have me just where I want to go, but with water lapping over my boot tops.

Although I own both types, I'd estimate I use chest waders 80 percent of the time. While they are hot and a bit heavy, you don't notice it when you're in the water. And even when I cuss them during a two-mile hike, five minutes in the water has me blessing them because of the freedom they afford.

Plan on spending at least $25 for chest waders, $10 for hip waders. Unless you know you're getting a real bargain, boots cheaper than this are bound to tear like an old sheet or crack and become porous after one season.

The best material is rubber with a canvas backing or, a more recent development, synthetic cloth with a layer of rubber sandwiched between the cloth and the backing. Both methods of construction resist snags and rips and, if stored in a cool, dry place, won't crack or deteriorate. Look for boots with reinforcement at the crotch and kneecap and in the foot. Most of the wear is at these points.

One welcome addition to the basic boot is felt soles. These cling to slick underwater rocks. Without them the sensation is a bit like walking on greased cannonballs.

If you do a lot of walking however, built-in felt soles will wear quickly. A simple solution is to buy slick-bottomed boots, and glue carpet to the soles with shoemaker's cement. Felt soles that lace on over your boot are also available commercially.

The shore-based angler often wears a wading vest, in which he can comfortably carry all the items he'll need, including hooks, floats, sinkers, flies, lures, insect repellent, an extra spool of line, and a fish stringer.

Fishing Vests

Fishing vests were originally designed for fly-fishing, but they serve the spin-fisherman admirably. When you do plenty of walking and wading, as opposed to fishing from a boat, you can carry all the gear you'll need on your back, leaving both hands free for fishing.

Vests that are cut short—they don't fall below the chest—are designed for the man with chest waders. Those that end around the waist are for hip-boot wearers.

Whatever style suits you, pick the product with the most pockets. It's a sure bet you'll have the gear to fill them. By judiciously selecting the tackle you'll be packing, it's quite easy to carry a more than basic selection of bait, artificial, and even fly-fishing spin gear. In short, a well-stocked fishing vest means you'll be prepared for any situation that arises on lake or stream.

Creels, Stringers, and Things That Hold Fish

In general, the creel is for the walking angler, the stringer for the boatman.

The most popular modern creels are canvas and rubber affairs, with a spring-loaded closure. When choosing a creel, remember that they must cool by evaporation. An unventilated plastic or rubber bag is a sure way to ruin a catch in a hurry.

Chain-type stringers carry my general stamp of approval. They keep fish from tangling with, or piling on top of, one another and thereby keep them alive longer.

The one exception I do make is with pike. These fish can twist, get a purchase on the chain, and snap open the clasps like a safety pin. On one pike-fishing trip in northeastern Montana, I lost a total of eight 6-pound-plus pike in three successive nights. I was sure someone was robbing my stringer, but hadn't seen a soul on vast Fort Peck Lake since arriving. I finally did run into another fisherman and he straightened me out. I've been using soft plastic stringers on pike ever since and have yet to have one "robbed."

Once your fishing is over, you should have some means to keep your catch cool between the water and your kitchen. Ice-packed coolers are one way, but in lieu of the bother of bringing a cooler and then finding ice, I just tote along a few gunny sacks. Put your fish in these, wet them down well, and they'll cool by evaporation.

Nets

Nets are important to the wading fisherman if he finds himself in situations where he can't beach his catch. They're a virtual necessity for the boating angler.

The best nets for wading are the collapsibles. They bend and fold to fist-size and are carried in a case. That way they don't snag on brush while you're fishing. When you need them, they automatically blossom into a broad-lipped pocket in the twinkling of an eye.

Boatmen need a long-handled net, but that long handle makes for some stowage problems when the net's not in use. For this reason I prefer a net with a telescoping handle. It's easy to store and quick to stretch out.

Any net you buy, be you a boatman or bank fisherman, should float. And the mesh should be woven from hard, synthetic plastic. This stuff is the only net material that won't snag a hook, a quality you'll immediately appreciate if you've ever put in time removing a three-trebled plug from a twisted cotton net.

A Tacklebox

A tacklebok is a wise investment whether you're a vested bank fisherman or unvested boatman. It provides a place for all your gear, and by virtue of its many compartments, some semblance of organization in an area that could easily be a chaos.

The best tackleboxes are made of high-impact plastic. These have a long life, and won't rust or corrode. One feature to demand is an automatic-lock arrangement which keeps the box from opening and spilling its contents all over the landscape, should you pick up the box unlatched.

Experience has proven that in fishing, at least, your equipment has a way of expanding to fill up all available space. So buy your box big. Mine measures 12 by 12 by 24 inches, with a lid that opens in the middle to reveal three folding trays on each side. When I bought it, I thought it was just the ticket to incorporate the contents of my two smaller tackleboxes.

At first, it was, but somehow, my equipment seemed to multiply. I bought a second large tacklebox within a month.

A Lure Retriever

A lure retriever helps when expensive plugs come in contact with brush, logs, rocks, or weeds as they eventually do. At two to three dollars a crack, it's a painful experience to lose a plug.

Lure retrievers amount to a heavy weight and tangle of chain attached to a stout nylon rope. The device snaps onto your line, and follows the line to the snag. Either the sock of the weight knocks the lure free, or hooks get entangled in the chain and the lure can be wrestled to the surface at the cost of a bent hook or two.

While these things don't *always* work, they've worked enough for me to have paid the price of their purchase many times over.

Boats

Boats are an area any serious fisherman is bound to eventually consider, and probably enter. Face it, there's no better platform from which to fish.

A topic this broad deserves a book, not a few paragraphs, but at least in terms of the average spin-fisherman, here are a few helpful hints:

Choose a boat first for lightness. By virtue of the fact that your first love is fishing, not boating, you'll probably do a lot of moving around from place to place with your craft. An aluminum cartopper 100 pounds or less is great for this.

Next, consider stability. You're not looking for wilderness or white-water ability, just for something that will keep you dry and on a comfortable keel while you float around and cast. This characteristic is most prominent with flat-bottomed craft.

Capacity should be a minimum of two anglers, with not much reason to demand a boat that can handle more than three. Even three anglers casting, trolling, or just bobber-fishing get in each others' way.

Admittedly, I'm prejudiced, because that description fits to a T the craft I currently own. It's a 14-foot, 85-pound aluminum jonboat that draws virtually no water. And I've used it to fish South Carolina's weedy bass lakes, to float Montana's Madison River, and on countless small lakes north and south. It's proven an admirable and able fishing companion in all but extreme cases of rough chop and white water.

Motors

Motors for the fisherman should be chosen with one function in mind: trolling. If an outboard can't be throttled down to a turtle-crawling whisper, you won't be able to cash in on the days when fish want their meals presented slow and easy. And those days are more frequent than most anglers imagine.

Once you're satisfied your boat will perform at a speed that approximates a slow drift, then shoot for power.

It's a pleasant advantage to have a boat that moves right along and gets you where you want to go in a hurry, so if you can find a high-horsepower engine that both sculls and scoots, buy it. But I doubt such an engine exists, so you'll probably end up with a motor of 4½ to 7½ horsepower.

Electric motors are a popular auxiliary with bass-buggers, and are the only motors allowed on some reservoirs and small lakes. Horsepower in these ranges from ¼ to 1, and they run for up to six hours, powered by a car battery.

Assuming you'll be using an electric for fishing, not transportation, low horsepower is fine and will give you the longest time span of operation. One feature to opt for is remote control. A foot pedal that controls both speed and direction, leaving both hands free to fish.

Fish Locators

Fish locators are electronic devices used in connection with a boat. Essentially a small, compact sonar unit, their real advantage isn't in spotting fish (most species lie too close to the bottom) but in the information they provide about the bottom. Once you learn how to interpret these gadgets, you not only can locate dropoffs, bars, and brush piles, but can also determine if a bottom is rock, mud, weed, or whatever.

By applying this information to species' habits and preferences, you'll have a very good idea of where concentrations of fish will be holed up.

Hemostats and Nail Clippers

Hemostats and nail clippers are two handy items to have dangling from your vest or stashed in your tacklebox.

Hemostats are surgical pliers that will grip the tiniest hook buried deep in a big fish's throat, saving wear and tear on both the fish and your fingers.

Nail clippers make knot-trimming and line-cutting neater and easier.

An electronic fish locator helped this pleased Ohio angler find the edge of the structure where this largemouth bass and some of its friends had been feeding. A plastic worm proved the bass' downfall.

While floating an Idaho river, this angler vacated his john boat and cast to a gravel bar where he hooked this fine rainbow trout. This is a crucial time in landing a fish; your drag should always be set light enough to permit the fish to take line should he make a last determined run.

2

FRESH-WATER
SPINNING
TECHNIQUES

There's a famous calendar picture that's made a million anglers crack a smile. It's a painting of a tweedy-looking trout fisherman with an expensive array of gear, sadly displaying an 8-inch brookie. The reason for his frustration is standing next to him: a freckle-faced farm boy with a cane pole and a stringer of fish that would choke a pelican.

The picture has its pros and cons. Setting the charm of the theme aside, I'd find it awfully hard to believe that an experienced fisherman with modern gear could ever be outfished by a kid with a cane pole. On the other side of the coin, if the older angler is a neophyte fresh from the tackleshop, the picture makes good sense.

The farm boy has fished all his life with a cane pole; he knows his equipment and how to use it. Chances are he lives near that stream and fishes it often; he knows where the holes are, when the fish will be feeding, what to use for bait, and how to present it naturally. Given that kind of situation, it's eminently possible for a cane pole to outproduce the most sophisticated fishing equipment money can buy.

Tackle doesn't make the fisherman. While it's true that good equipment is an important intermediary, how to use it—technique—is and always will be the telling factor in fishing success.

RIGGING TERMINAL TACKLE

Terminal tackle and how you tie it together has a lot to do with your bait or lure's performance and its appeal. But before we get into the rigging tricks that encourage fish to hit, let's first make sure your offering holds together under angling pressure.

Knots

Knots are the weakest link in your hook-line-reel-rod chain. Monofilament is quite different stuff from other line material, and many conventional fishing knots will either slip or self-cut when applied to mono.

Although no knot offers 100 percent line strength, one terminal knot comes close to 95 percent. Chances are you'll be using this knot 95 percent of the time too. It's called the double improved clinch knot.

To tie it, measure off 18 inches of line. Double that line over so you have two parallel strands of mono 9 inches long.

The principle behind the use of doubled line isn't what at first seems obvious. The second strand of mono only acts as a cushion and a deterrent to critically sharp bends at the knot. So think of this double strand of line as if it were one when you're tying on. You'll avoid quite a few complications.

To connect your line to the eye of a hook, pass the working end of the line—the point where it doubles around—through the hook-eye *twice*. Draw it back so it's even with the single loose end. This should fall around 4½ inches away from the hook-eye.

Take five turns with the working end around the two strands of line that have not passed through the hook-eye.

There will be a hole at the starting point of the five twists, where the line first passed through the hook-eye. Double back and thread the working end through that hole.

You will note that another loop or hole has now been created. It begins where your twists end, runs back parallel to them, and ends where the double line passes in front of the hook-eye. Slip the working end through this hole.

Draw all ends up tight by pulling simultaneously on hook and line, then on every strand of mono. On all strands but the one connected to your reel, you can use pliers or your teeth for a grip. On the connecting line use only your hands so you don't bruise the mono.

Clip all ends close to the knot, making sure you don't inadvertently cut your line.

Use this knot whenever you're tying onto a lure, hook, sinker, or snapswivel. Since it slides like a hangman's knot, use it also to anchor new line to an empty spool. This covers virtually all situations but one, tieing line to line.

If you've mastered the clinch knot, this tie, called a blood knot, should be easy.

Take the lines to be joined, and overlap them 6 inches. At the center of the lap, 3 inches from either loose end, insert a twig, nail, or finger between them. Twist each loose end five times around the line it's lapping. Bring each loose end back through the hole made by the twig. Tighten up, clip ends close, and you've got it.

One useful variation on this knot is for tieing extremely stout leader material to light spinning line. Because the heavy line isn't as supple as the light line, it doesn't nest snugly and tends to slip. To overcome this problem, double only the light line back over itself, as in the clinch knot. Tie the blood knot just as before.

The blood knot is best for tying onto monofilament leaders and shock cords. While I've seen many fishermen use the blood knot to splice on 50 yards or so of fresh line, I'm solidly against it.

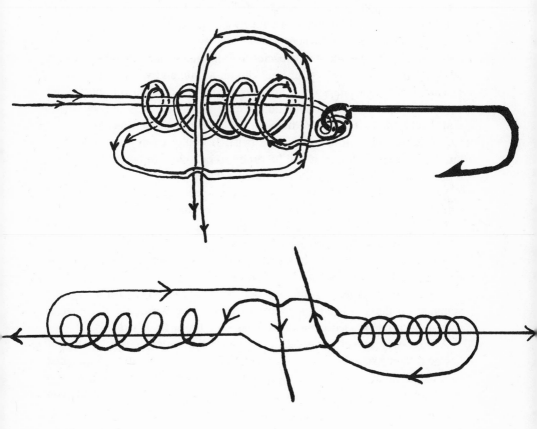

For one thing, any knot looses strength with age. Hook onto some big, old soaker a week after you've made the splice and you can virtually say good-bye if he peels line off up to or beyond the knot.

A more frequent problem will be that the knot will catch line as it spins off your spool and do some funny things to a cast. At worst, the knot will hang up in a line on the move, and peel off several turns of under-line. Should this happen, figure on five minutes minimum to un-snarl the mess—if it can be undone at all.

The blood and clinch knots give you the greatest integral strength when used with mono, but don't assume they're indestructible. Not only will they weaken with age, but also after the repeated strain of fighting a fish, pulling free from a snag or just normal casting. You'd be wise to test them often, and get in the habit of breaking and retying every time real pressure has been put on the knot.

Rigging the Artificial

Because monofilament is largely invisible under water, leaders aren't used as frequently in spinning as with fly or bait-casting. A steel or heavy mono leader is advisable when you're deep-trolling, jigging around sharp rocks, or after a sharp-toothed species like the pikes, but generally you just tie a snapswivel directly to your line, clip on a lure, and you're ready to go.

That basic rig—snapswivel and hardware—is the most popular and consistently productive combination. There are however, some variations that deserve note. They often turn the trick when fish seem uncooperative.

· Adding weight to a lure is one twist. If you're casting a light, flashy lure in any kind of water, it will be prone to ride close to the surface. Even a heavy lure will ride high in fast-moving water.

Since the majority of a gamefish's time is spent hugging bottom, adding extra weight at least means you'll get closer to him.

The added weight could be a keel sinker, but I prefer the rubber-core type since they can be changed quickly and don't have to be tied on. Twist the sinker right on your line, between 9 and 12 inches from your lure. A weight closer to your lure than this cuts down on action.

· Three-way rigging is another way to get deep. This trick is quite common on the steelhead and salmon rivers of the West, and I've used it with quite a bit of success in deep holes on eastern trout streams.

A three-way swivel is needed, the smaller the better. The end of your line goes to one swivel eye, a foot or better of mono leader with lure attached to another, and a third mono leader tied to a weight to the other. The length of your sinker leader is dependent upon the depth at which you want your lure to work. The best sinker here is the pencil lead, since it resists snagging.

A useful variation on this rig is to tie your lead on with line lighter than that on your reel. That way, should the lead snag up, you lose only it and not the entire terminal rig.

· The teaser method of rigging amounts to using two lures at once. At its simplest, this arrangement is nothing more than a supplemental hookless spinner, preceding a lure, fly or bait.

More complex variations include a fly tied 6 inches above a lure or jig. This simulates a small baitfish chasing down a meal. A trailer rig finds the secondary lure following behind. This is usually done with a 6- to 12-inch leader, tied to the rearmost hook ring on a plug or spoon.

One particularly interesting application of this multilure is in using it to fish for two species at once. For example, a topwater bass plug can be fished in conjunction with a fly for panfish. On Florida's St. John's River, a common tactic is to fish for bass with an underwater plug that trails a small dart. The plug catches the bass, the dart, shad.

Rigging Naturals

Rigging naturals is a matter of putting together a hook-line-sinker combination that will present your bait in its most natural light.

Hooks

Hooks play an important part. Size them according to the bait, not the quarry. A big, juicy nightcrawler fits a number-8 baitholder like a glove. A small mayfly nymph requires sizing around number 14. If you're fishing a big sucker minnow for pike, a 2/0 will probably be in order.

Basing your hooks on bait size offers practical advantages. Since a fish that picks up a natural will usually chew for a while, a hook larger than the object he's mouthing might cause him to spit it out.

Appearance is another consideration. A bait with a pound of bare steel in plain sight is bound to work against you. That protruding point is also prone to snag up.

On the other end of the scale it's not wise to have a hook so small it disappears into the bait entirely. The point of the hook should just emerge from the bait; it's more likely to penetrate a fish's mouth that way.

Weights

Weights work best when they're on the light side—just heavy enough to give you some reach, or hold you close to or on bottom. Too heavy a weight will cost you fish; they'll either prevent your sensing a bite or spook a nibbling fish or put up so much resistance that you won't be able to set the hook.

There are two basic methods of rigging a hook and weight. The standard still-fishing rig amounts to a weight at the end of your line, with a hook on a leader 6 to 12 inches above it. The beauty of this rigging is that a fish can transmit a nibble to you without first having to move the weight. This arrangement is best when put together with the help of a three-way swivel and is employed when you want your bait to remain immobile.

Drift style fishing, which includes all presentations that find a sunken bait on the move, requires a rig with the sinker above the hook and on the same line. In this arrangement the bait flutters freely behind the weight, and does not foul around your line, as frequently happens with a still-fishing rig.

There are of course, many variations on the basic design of these rigs. Some you might find useful include:

· Spreaders for still-fishing. This amounts to a rigid arm that stands at right angles to your line. Tie a hook and leader to the arm and it helps keep your bait from becoming entangled with your line.

· Floatants that float your bait up off the bottom. The addition of a small piece of marshmallow or a cork will do this. Worms can be "blown"— injected with air by way of a hypodermic needle, or commercial worm-blower. This trick is especially useful for getting a bait above obscuring lake-bottom weeds (see *Spinning On a Lake*, page 90).

· Slip sinkers, used both for drift- or still-fishing. A hook is tied to a 2-foot leader, the leader to a swivel. A sliding egg sinker is threaded on your spinning line, then the line tied to the swivel. The swivel keeps the sinker from sliding down to your hook. When a fish picks up the bait, he can run free on a slack line without having to drag a hunk of lead around.

· Staggered weighting. When drift-fishing a river from shore—allowing your bait to be carried by the current—a single blob of lead will snag more often than several small chunks of equal total weight, spaced 2 to 4 inches apart.

Baits

Baits and where you hook them are just as important as your hook-sinker arrangement. For example, if you're using crawfish, you should run the point of your hook through the tail. These creatures always move backwards, so when you retrieve, your bait will have a more natural appearance. Even when still-fishing, a hooked tail has its advantages; piercing the head or thorax region of a live crawdad will kill him quickly.

Other commonly used baits have similar areas where its best to bury your hook:

· Insects, such as grasshoppers, crickets, hellgrammites, and mayfly nymphs, should have the point of the hook driven into their thorax from the direction of the abdomen. The thorax is their shell-hard segment lying about midbody. While this doesn't do their health any good, it's about the only way you'll get them to stay on a hook without painstaking tieing jobs.

· Minnows can be hooked in the lip, tail or back. Soft-spined minnows, fished without a float, should be hooked in the lip. This keeps them alive the longest. Stickle-spined minnows like perch and sculpin should be hooked in the tail. Gamefish get them headfirst. Minnows dangled from a float should be hooked through the back. Make sure to run the point through the flesh *above* the backbone, or they'll die quickly. Dead minnows are best fished with a needle-type hook sewn through their body.

· Worms should·be hooked once through their light-colored collar. If you can't find a collar, hook them a third of their length from their head. If you can't find their head, make an educated guess; you should be right half the time!

Threading a worm around and around the shank of a hook helps prevent bait-stealing, but unless that's a recurrent problem, don't do it. A worm with seven right angles hardly looks natural.

· Frogs and salamanders stay alive the longest hooked through the lip. This also makes them look most natural underway. Hook harnesses are made for these critters, but they show an awful lot of bare steel.

· Meat baits like beef, pike-belly, and sucker meat work best cut in a tapered strip. Place the hook at the thick end of the taper.

Rigging a float

Rigging a float to your line is usually done in one of three ways. Either the line is threaded through the center of the float and a wedge inserted to lock the line in place, or the line is tied to one side of the float and a leader to the other, or the float simply snaps on.

The latter is the simplest, though it presents a few problems. First, mono is slippery and often slides in the snap. To overcome this tendency, take a few turns of line around the extended snap before returning it to the closed position.

The buoyancy of these floats also bothers me; ideally, a float should be almost as heavy as the water. That way, when a fish yanks, there isn't too much resistance up there yanking back. You can accomplish this effect by adding water to a float if it has this feature. If not, add a rubber-core sinker to the line just below the float. In that position, it won't hinder a free-swimming bait. You'll also be able to make a longer cast.

Occasionally, a weight close to the bait can be useful, most notably when you want to get it down past surface-feeding rough or small fish in a hurry.

The average float can't be fished with a leader longer than your rod. You can't cast both bobber and bait effectively. You can rig a deep-fishing float however, handy for working close to bottom when that bottom is a nightmare of snags.

Use the type of float designed to hold your line in place by way of a wedge, but don't insert the wedge. Let the float slide free on your line like a slip sinker.

Place a light weight 6 inches above your hook. This weight helps to sink your bait and prevents the float from snugging up against your hook.

Next, measure off the desired depth of line. At that point, tie a tight knot above the float with a rubber band, and clip ends close. The knot should be large enough so it doesn't slide through the hole in the float.

Reel in slack to within 6 inches of the float and cast. When it hits the water, the weight will carry your line through the float until it's stopped by the rubber band.

Fishing artificials with a bobber is also a useful technique. There will be times when you want a lure to work quite close to the top.

The best floats for this particular job are bullet-shaped and can be filled with water for extra weight. Fill them to the point where they'll barely sink. When you retrieve them, they'll ride just under the surface, keeping your lure high, but creating virtually no disturbance on top.

Rigging Rubber Worms

Rigging rubber worms requires that you first thread them on a hook. Use long-shanked hooks in the number 2 to 1/0 category and carry a

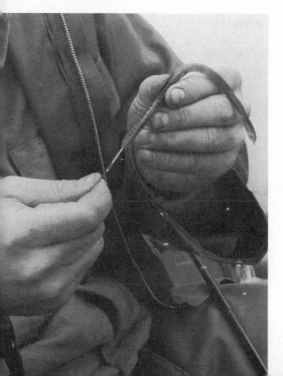

There are many ways of rigging a plastic worm. Some anglers use a needle and run a piece of monofilament through the worm, and then tie on their hook, pulling the hook back into the worm. This keeps the worm well back in the hook.

long upholstery needle with you. Knot a 2-foot leader to the eye of the hook and thread it through the needle. Lay the hook so the eye is directly under the front tip of the worm, and note where the bend of the hook begins in relation to the worm. Insert the needle at this point and push it through the center of the worm toward the head. Pull it and the leader through. The hook shank will follow the leader with some pulling and pushing. The bend of the hook should protrude from under the flat side of the worm if this feature is cast into the rubber. If you want to fish these worms with a weight, use a sliding sinker rig. If you plan to work them weightless, join line to leader with a blood knot.

Rubber worming has reached a point in popularity where rigging the things is a craft unto itself. Although there are infinite twists to putting them together, two major variations I've found useful include:

· Gang hooks, usually two, with the second threaded into the last third of the tail. This is accomplished by first threading the rearward hook with a leader attached through the worm, then threading the forward hook through without a leader. Tie the leader from the second hook to the eye of the first with the following knot.

Pass the leader through the eye of the hook and draw it tight. With a pencil or nail parallel to the shank, take five turns of line back from the eye.

Pass the end of the leader through the turns (between line and shank) and back through the eye.

Carefully remove the nail and draw the leader up tight.

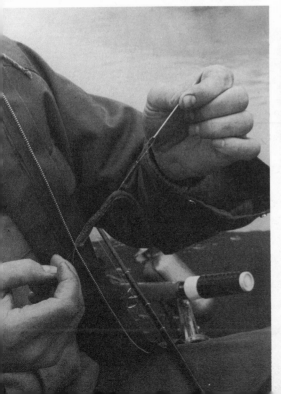
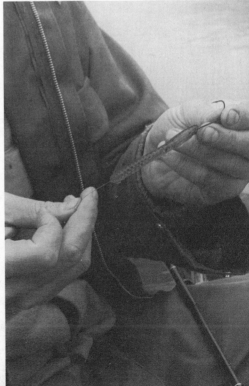

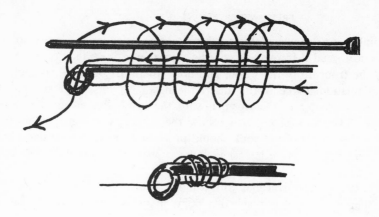

· Snag-proofing a rubber worm is often a necessity, since big bass love to hang around weeds and brush. You can do this by rigging up with a weedless hook or by reversing a normal hook.

This operation requires that you rig your worm so the point of your hook angles toward the belly of the worm. Bury the point up to the barb, and you've got a snagless, weedless worm.

CASTING

Although specialized casts go by many names, there are only two types of spin-casts. All the rest are variations on the theme.

Here Norman Strung demonstrates the popular snap cast used by many spin-fishermen. Beginning with the rod pointed where you wish to cast, sweep it back over your shoulder and then snap it forward, releasing the line and sending the lure to its target.

The Snap Cast

The snap cast is the most popular and is accomplished in much the same way as cracking a whip. This cast depends largely on wrist action and makes full use of the recoil power of the rod.

Face your target and point your rod tip in its direction. The rod should angle forward anywhere from 45 to 60 degrees from parallel with your body, and your lure should dangle from 4 to 8 inches away from your rod tip.

Make a false back-cast that puts a deep reverse bend in your shaft.

Snap the rod forward sharply. As it recoils, you'll note the shaft imparts extra velocity to the lure.

Release when your rod returns to its approximate starting position.

The physical nature of this cast makes it the mate of fast-taper rods and lures that balance perfectly with shaft and line weight. Soft baits or overweight lures will pop free under the tremendous strain.

The Soft Cast

The soft cast launches its payload in something of an opposite manner; like a catapult rather than a whip. This casting technique works best with a slow rod and begins not with a snap, but with a steady building of velocity.

At the start of the cast, lure and rod-tip angle approximately 45 degrees behind you. Make a habit of checking over your shoulder; your bait

When using delicate baits such as minnows, worms, frogs or other natural baits, a soft cast is required. Here Norman Strung begins with the rod behind him and gently sweeps the rod forward, following through as the bait sails to the target softly, and thus preventing it from being ripped from the hook.

shouldn't be swinging, and it should dangle from 12 to 18 inches of line. Where there is overhead brush, use this position to make sure you won't collide with a branch on the forward stroke.

Start the cast slowly and gradually increase its velocity. Initially, your forearm does all the work, then as your rod tip approaches the point of release, your wrist should spring into action, adding an extra flick of speed.

The execution of a soft cast is much like the forward cast of a fly rod. It's useful because its slow buildup of power allows for plenty of reach, but won't snap off a delicate bait or heavy lure. This is also the cast to employ when you've got two weights in different positions on your line: a float and bait, or lure with an extra weight. A soft cast keeps the two weights from cartwheeling in the air and the hooks from fouling with line.

Distance and Accuracy

Distance and accuracy are two arts a caster must master. In the distance department, how your equipment is put together plays an important part. A full spool of line, large butt guide, and long rod all lend themselves to reach. A light line does too; there's less weight and friction to overcome with 4-pound test than 8.

· Line release must occur the split second your rod straightens out. At this time, the moving weight is floating free between your slowing rod tip and the end of your finger-held line. Release before this time doesn't utilize the full power of the rod. Release after this time slows the lure down since it must briefly drag your rod tip along with it.

· Loft is another important component of a long cast. As a weight sails through the air, it's pulled down by the force of gravity. Release a cast weight when your rod shaft is roughly parallel to the surface of the water, and gravity will have it striking the water long before it's reached its greatest potential distance. The idea then, is to release when your rod reaches an angle that will arc your lure up and out and keep it from striking the water until it's used up all energy by dragging line from your spool. Theoretically this means release when your rod hits 45 degrees.

This loft rule doesn't apply on windy days. Perfect loft on such a day doesn't achieve ultimate distance. Wind resistance on the bellied line is the culprit. In general, the harder the wind blows, the closer to parallel with level your rod shaft should be at the point of release.

How do you tell if your timing, both of release and loft, is on? The way a lure hits the water is one sign. If it makes a big splash, or skitters across the surface, you're wasting energy that could give you more distance. Try releasing earlier.

If you find your lure sailing straight up in the air, entering the water at a near 90-degree angle, and must take in a huge belly of slack line before your lure starts to move, try holding your release longer.

When your lure angles well above the water in a graceful arc, then hits with a clean *blip* and only requires a turn or two of the reel to get moving, you're safe to assume you've made the most out of a cast.

Accuracy

Accuracy—placing a bait right where you want it—is made up of two components. One of them is lateral accuracy.

The commonly accepted way to achieve lateral accuracy is to line up your rod between eye and target and keep the shaft on that one plane while casting. Ideally, if you do this, the weight must stay on that plane during flight.

Of course, ideal situations are great in theory but seldom in practice. A third of the problem is that there will be many times when it will be impossible to cast from this position.

Another third is the possibility of wind drift.

And the final third is the same quirk faced by golfers, shooters, and ballplayers: no one drives, nestles a gunstock against his arm, pitches a ball, or casts a lure in exactly the same way. Take me for an example: as a left-hander, when I wind up for an overhead cast I can feel my lure swinging slightly to the left. I also feel uncomfortable casting a rod directly overhead, so my shaft is usually cocked five degrees left of center. Near the point of release, I also find my wrist going through a curious little half-twist. Probably, if you study your casting carefully, you'll discover similar but not identical physical quirks.

Rather than trying to overcome natural tendencies, use them to your advantage. Line up by pointing your rod tip toward your target, and cast naturally, comfortably. During the cast, never take your eyes off the target. Eventually, you'll see a pattern begin to develop; you'll either be consistently left or right to some degree.

Correct this by compensation; by consciously aiming 5 feet to the left of your target or to whatever distance and direction are needed to put you right on the money.

One real advantage to this technique is when you run into a stiff side-wind. All it takes is a cast to test where your lure's going to go. Once you determine that lateral deviation, you'll enjoy the accuracy of a real pro.

The second half of placing a lure where you want it brings us back to distance. While extremely short casts are better handled by other means, in most cases this area of accuracy is achieved by making a pitch slightly longer than necessary, then feathering it to draw it up short.

Minimum feathering effect is a matter of dropping your index finger to the moving line, thereby slowing it down. More positive results can be obtained by nesting the spinning coils in your half-closed free hand. You increase the friction as you close your hand.

The difficult part of distance accuracy lies in your eyes. You've got to learn how to judge the range between you and your target, and between that target and a lure on its way. To learn this skill, there's no easy trick, only an old maxim about practice making perfect.

Casting Position

Casting position yields most accuracy when you place one foot a half-pace in front of the other (left foot first if you're right-handed), and align your shoulders along that plane. If you're right-handed, your target area will fall roughly 45 degrees to the right of that imaginary line. Of course, in 90 percent of your casting situations, you'll be wrapped around a tree trunk, fighting the current for a grip on a slippery rock, or bent to the knees, trying to slap a lure home under an overhanging limb.

The Grip

The reel foot should fall between your ring finger and middle finger. This leaves your index finger free for line control, while your middle finger prevents the rod from slipping. Just between us, I do it all wrong, cradling the foot between my index and middle finger. It upsets my fishing buddies no end.

On a spin-cast (closed-face) reel, the correct grip finds the reel on top of the rod rather than underneath. Place your hand behind the reel mount, and use your thumb for release control.

Specialized Casts

Specialized casts are useful tools since they allow you to adapt to difficult conditions. Most of these casts can be executed as either snap or soft, depending on whether you're using bait or lures. In general, you'll also find the snap cast best for relatively open areas, and the soft cast most practical when there's brush or other obstructions that bar a clear swing.

· The overhead cast finds your rod inscribing in semicircle directly overhead. It's the most popular of all casts, since you get a lot of power behind your lure or your bait. However, an overhead cast requires lots of operating room.

· A sidearm cast is the best if there is not enough operating room. This approach requires your rod to be at right angles to your body. It's nearly as powerful as the overhead cast, but unless you're ambidextrous, you'll only be able to execute it on one side. Don't forget to angle your cast upward for loft—sidearmers have a tendency to cast parallel to the water and cut their distance. Realize however, that because of this natural tendency, a sidearm cast is good on a windy day since it keeps weight and line close to the surface of the water. It's also an effective technique when you want to place a bait under an overhead obstruction.

· The backhand cast enables you to work from your off side. Your casting arm comes across in front of your body, with your rod at a right angle to you. If there's no interfering brush, you can execute a snap cast

The backhand cast proves very useful on small, brushy streams where it's impractical to sweep the rod back over your shoulder as you cast.

The pendulum cast is especially useful when you want to cast a lure or bait up along a deeply cut bank where there are branches hanging low over the water. It's a cast that is easily controlled and will get your offering into tight spots.

from this position and get fair distance. Should there be an obstacle, a soft cast is the only way out.

· The pendulum cast is another possible solution to nearby brush. It's also effective on a nearby target. Position for this one finds your rod pointing toward your target and your lure dangling on a length of line at least half as long as your rod. The lure swings like a pendulum. Halfway through the forward swing, give your rod tip an extra flick for added power and distance. You can also manipulate your line like a fly rod, giving the line a quick jerk at release. This adds even more distance.

· The bow-and-arrow cast conjures up mixed emotions on my part. It's best suited for brushy situations in the extreme, and is accomplished by holding your lure in hand. Draw it back to put a deep bend in your rod, let the lure go, and, like a bow driving an arrow, it sails out. My number of doubts about this cast are directly proportional to the times I've ended up with a hook in my finger. Frankly, I'm a little nervous—at least to the point where I never try the bow-and-arrow with lures that sport more than one treble hook.

· The circle cast develops power by whirling your rod tip and lure in a tight circle. This can be done from an overhead, sidearm, backhand, out in front, or, should you be on top of a bridge or culvert, a straight-down position. Timing of release is extremely tricky on this one, so practice up with a hookless dummy, or plan to lose a lot of lures in trees.

· The snub cast isn't really a cast, it's a way of ending one. Send the lure on its way by whatever means is appropriate. Before it hits the water, close your bail and start reeling. The lure enters the water already on its way toward you. This technique is useful in extremely shallow waters, since the lure doesn't have time to sink. If you want the hardware to remain high, hold your rod high above your head.

The bow-and-arrow cast utilizes the rod as a bow and shoots your lure to the target.

· The skip cast isn't really a cast either, but another way of laying your bait down. By intentionally putting more power behind your lure than is needed to reach your target, you can skip a lure across the surface like a smooth, flat stone. This cast is often the only way into tight spots, protected by overhanging brush or other obstacles.

Retrieving Once Your Bait Hits the Water

Retrieving once your bait hits the water. It's a good idea to pause before beginning a retrieve. There are of course, circumstances where this is unwise, say, where you have a fast-sinking lure and a shallow, snaggy bottom. But as a rule of thumb, the pause has merit.

First, a fish near the vicinity of the dimpling lure is sure to be spooked by a splash. He won't leave the country, but he will scoot away. Waiting before you crank the handle gives him a chance to size up the situation, to imagine there's no apparent danger, and perhaps to come over and investigate that shiny thing fluttering down toward the bottom. If you begin the retrieve immediately, the fish might never see the lure. It could be out of his range before he overcomes his initial reaction.

Depth is another factor in the retrieve-pause rule. There are times when fish will be actively feeding on the surface, but for the most part, all species look for their meals close to the bottom. Giving your lure time to sink gets your offering down where the action is.

Pausing serves a third purpose. It gives you time to take slack out of your line and wind those first few turns of mono tight onto your spool. If you don't make this a regular practice, you'll find loops of loose line forming on your spool that will interfere with your casting.

Rod Position

Rod position during an artificial retrieve should generally be on a straight plane with your line. The idea is striking power; when a fish hits, you then have the full arc of your rod, about 12 feet on a 6-foot shaft, to yank in line and set the hook.

This isn't an ironclad rule, since it's often necessary to keep your lure shallow, and a high-held rod is one way to accomplish this. There's also the matter of possible obstacles and jigging. But try not to get caught by a fish with your rod high in the air. Unless you've got a very short line, you'll either miss the strike entirely or fail to set the hook deeply enough.

One further advantage to a rod held low is that some fish will follow you right up to shore. In this position, you'll keep your lure in the water longer, and increase the chances of catching the trailing fish.

When You're Retrieving Bait

· When you're retrieving bait, the opposite holds true. Hold your rod roughly at 12 o'clock. In most bait-fishing situations, you want slack in a hurry, so a nibbling fish won't feel you on the other end until you're good and ready. Drop your rod tip and you've got it. When you're ready to strike, *then* get your rod on an even plane with your line and sock it to 'em.

Beyond those generalizations, specific types of terminal tackle have a few quirks common to their kind. So let's take a look at individuals:

· Spoons are perhaps the most difficult to work, since they exhibit a variety of characteristics at different speeds. For example, a wobbling spoon is designed to swing from side to side, looking very much like a swimming fish. Reel too fast, and they'll whirl like a spinner, losing some of their appeal. Learn to feel that speed at which they first start to work and maintain it. Spoons of all varieties are among the lures that respond well to a jerky retrieve; it gives them a lot of flutter and flash.

· Spinners exhibit more predictable characteristics. Once they begin to whirl (and the motion is easy to feel), they're working. Reel too fast and they'll pop out of the water. Generally, I've found a slow steady retrieve the most productive, but don't overlook the possibility of occasionally jigging; they flutter attractively as they sink.

· Underwater plugs seem to produce best when you vary the rate of retrieve. While taking in line, they should always move fast enough to produce the action common to their design, but frequent pauses, then sudden spurts of energy, do seem to add appreciable attraction.

· Surface plugs have no optimum rate of retrieve. They're most effective when made to behave erratically. Pop them, burble them, dive them, then let them sit. Skitter them across the surface, then stop. You'll find fish are as prone to hit during periods of inactivity as when the baits are on their irritating way, so don't take time off when your plug's at rest.

· Jigs take some getting used to. It's not a matter of a correct rate of retrieve, but rather correct technique. A jig's appeal lies in the way it's worked; up-down, up-down. The lure rises and it falls, rises and falls. The temptation here is to use the rod for the rise and the reel to take in slack during the fall. The problem is that it's difficult to feel a strike on the fall when you have slack line.

Instead of using the rod to jig, I rely only on the reel. Holding the rod at about a 45-degree angle, take in a few turns of line and stop, take in a few turns of line and stop. Using this technique, you'll keep all slack out of your line, and will be able to feel the lightest tap, even on the fall.

Another method of jigging involves no retrieve. When fishing from a boat, you simply lower the lure to where you think the fish are and work it in that one spot. In this situation, you've got to have a good idea of the speed at which the jig sinks to keep slack out on the fall.

When working any jig, remember that like a topwater plug, fish will strike these lures when they're at rest. So stop jigging entirely every once in a while, leaving the lure either suspended or resting on the bottom.

· Bait fished in any kind of current is best not retrieved at all. Do your fishing while the bait is being nursed along by the water and use your reel only to direct the bait or to retrieve when you're ready to cast again.

In lakes (and here I include the rubber worm), bait is most effective when retrieved at a plodding pace. Live bait fishermen are prone to leave their bait immobile, either on bottom or under a bobber, but I'm not a believer. You're cutting your odds because you're not covering territory.

While it's a good idea to let a bait sit for a minute after the cast if you don't get any takers, slowly draw in a few feet of line and let it sit again. Chances are that somewhere along its route you'll drag that bait right by the nose of a waiting fish.

TROLLING

Basic to trolling is a boat and motor that can be throttled to a crawl. Although not all trolling situations require extremely slow speeds, they're needed often enough to count heavily in the size of your stringer.

Spinning isn't well-suited to deep-water trolling. This pastime requires heavy lead core or wire line, large-capacity reels, and stout rods. But spinning gear is eminently capable of trolling at depths down to 30 feet, the range where most fresh-water action is anyway.

Obviously, the principle behind trolling is to let your motor do the job of working your lure. Let your offering drift out behind the boat, close your bail, and settle down. Beyond those simplistics however, lies a whole world of absorbing nuances and nuisances.

Proper depth is important. All species of fish prefer a particular temperature: trout fare best at around 50 degrees, bass around 72. Since lakes exhibit thermal stratification—layers of temperatures that decrease as you approach bottom—trollers do well to lower a thermometer into the water, find the depth of their quarry's preferred temperature and work their lures at that level.

No special savvy is needed to troll near the surface. That's where most lures normally work. When the fish are deep however, you've got to know how to get down to them. An important part of that art is determining where your lure is riding.

You Can Tell How Deep Your Lure Is Working

You can tell how deep your lure is working if you first use color-coded line; line that changes to a different color at regular intervals. There is no standard for the length of each color, but the particular product you buy will be labeled as to its rate of change.

Obviously, when you're running a hundred feet of line behind your boat, that doesn't mean your lure is down a hundred feet. The only way you can determine the depth at which your line is working is by trigonometry.

It might strike your buddies as funny when a table of sines and a protractor pops out of your fishing box, but they're guaranteed to stop laughing when they know the fish are at 25 feet, and you're the only one who can tell them what color line that requires.

To find lure depth, you'll have to measure the angle at which your trolling line enters the water, then multiply the sine of that angle by the number of feet of line you have out. The resulting figure gives you your depth. You won't need a whole table of sines—just those for angles from 10 to 40 degrees.

Should you forget that mathematical paraphernalia, there's another way to guesstimate lure depth if you have a 12-inch ruler (check the handle of your landing net).

· Measure your line to a point 12 inches from the spot where it enters the water.

· Measure the distance from that point straight down to the surface of the water.

Multiply the second figure by the number of feet of line you have out and divide that number by 12.

For illustration, let's say your line is 3 inches above the water, 12 inches from the point where it enters the water. And that you have 100 feet of line out.

3 × 100 is 300. 12 into 300 is 25.

Your lure is running approximately 25 feet under the surface.

Achieving Trolling Depth

Achieving trolling depth requires fewer mental gymnastics, but still takes some savvy.

First, consider letting out more line. Thirty feet of trolled line will ride around 10 feet higher than 100 feet of trolled line (using the same lure). However, at the 100-foot point, letting out still more line won't do a thing. The problem is mono's lightness. Water pressure on the moving line holds it up.

Consider dropping your trolling speed. The slower you go, the deeper your lure will run. If your boat won't throttle way down, try trolling backward, throwing a bucket overboard as a drag, or both.

Perhaps that speed is too slow to set the lure in action. Next, consider a deep-diving lure.

The many brands of deep-divers have one thing in common, a long lip that digs into the water and acts like a plane to drive the lure down. If the fish don't seem to favor that offering, or the plug still isn't working deep enough, try adding weight.

Drail or keel-type sinkers work best for this job since they don't put up much water resistance. Place them well ahead of your lure so they don't cut down on action.

If you still aren't getting down to the fish, you have three options: (1) use braided Dacron line for trolling which naturally runs deeper than monofilament, (2) drift and try some deep jigging, (3) invest in a conventional trolling outfit with wire or leadcore line.

Trolling Techniques

Trolling techniques are largely based on the preferences of the species you're after. In general, you'll find the most takers not far out in the middle of a lake, but close to weedy shores, over abrupt dropoffs and around underwater obstructions like rock dikes and brush piles. Finding these underwater havens without some previous knowledge of the bottom is a matter of by guess and by gosh unless you have an electronic fishfinder, so these gadgets amount to a good investment for the guy that trolls a lot.

While underway, it pays to hold your rod in your hand rather than resting it in a rod holder. You can jig the lure or bait, thereby making it more attractive to fish and you're in a position to set the hook should a fish strike.

When you're running more than one line, be quite careful on turns; make them wide, or you'll cross your partner and probably end up with an impossible snarl of line. This problem becomes more in evidence as you increase the number of trolled lines.

It's virtually impossible to troll with more than four lines, and even with that number, you'll have to pay close attention to their positioning. Two rods should point straight back over the water from the stern quarters. Two other rods should jut from amidships at right angles to the keel. The rods in the stern should run shorter lines than those bristling out each side.

When trolling with four lines, it's mandatory that when someone gets a fish on, everyone else reels in.

Line twist often occurs while trolling (and while retrieving against a current). The problem either stems from lack of or improper function of a snapswivel; a whirling lure like a spinner or fast-retrieved wobbler then puts a turn in your line for each revolution it makes.

The results are easy to spot. When you let your line go slack, it comes alive, literally jumping into swirls and curlicues that will eventually become an impossible bird's nest.

Luckily, the solution is as simple as the cause. Remove your lure and let your empty line feed over the stern (or downstream). You might have to urge the first few coils of line off your reel by hand.

Let the same amount of line out as you've been trolling or casting. You can double-check your judgment by slacking up on a few feet of line. If it falls into a twist, let more out. If it stays straight, you've passed the point of curling.

Snap your bail in place and wait a minute or so. The water resistance will take all the curls and swirls out of your line.

THE STRIKE AND SET

Assuming a fish has your lure or bait in his mouth, the object is then to take in line so fast and with such force that your hook is imbedded or "set" beyond the barb. This is usually accomplished by snapping the rod tip up or to the side. Simple enough. But there are several factors often entering the picture that make an effective strike a bit more difficult.

One problem stems from elasticity. When you make a long cast and get a hit almost immediately, the span of mono is bound to stretch and in so doing, blunt the force of your strike. This is particularly true when using light lines; 2-, 4-, or 6-pound test.

The problem is further compounded should you be using a light or soft rod. Rather than drawing up your line in a hurry, your outfit bends and bows like a palm in the wind.

To rectify this situation, make a habit of striking extra-hard when you know you've got a lot of line out. You might even take a step backward as you snap that rod tip up. Another practice to learn so well that it becomes a reflex is to retrieve during a way-out-there strike—crank your reel handle and take in line. The combination of a hard pull, a step backward and a working reel will set your hook in even the hardest mouth.

It's also a good idea to keep your antireverse in gear any time you're not fighting a fish. The split-second surprise of a strike and your instant reaction is often a combination that jerks the reel handle from your grasp. Without antireverse, the handle will spin like a top and more often than not, give your fish the slack he needs to get free.

When you get a hit at moderate distances between you and your hook, say between 20 and 60 feet, a mighty tug is hardly necessary. As a matter of fact, laying into your rod like a tuna fisherman at this stage might lose you your fish. You'll either yank your lure clear of his mouth or open up a hole in the fish's jaw that will later allow him to throw the hook. The best reaction at this range is nothing more than one sharp snag.

The fish that takes a swipe at your hook at close range is the one who's most likely to get away. Your reflexes are so keyed up to responding to that sudden tug, that more often than not you strike too soon and too hard. Don't forget that at longer ranges, it takes a little while for the sensation of a mouthing fish to be telegraphed along your line, down your rod, to your hands, brain and back to your arms. At a short range, your line and rod are more sensitive, the tug more pronounced, and usually, so is your reaction. This is particularly true when you can actually see a follow-up; when some big pike or bass suddenly looms up behind your lure and opens his mouth. It's a sure thing to set the most experienced angler on the tip of his toes and has proven so unnerving to me that there have been times when I've struck even before the fish hit!

It's tough to do, but if you can keep your cool, delay your response to that tug. Even at close ranges, a strike should be *almost* an instantaneous reaction, so there's no formula about counting off seconds. If you can see your lure and fish, ignore the tug and wait until you actually see the lure in his mouth before pulling. The delay in human reaction time should have you right on the money. If you can't see your fish, you'll probably be so surprised that you'll yank back, and the lure will come rocketing out of the water. There's no way to overcome that reaction, so I've learned to make a practice of holding my rod very loosely when I get down to those last 12 feet of retrieve. Then, if a fish strikes, the rod has some seesaw give. Once I gather my wits, get a better grip on the rod, and strike back—still a matter of a split second—the fish usually has had enough time to clamp down on the hook.

The Strike With Bait

The strike with bait is a slightly different cup of tea. When a fish takes a swipe at cold metal, it doesn't take him too long to figure out he's hanging on to an inedible. With natural bait, he's got something to chew on.

Striking at the first nibble will usually miss you your fish. Most predaceous species first try to kill, stun, or be assured of capturing their prospective meal, then get around to eating it.

Pike, for instance, slap viciously at a bait. When using a lure, keep track of how often you hook them in the side of the head. Bass will pick up a rubber worm sideways, run with it for a while, stop, and get it in a better position for ingestion. Walleye will mouth a minnow, gnaw for a while, then swallow.

When you're using bait, give them time to get these preliminaries over. Drop your rod tip on that first hit, open your bail and let them run. How long to let them run varies with each fish; I usually give them free rein until they stop, then close the bail, and slowly take in line until I can again feel them working.

At this point, all the rules of setting apply: when they're way out there, lay into them. At moderate ranges, a sharp snap. Close in, a small jerk should drive the hook home.

There is one time, however, that I don't abide by the "let 'em run" rule. If you don't want to keep the fish, strike right away. You'll miss quite a few, but those you catch will be hooked in the mouth, and will live if released.

PLAYING THE FISH

The term "playing" when used in this sense is the ultimate misnomer. You don't need any special knowledge or technique to "play" with a fish—it's all a matter of what you enjoy most.

Some anglers get a kick out of hearing their drag scream when they hook into a modest- or medium-sized fish. Speaking for myself, I prefer a tight drag and a technique that comes close to horsing. I like to feel them work; shuddering on the end of my line, taxing my wrist with spurts of energy. Ninety-five percent of my fish are fought that way, "playing" to get the most personal enjoyment out of a fight.

Of course, there comes a time when the tables turn. It might be a 3-pound brookie tail-dancing on the end of a 2-pound test ultralight rig, or a 25-pound northern, lunging against the strain of 12-pound test. Whatever the specifics, when I hook a fish that's capable of beating me and my gear through brute force, I no longer "play." I get downright serious.

Actually, you should get serious long before the battle ever begins. Anticipating that it just might happen, you should have fresh line; strong, frequently checked knots; and a perfectly adjusted drag. Assuming all these physical aspects are in order, it's then all up to you.

The set is when it all begins. You feel a strike, or watch as your baited line moves off, then lean back with a snap. For a split second you think you have a snag. Your rod tip is at 12 o'clock, your wrists straining. You wait hopefully for a reaction, then all hell breaks loose.

A fish just hooked will react in one of two ways: he'll either jump or run.

· A jumping fish is most often lost because he throws the hook. He dances, vibrates, rattles, and works the lure free so it sails back at you as if spit out in a gesture of contempt. The only way to overcome this tactic is to keep slack out of your line. Reel, snap your rod tip far behind your shoulder, backpedal—any trick that will keep a taut line. When the fish reenters the water, return your rod to a 12 o'clock position.

· A running fish deserves the opposite reaction. A boring dash that peels off yards of line in the twinkling of an eye raises the immediate possibility of a broken line. There's tremendous friction being generated

When you're using extremely light line, like this winter crappie angler fishing a southern impoundment, it's best to use a landing net to get your fish aboard. Otherwise you might suffer a broken line or rip the hook from the fish's jaw.

against your guides and reel-roller. Your drag is turning so fast that a speck of dust could create resistance in excess of your line strength. The sheer weight and drag of your line cutting through the water is a further strain. To alleviate some of it, point your rod directly at the running fish, and if it's possible, slacken up a half-turn on your drag.

This position also puts you in great shape for taking up slack should the fish decide to jump—a tactic that often caps a searing run.

· The initial run is always the heart-pounder. After it, a big fish will usually settle down and fight. There will be other runs, other jumps, but somehow they won't exhibit the brute power and potential loss of that first one.

At this time, I always snap off my antireverse. While I don't recommend this for everyone, it's a practice that deserves consideration. For one thing, I don't trust a drag implicitly. I'd much rather use my fingertips to judge the breaking point of line, reeling backward when I feel the strain is too great. If the fish moves out faster than my hand will turn, I'll just lock my hand in position, depend on the drag, and pray. I've never had a fish tear a handle from my hand once I knew he was on. They will in the surprise of the first strike, and that's the only time I count on both drag and antireverse.

When you're neither gaining nor losing line, keep your rod at about the

11 o'clock position. Let it do all the work, bending to cushion runs, re-coiling to bring the fish closer. View your reel as a receptacle for your line and nothing more.

Pump the fish in when he begins to tire. Lower your rod to 10 o'clock, reeling in whatever slack you can get. Raise it to 12 o'clock slowly, then drop it to 10, again adding line to your spool.

· Turning a fish is another heart-pounder. When a lunker heads for a brushpile, stump, weedbed, or snaggy bottom, you know he's got one thing in mind: to get you wound around something so he can break off.

The only sure way you can stop him is by brute force, by applying pressure until he gives up and goes the other way. You of course run the risk of applying too much beef and breaking off, but you can cut the chances of this happening if you anticipate his move and begin applying modest pressure long before he ever nears his destination, thereby gradually tiring him out.

Do this by keeping your rod tip high and dropping your index finger to the turning spool, pressing against it. The harder you press, the more pressure you're putting on line and fish. This situation is where skirted spools come in handy. They're easier to control because the skirt is more accessible to your finger. It's possible to get a burn on your fingertip doing this, but if a fish is big enough to burn you, landing him will be worth the pain.

One other trick worth trying is striking your line with a fingertip like a bass player in a jazz quartet. Sometimes this irritates a hooked fish enough so he forgets where he wanted to go.

LANDING THE FISH

Those last heady minutes before a fish is in hand are easily as critical as those following the initial strike. Perhaps more so because there's less margin for error.

All but a few feet of line has been taken out of play. You can't depend on its shock-absorbing qualities. Your rod is at an awkward angle where it too, is limited in the amount of bend and bow it can contribute to check a sudden surge of power.

Even the angler is at a distinct disadvantage, for his fish is now close to all kinds of potential foul-ups; afloat there are fish stringers and anchor lines; ashore or wading, you've got to contend with streamside brush and the most embarrassing offender of all, your own two feet.

There are, of course, ways to at least reduce the chances of losing your fish just as the battle is nearing its end. A great deal depends on how you've played the fish.

Make certain you permit any fish to tire itself well away from where you're standing. Then, as it tires, work it towards you and prepare to net it.

No matter the species, a fish that's been horsed in or underplayed stands the best chance of getting away during an attempted capture. He's got plenty of wind for a hard-boring run that might snap your line or lead you into a nearby snag. Fish prone to jump—trout and bass, for instance—can be counted on to do some tail-walking if they're not exhausted. It's exciting to watch, but the performance is usually capped by the fish throwing the hook.

So before you ever bring a catch close to you or a boat, make sure your fish has been put through its paces first. That way, you stand at least an even chance of winning the argument.

To overcome the potential loss inherent in a line that's too short and a rod that's not in a position to bend, use the most of both that you can. In other words, the position that affords you the greatest latitude in checking a sudden shock is hands over head, rod in the 11 o'clock position, and standing on your own two feet. Obviously, this is only possible if you have someone else to net your fish, and, often, it's impractical, as, for instance, when you are fishing from a canoe.

But keep that position in mind and strive to come as close to it as conditions allow.

Once the fish is alongside, one cardinal rule applies: keep his head up. Badgers, a burrowing member of the weasel family, are famed for their ability to resist being pulled from a hole once they get their head and front feet in. Even a horse and lasso can't get them out. On a smaller scale, that's the same advantage a fish has once he gets his head pointed toward bottom. Every muscle and propelling fin in his body is now in a position to work against you. So before you ever bring a net to play, make sure your trophy's eye is on the sky. That way, should he find his second wind, he's got no place to go but up.

NETTING

You shouldn't even look at a net until these three conditions have been satisfied. But even then, there are a few more tricks to the trade.

Just for the sake of experimentation someday, see how fast you can move a net underwater. You'll find quite a bit of resistance and very little speed, especially when compared with the frantic darting of a hooked fish. Yet this is the way most anglers get their netting done, by powering a series of zigzags through the water until by luck as much as anything, the fish happens to wander into the mesh.

There is of course, a better way. Using a net a little bit like a spear, stab down into the water at an angle that will take the rim of the net under the

Draw the fish towards the mouth of your net. When the fish is in the bag of the net, lift it swiftly and get the fish aboard, as these anglers are doing on this picturesque Wyoming river.

fish. Bring the rim up sharply around the fish, and you'll have him in the twinkling of an eye. This speed is achieved because you don't have to fight the resistance of water on the mesh of the net. On the initial stab, the net is collapsed, laid flat against the body of the rim. As you scoop up, the rim is fully out of the water, and around the fish, before the net has a chance to balloon out and slow you down. Now you can go as slowly as you like, because your fish is inside and yours for the taking.

Wading and Beaching

Wading and beaching require some specialized savvy to land a fish. When you're wading, your biggest problem will be your own two feet. I wouldn't want to count the times when a last-ditch effort on the part of a hefty fish had me reeling and jigging, one-legged, in the middle of a stream while I tried to get the two of us disentangled.

Again, the best way to avoid this is to play your fish out completely, so he doesn't have the poop to wind you up like a spider does a fly.

Another good rule when you're playing a fish close is to keep your feet together. You can whirl and turn to fight a fish in any direction and don't have to worry about him shooting between your legs.

Finally, if you're in a river or a stream with any kind of current, don't attempt to net your fish until he's downstream from you. An upstream netting attempt has the water working in the fish's favor.

There will be times when you won't be able to use a net, most notably, should you be fishing from a shallow shore without a pair of waders. In this case, beaching is the only answer.

The trick in beaching a fish successfully is to let him do all the work. Be patient and keep a constant bow in your rod and the pressure up, and every twist and flop will drive the fish closer and closer to shore. Don't relax the pressure until you're sure the fish is within reach, or far enough into shallows so he can't turn and run. A good friend of mine lost a beautiful fresh-water striper, and very nearly his entire outfit, when he laid his rod down to haul the "whipped" fish ashore, and it took off for the other side of Santee Cooper Reservoir.

Other Means of Landing

Other means of landing are sometimes useful, but if there's a net around, reach for that first.

· Bass can be landed by squeezing their lower jaw between thumb and forefinger. As you lift them from the water, bend the jaw down. This paralyzes them. It paralyzes most other fish too, but thanks to the abundant dental work common with more toothy gamefish, this landing technique is a good way to lose a thumb on fish other than bass.

· Pike will be quieted if you jam thumb and middle finger into their eyes. Come down from the top of the head and be *very* careful. They're one of those species who delight in a tasty thumb.

· Walleye will come ashore if you get a grip on their gill plate. Grab the gill close to the fish's underside. High on their head their plates are knife-sharp.

· Trout of all species and most cold-water fish are tough to land without a net. Big salmon, steelhead, and Dolly Varden can be wrestled ashore by a hand-hold on their tail, but most others are too small and slippery to hang on to. You might remember that no cold-water fish has sharp fins or gills—only teeth. Keep your fingers away from their mouths, and have at it as best you can.

SPINNING TECHNIQUE ON A RIVER

Many of my boyhood memories are wrapped up in the Connetquot River, a flowage that seldom got wider than 15 feet before it entered a brackish estuary. Cottonwood Creek, bubbling by my present home in Montana, carries five times as much water as Connetquot did, and is just about as wide. New Jersey's Flat Brook surprised me when I first fished it. I'd expected a trickle, and found water 25 yards wide in places.

By way of definition, let's call a stretch of moving water 50 feet or more across, a river. This essentially means that long casts are possible, largely eliminating the possibility of spooking fish by your physical presence.

LURE FISHING

In 75 percent of your fishing situations on a river, you'll find your best approach to be a quartered cast. You stand with your shoulders parallel to to the bank, and peg a cast upstream at an approximate 45-degree angle. The last few yards of your retrieve should find your lure returning on a path that angles 45 degrees downstream.

This technique is effective because it naturally covers a broad spectrum of lure-presentation, action and water. At first, your lure runs with the current, fast and deep. As it swings past you, it loses speed, increases its action, and begins to lift off the bottom. Toward the end of your retrieve, it's close to the surface, moving slowly, and flashing frantically. The chances are good that one of those many combinations will prove appealing to a fish somewhere along the route.

A quartered cast is also a natural way to thoroughly work out a patch of water. Make one cast for each pace, and the odds say that your hardware will have to pass within striking distance of every nook and cranny in the river.

Realize that you'll have to match the angle of your cast to the speed at which the river is flowing. A fast, strong current requires a greater upstream reach, and a slow current means a cast closer to a right angle from the riverbank.

Fishing upriver requires a very fast retrieve, not only to keep your lure in action but to prevent hanging up on the bottom. If you frequently find yourself in the situation, consider using a fast-retrieve reel; it'll save a lot of frenzied cranking.

Casting against a current is one way to make sure your lure will work deep. It does it quite naturally. When you're plunking down in shallows or a real raging torrent, use the snub cast. In shallows you won't hang up, and in rapids you won't end up with your lure drifting faster than you can take in line.

Except in a slow-moving river—I'd say a flow three knots or under—fishing directly downstream won't prove too productive. Your lure will ride high, and probably it will be impossible to maintain the correct rate of retrieve. Remember again that changing currents make this a flexible rule. In rivers of seven knots or more, an underwater rock can slow the flow behind it to a snail's pace—fishy water, indeed, for a downstream cast.

The faster water is moving, the more prone fish will be to lie behind some breakwater—a rock, snag, or in an eddy—so an important part of river fishing is learning to read water.

The cold water outlet below Greer's Ferry Lake in Arkansas provides fine trout fishing; here Keith Gardner works his lure across the swift current.

Rivers are big water; in order to score you've got to study the water and think like a fish. Find the spots where the fish are apt to wait for a meal and work them thoroughly.

Although every inch of water in a river has the potential to hold a fish, another place to pay particular attention to is the opposite bank. A presentation that finds your lure working from shore out will always be the most effective. For that reason, float-fishing or deep wading with chest-high boots are favored techniques for spinning on big rivers.

Bait Fishing

Bait fishing involves one of two techniques: still-fishing or drift-fishing.

Still-fishing amounts to first identifying a fishy spot: the meeting of two currents, a quiet pocket behind a rock, or a deep, slow hole. Sufficient weight is added to your hook to anchor it in one place, you bait up, cast out, and wait.

While still-fishing is a pleasant way to pass away a lazy Sunday afternoon, it's not too exciting and not nearly as productive as drift-fishing.

Drift-fishing involves working out the same fishy spots, but instead of an immobile bait, yours is always on the move. Not only does this mean you'll be covering more ground and thereby tempting more fish; it's also an eminently natural presentation, and extremely effective in hard-fished waters.

The two tricks to drift fishing involve your weighting and the ability to determine the difference between bottom and a bite.

You should have just enough weight so that you frequently feel your bait hitting bottom, but not so much that it constantly hangs up or snags. This weighting will change with the speed of the water you're fishing: the faster the water, the more weight you'll need.

Identifying a bite as such is a matter of educating your fingers. A snag will feel like a hard knock as your lead hits an object, then a gradual easing as it slides up and over. A bite is the exact opposite: a gradual easing to a stop as the fish picks up the bait, then hard raps as he starts to tear away.

A good rule for the beginning drift-fisherman is to keep your eye on the point where line enters water. If it's not moving with the current, and you feel some hard knocks, there's a fish down there eating. Another wise move is to keep your rod tip high. It reduces line drag in the water and telegraphs a delicate nibble more clearly.

The area you work is essentially the same as that for lure fishing: a quartered cast 45 degrees upstream. But don't retrieve. Let the water carry your bait where it will.

Since bait takes some time to sink, you'll actually only be working out a 60-degree pie-slice of water. The time when a fish is most likely to pick up starts when you feel the first rap of a rock to indicate you're close to bottom, and ends when the bait lifts off the bottom. At that point, retrieve and cast again.

Drift-fishing while working directly upstream or down requires different weighting. An upstream cast needs little, if any weight. There's virtually no pressure being exerted on line or bait, by the moving water, so a mere pinch of shot will quickly carry your offering close to the bottom. Too much weight in this situation will result in frequent snags.

When fishing downstream, the opposite is largely true. Your bait will be moving slower than the current, which will hold it off the bottom. Add enough weight to pick up the feel of the bottom.

When fishing upstream, keep a taut line as the bait tumbles down toward you—it's the only way you'll feel a bite.

Except in very slow-moving currents (where no weight should be needed), you're better off to feed out line on a downstream drift, rather than letting it run on an open bail. Again, you'll stand a better chance of feeling a bite.

Occasionally, you might want to float a bait, as is sometimes the case with grasshoppers, crickets, and huge salmon flies. Do this in conjunction with a clear plastic bubble, using the same techniques described for dry flies in *Spinning With a Fly* (page 93).

SPINNING IN A STREAM

Streams—flowages of water less than 50 feet wide—are essentially small versions of rivers. In other words, you'll find fish in the same places and fool them with the same techniques that work on larger water.

Some problems arise however, in that you won't have a lot of room to work. To overcome this disadvantage, consider using medium-light to ultra-light reels mounted on short 4½- to 6-foot rods. They require only a short swing to send a lure on its way, compensating to some extent for the lack of elbow room.

In the spring, streams are usually muddy or roily. This is the best time for bait and the time you can cover their waters from any direction; upstream, downstream, across the current—whatever approach will place your bait or lure in the proper position for a potential strike.

In the summer and fall however, you can expect streams to be gin-clear. In this condition, fish will often be able to see you—and spook—if you're working across or downstream.

Under clear-water conditions, lures will prove the best producers. Make it a practice to work them upstream. This approach doesn't dislodge muck that might alarm a feeding fish, and it conceals your physical presence more effectively. Most fish will be facing the current, not you. In addition, the stream's gradient will keep at least part of you out of sight.

Like big water, plan on fish being in slow pockets, deep runs, and eddies. Guesstimate where they'll lie and place your cast well ahead of that point so they won't be spooked by a splash.

Remember that when fishing clear water in close quarters, exposure is always an important and telling factor in success. Use shore brush for camouflage. Stalk fish like an Indian scout without a lot of splash or slosh as you move through the water. Keep low, and wear clothes of neutral shade: khakis, browns, and greens.

You'll discover that streams and their close-in brush will be the place where specialized casts and their correct execution will catch you more fish: the bow-and-arrow, backhand, pendulum, snub, and skip-cast.

When your position or the stream's characteristic prohibits a drift with bait, cast directly into a promising pocket and let it sit there for a moment. Begin a very slow retrieve until the bait works out of the pocket. Try this two or three times. If no takers come along, move on to the next possibility.

Occasionally you'll find yourself in a position where the water can work for you—say, you're trying to reach a deep hole under a tangle of brush. Don't overlook the possibility of penetrating that hideout by placing your offering atop a floating piece of wood, opening your bail, and letting the current carry it there for you. Slip it off the piece of wood when your bait reaches the position you think attractive.

Fish in streams seem to react faster to changes in feeding patterns than those in rivers or lakes. For example, a good, heavy rain will encourage any fish to look for worms, but you'll find stream inhabitants actively feeding on them long before their big-water cousins. On rivers and lakes, a fly-feeding binge takes quite a while to get underway—and stop. On a stream, the dimpling fish turn on and off like a passing shower.

Because they're easily influenced, you can occasionally urge a strike from a stream fish with unusual tactics. For example:

When you drift a worm through a hole, consider powdering some dirt in the water first. This simulates a bank caving in and just might whet a lunker's appetite for a juicy crawler.

When fishing nymphs, dislodge a few rocks with your feet well above the hole to send some hors d'oeuvres down before the main course.

If insects—crickets, willow flies, grasshoppers, etc.—are clinging to the bank brush, regularly knock a few into the water. Even if you're not using them for bait, it still might encourage fish to start thinking about food.

Small Streams

Small streams, tiny rivulets you can jump across, deserve some special consideration. They're often fantastic fish-producers, especially for trout, and are usually overlooked by other anglers.

Their size virtually precludes lure fishing, so you'll have to think bait. For fishing naturals on these small streams, I favor a long rod, used roughly like a cane pole.

There will seldom be enough room for casting, so fish these rivulets using your rod like a probe, dropping a bait in front of some undercut bank or letting it drift through a deep run. You can open your bail and let the current carry your offering into unreachable spots—through a tangle of brush or under a log, for instance.

These young lads enjoy an opening day of trout fishing on a crowded eastern stream. Spinning succeeded in placing their worm-baited hook out in the deeper part of the stream where the trout were holding in an eddy.

When you feel the tap-tap-tap of a nibbling fish, it's time to strike, but you might not have the clearance needed to snap your rod up. Set the hook by taking line in fast. Either crank your reel, or handle your line manually, using your mono like fly line.

If it's at all possible, stay out of the water and back from the bank. If there's too much shorebrush for bank fishing, wade downstream quietly, with your rod and bait in front of you. You might raise some muck and moil, but the advantages of silent wading and letting the current place your bait for you far outweigh the color of the water.

SPINNING ON A LAKE

A lake is the place where the long cast comes into its own. You've got a lot of room to work, and the more water you can cover with each flip of a bait or lure, the better your chances of connecting.

Lakes have their hot spots, too—places where fish like to congregate. These should be the focal point of your exploratory casts.

Although what amounts to a hot spot has a lot to do with the species you're after—bass like weedbeds and trout don't, for example—it is pos-

Spinning is contemplative. This lone angler is working a productive beat of water, the morning mist still hanging low.

Maine's big Lake Sebago produced this fine landlocked salmon to an angler who patiently probed its depths with light spinning tackle and a miniature wobbler.

sible to make some generalizations about places that are bound to produce, no matter your quarry:

· Sharp dropoffs deserve special consideration. These can either be an underwater cliff or some sort of submerged island, a gravel or sandbar, or point of rocks. Bait fish like to congregate around these places, and anywhere there's food, you'll find larger predaceous species.

· Brushpiles and snags are good for the same reason. Both insects and small minnows frequent them for the protection their maze of branches provide.

· Lake inlets, outlets, and underwater springs are especially productive. The moving water carries food with it, and the temperature differential between a cool stream or spring and warm lake provides double attraction.

· Channels and old riverbeds in man-made impoundments can be counted on to hold concentrations of fish. Their submerged banks amount to a dropoff, and they'll carry more current than other parts of the lake.

Lure-Fishing

Lure-fishing in a lake will be most productive if you choose hardware that generates a lot of action with a minimum of movement. Wide-bladed spinners; light, stamped metal spoons; and frantically active plugs all lend themselves to a slow retrieve that seems to anger a fish as much as tempt his hunger.

Another generalization that will prove its worth is to go deep first. The bulk of a big fish's life is spent close to the bottom, so unless your quarry is obviously on a surface-feeding binge, that's the place you'll find the most action.

The most effective way to cover a possibly productive patch of water from shore is to imagine the range of your cast as a semicircle reaching out into the lake, with you at the center. Peg at least seven casts toward the rim of the circle, beginning close to one bank and ending close to the other.

Let's say the radius of that circle is 100 feet. After those seven casts— or more, if the spirit moves you—move 25 feet and cast again. Keep moving in the same direction and you'll be crisscrossing fishy spots with enough variety in approach to tempt even a vaguely interested fish.

Bait Fishing

Bait fishing on top means a bobber. When you're working water with 3 feet or less depth between float and bait, the push-button float that snaps onto your line is fine. If you'll have a longer leader than that, casting is extremely difficult unless you use the sliding float.

Whatever float you're using, it should come as close to neutral buoyancy as possible. This can be achieved by adding weight to your line, or by using a bubble float that can be filled with water.

Should you want a free-swimming bait, say a live minnow, add the required amount of weight close to the float. If you want your bait to sink fast, add it near the hook.

With near-neutral buoyancy, a fish can pull a float under with little trouble, and there is less chance of its being spooked off by unusual resistance.

Fishing a lake bottom carries with it one inherent problem: most lakes have thick weed growth that reaches up several feet, obscuring your offering. To counter that disadvantage, try floating your bait up off the bottom. Estimate the depth of the weeds and arrange the leader between

When working a shoreline with spinning tackle, make certain you are thorough. Fat Florida largemouth bass feed right up in the grass along the shoreline; if you don't get your lures right in close, you simply won't catch them.

Whether fishing a feeder stream emptying into a lake or the broad expanse of a lake, use a stealthy approach and you'll catch more fish. This angler knelt along the bank in order not to cast a shadow on the water and hooked this fine cutthroat trout from a high mountain feeder stream.

sinker and hook so your bait is riding anywhere from 6 inches to a foot above these vegetables.

Add a floatant to your hook; a marshmallow, small chunk of cork, or best of all, if it's possible, "blow" your bait. This technique involves injecting air into a worm or dead minnow so it's lighter than water. Commercial worm-blowers are available, or a hypodermic syringe can be used.

The net effect is a meal that dangles well above obscuring weeds, more attractive to fish if for no other reason than it's easily seen.

Don't overlook the possibility of working a bait fished on or off the bottom, much as you would a lure. Your retrieve should be agonizingly slow, and don't worry too much about action. But by giving your bait some movement, you add an extra measure of attraction and increase its exposure. Both factors increase the odds that you'll run across a taker.

SPINNING WITH A FLY

Fly-fishing has long been considered the most "sporting" of angling techniques. Subjective judgments aside, the form is eminently practical for the spin-fisherman. For one thing, learning this technique opens up some "fly-fishing only" waters to him—a designation of choice streams that's becoming more predominant these days.

Then too, a fly is often a most effective bait on heavily fished waters. I can remember a little pond near New York City that was whipped to death by worm fishermen and hardware merchants, usually with meager success. Everyone assumed the place was fished out, but very quietly, I took regular limits of brookies there.

A little black fly and bubble float was my secret weapon, and I'm sure to this day that the rig was so unfamiliar, yet, so natural, that those "educated" fish just couldn't pass it up.

Spinning with a fly is a technique that lends itself well to light equipment. While it is possible with rods and reels in the medium to heavy category, light line is a virtual necessity, since casting weights will be at a minimum.

Soft rods from 6 feet to 4½ and reels weighing no more than 4 ounces are my favorites for this form. Line weights should center around 4-pound test, though you can go another 2 pounds in either direction.

The type of terminal tackle you employ is determined by the class of fly you're fishing. Flies fall into four categories: nymphs, streamers, wets, and dries. Since the fly will decide your approach, let's center this discussion on them:

· Nymphs are designed to imitate the larval or pupal stages of aquatic insects. In terms of the trouts, they make up the bulk of their diet, and consequently these insects are of major importance to the trout angler.

Except for a few hours out of an entire year when they're emerging to become adults, nymphs stick pretty close to the bottom, and that's where they're most effectively fished.

To do this, simply add sufficient casting weight two feet or so above the fly. Remember that nymphs don't swim, dart, or dash, so a "dead" drift, much like drift-fishing with bait, is the most effective way to present them. This simply means you've got to keep them moving with the current in a stream or slowly crawling across the bottom of a lake.

Realize that in a stream you can't use so much weight that you hang up on bottom. That's one of the reasons for employing the light tackle that will cast light weights. And don't get too enthused about preweighted nymphs, flies tied with casting weight incorporated in their body.

A normal nymph is just a bit heavier than water. When he's dislodged from his home on the bottom, he tumbles quietly through the water. That's the same effect you'll get with the near-neutral-bouyancy standard fly, weighted well above the hook.

· Streamers or bucktails imitate a minnow. As such, they'll be attractive to a wide variety of gamefish. They're also the easiest of all flies to work with a spinning rig. Like lures and plugs, these streamers should have plenty of action. Weight them as heavy as you'd like, but again with your lead a few feet above the fly. Jerk and reel them through attractive lies. I've found streamers to perform well when they're tied preweighted, but I still favor the unweighted fly with a weight on the leader. Rigged this way, the streamer behaves more erratically and, I think, more attractively to fish.

· Wet flies imitate either an emerging adult stage or a spent adult that has sunk. They're effective not only on trout, but panfish as well. Wets are easiest to fish with a plastic bubble, the kind that can be weighted with water. I prefer the elongated, oval kind, shaped roughly like a bullet.

To rig a float with a fly, clip a snapswivel with your line attached to the float's slim end. Tie a leader at least 4 feet long to its large end and, on the end of that, your fly.

Wets should be worked in quiet rivers or a lake—a slow, measured retrieve will do the job. You can also use this method of presentation with nymphs if you know they're beginning to emerge for a hatch. On fast water, imparting movement to these flies is unnecessary. Fish them on a drift.

· Dry flies imitate adult insects, alighting on the water to lay their eggs or floating on the surface after they expire. They're the toughest to present, since they must be kept floating, and well away from the bubble, but they're by far the most exciting feathers to use.

To keep your fly floating, cover it with one of the many commercial preparations designed to prevent it from absorbing water. Mucilin is one old standby that comes to mind. Apply it before your fly is wet.

Avoid getting your fly too close to your float by feathering the last few feet of your cast. This draws the bubble up short and plunks the fly down beyond it. While it's drifting, you can keep some distance between the two by occasionally reeling in a few feet of line.

Except for terrestial imitations—floating grasshoppers, crickets, panfish poppers, and the like—a dry needs no action. Just let it float along in the current or rest on the lake until some obliging fish gulps it down.

All varieties of fly-fishing require an immediate strike on your part. Once a fish discovers he's got a mouthful of feathers instead of a meal, he drops his mistake in a hurry.

Unlike lures, flies aren't produced by brand names. They come in different designs called patterns. There are over five thousand fly patterns on the books and infinite variations on those patterns. Knowing this, I always feel a bit presumptuous when I start citing specific flies as "best," but doggone it, there are some patterns I always seem to reach for first. They are:

—Nymphs; insect green, gray, or brown woolly worms; Montana nymphs; gold-ribbed hare's ear; caddis; and grub-worm.

Streamers; muddler and spuddler minnow; mickey finn, spruce fly; grey ghost; light and dark Edson tiger.

Wets; black gnat; royal coachman; leadwing coachman; gentry; gold-ribbed hare's ear.

Dries; Renegade; bivisible; adams; grey wulff; catskill; joe's hopper; muddler; black gnat; iron blue dun.

ULTRALIGHT SPINNING

Spinning with gossamer lines, wandlike rods and feather-weight reels is more than just a gimmick to pit yourself against a heavy fish with odds in his favor.

In heavily pressured areas and gin-clear water the invisible lines and thumbtack-size lures common to this form will often fool a fish when other tackle won't.

In terms of pure sport, ultralight amounts to an equalizer between you and fish too small to be exciting on medium-weight tackle.

Finally, ultralight finds a welcome home on little water—streams with close-in brush that limits the swing of your cast. While this technique could never be called the core of spin-fishing, it's certainly an important offshoot and an intriguing way to catch more fish.

The Ultralight Reel

The ultralight reel should weigh in the neighborhood of two to four ounces. All the quality features of the standard spinning reel should be incorporated into the featherweights, but on this reel, the importance of a top-notch tension device is critical.

When you're using 8-pound test, a drag adjustment that's off a half-pound or so presents no real problem. However, on 2-pound test, that margin of error accounts for 25 percent of your line strength—an understandably important edge when you tie into a heavy fish.

So double-check for quality in your drag: smooth, chatter-free operation and release that's triggered at the precise pound-setting.

One way you can do this is to rig your rod and tie the tag end of your line to a weight. Let's say you're using 2½-pound test and want your drag set at 2 pounds. When you try to lift a 2-pound weight, your rod tip should dip to a certain point before the drag springs to action. As line continues to be stripped off, the rod should not change its bend appreciably—in other words, the force required to keep your drag in motion should not be significantly less than that required to start it in motion.

A high-speed retrieve is another desirable feature with UL. Your spool is small to begin with, and this cuts the rate at which you can retrieve a line. Stream-fishing in the low water of summer is one place where UL is especially effective, and this situation is best dealt with by casting upstream. A fast retrieve means you'll be able to stay ahead of the pace of your lure.

The Ultralight Rod

The ultralight rod should weight between 1 and 2 ounces. This means the total weight of your rig should fall between 3 and 6 ounces, with a 4½-ounce combination falling right in the middle.

The length of the rod should be 4 to 5 feet, and the shaft should be quite slow and soft in action. The lures you'll be casting aren't heavy enough to put a fast taper to work, so your stick must bend to the corks.

Ultra-light spinning tackle is designed for delicate fishing situations such as in this brush-lined stream. Trout that are wise to casual fishermen will only take a lure presented on hair-thin, almost invisible, two to four pound test lines.

Because of the weight factor, tapered sliding rings for a reel seat are preferred.

Ideally, your butt guide should be close to the diameter of your reel spool for minimum line-friction. Because the rod is so small, one-piece construction or a ferrule between blank and butt will deliver the best performance.

Ultralight Line

Ultralight line is generally considered as falling below 4-pound test. Although strengths as low as ¾ of a pound can be purchased, such sophistication is required to use the stuff that few anglers can use—much less master—such spidery mono.

As a rule, I seldom use line lighter than 2-pound test. When clear water isn't too much of a factor, I'll go to 3. If I'm not trying to cast the smallest lures available I'll occasionally go to 4.

Whatever line-rod-reel combination you decide on, it should be capable of casting a 1/16-ounce lure between 50 and 60 feet.

Lures

Lures for ultralight will weigh between ⅛ and ½₀ of an ounce. Essentially, they're pint-sized versions of the standard weights, but they should be capable of producing a lot of flutter and flash at slower speeds than their big brothers. UL lures are available in all popular types: spoons, spinners, jigs, and plugs.

Generally, snapswivels shouldn't be used. The smallest snapswivel made is often bigger than the lure you're using, so make sure any UL lure you buy doesn't have a sharp edge around the tie-on point and frequently check the strength of your knot.

Twisted line is a common headache with UL, as much for the lack of snapswivels as incorrect playing of fish. With hairline diameters, the smallest snarl is impossible to get out. If you find twisting in your line, let it drift lureless downstream. Close your bail when it reaches the farthest limit of your casts, and hold it there for a minute. The moving water will take out the corkscrews.

Bait-Fishing

Bait-fishing is great with UL. In most situations, you won't need extra weighting. Just thread a worm or minnow on a hook and put it to work. Remember too, that this extra-light tackle is perfectly matched to spinning with a fly.

Casting

Casting requires a great deal of practice. Lures are so light that they generate little resistance. Your finger won't be sensitive to the precise moment of release, so you've got to do some educated guessing until you get the timing down pat.

Fishing hardware, the rod, has to do virtually all the work, so really put some snap in the cast. Bait, as in standard spinning, requires a soft cast to keep it intact.

In low, clearwater situations, or in waters where the fish are superspooky, cast beyond the point you think they might be at, and feather the cast just before the lure strikes the water.

This creates an entry of lure to water close to 90 degrees and results in a clean blip rather than a loud splash.

Playing the Fish

Playing the fish takes some special savvy too. Your drag should be set on the light side. Remember that a pound can represent half your line strength, not much of a margin for error considering a searing strike, a hard-running fish, and your inevitable temptation to pressure him too much.

So make it a rule to play the fish *only* with the rod. When his run is over, pump him in by slowly raising the rod tip and retrieving line as you drop it.

Don't try to reel unless you're sure you'll be taking in line. Cranking the handle while the drag is in play is one way to get maddening line-twist.

If you have to brake a run, do it by dropping a finger to the turning line-spool. Do this only if the fish is heading for an obvious breakoff: the lip of a falls, a brushy snag, or a sharp rock.

Be particularly careful when landing a fish. You virtually have to use a net for this. The light pressure brought to bear usually means a fish will get his second wind as soon as he sees you.

3

SPINNING
BY SPECIES:
FRESH
WATER

The sections on tackle and techniques were a broad look at the ways and wiles of the spin-fisherman. However, individual species of fish require individual attention. Many of them differ in the baits, rigging, lures, and tackle to which they're most susceptible and in the type of surroundings they call home.

Here then, is a rundown on America's most popular fresh-water game-fish and some common and not-so-common tricks that will put them on the end of your line.

LARGEMOUTH BASS

The bigmouth bass is America's number-one fresh-water gamefish, and after a brief look at his background, it's easy to understand why.

The largemouth is native or has been successfully introduced to waters in every state in the union with the exception of Alaska. He grows big too. The world's record is 22 pounds 4 ounces, and fish weighing in between 9 and 12 pounds aren't uncommon.

Add to this an appetite for virtually anything that swims, his reputation as a bulldog battler on the end of a line, and a tendency toward aerial acrobatics, and you have an exciting opponent that lures millions of anglers annually.

Tackle for bigmouth should be stout, as much because of his bulk and tough mouth as the kind of water he calls home. A largemouth's lair is more often than not a tangle of weeds, bristling brush, or a knotty snag. Once he's hooked, that's the place he'll head, so stiff rods and heavy lines are needed to snub that run.

Favored lines run 6 to 20 pounds. Six-pound test is the lightest line used in the northern states where the bass average 2 to 4 pounds. Down South, particularly in Florida, natives chuckle when you show up with any line weight under 12.

Rod actions for bass should be medium-heavy to heavy. Many anglers favor a fast tip incorporated into the rod since it makes for easy plug-casting, but still gives them the backbone needed to turn a bull bass. Several manufacturers offer special worm rods with actions specifically adapted to rubber worming, one of the deadliest bass techniques employed today.

Like the rods, reels should be medium to heavyweight by fresh-water standards, and capable of holding at least 100 yards of 15-pound test. Many experienced bass addicts (a breed not unlike the tweedy trout fisherman) swear by the closed-face reel, since they often fish at night.

Mono leaders, or *shock cords*, are advisable, especially when fishing with the lighter lines. A bass doesn't have a toothy mouth, but his jaws are extremely abrasive. A 15- to 20-pound test leader helps keep him from sawing his way free. Even with these heavy leaders, keep checking for obvious weakening.

Artificials that work best are plugs and rubber worms. In the plug department, underwater lures are the most productive. The depth at which you work them should be a function of the water you're fishing. You'll seldom find a bigmouth far from the protection of vegetation, so a lure that just skims across the top of bottom growth will at least be in the best position to interest a bass. Remember too, that weeds seldom grow in water deeper than 20 feet, so this becomes something of a cutoff point for resident fish.

Bass seem to strike as much by sound as sight, so many of the best lures incorporate rattles, spluttering propellers, and vibrating fins to attract attention.

Topwater plugs, while not quite the producers divers are, amount to the most exciting fishing. When hitting one of these lures, a bass will often clear the water by a foot or more in a flurry of spray, enough to put the most relaxed angler on the balls of his feet. Topwater plugs are also advantageous in that they can be worked through protruding reeds and around pods of lilies, two of a bass's favorite hangouts. They're also first choice for night fishermen, since the noisy burbling and splashing and the ripples they create make them easy for a feeding fish to locate.

A few other rules of thumb for bugging a bass; when the water's cool, bigmouth will be most prone to take an underwater bait. When it's warm, he'll tend to look toward the top. Seventy-two degrees is about the perfect temperature for this species.

Many of the serious bass fishermen I've spoken to theorize that bass feed according to their stomachs and not on a predictable schedule. When their stomachs become empty, they gorge themselves, then remain inactive until they again get hungry. The rate of digestion, and consequently the frequency of feeding periods, is determined by things like water temperature, rate of growth, and energy expended.

This would explain in part a bass's unpredictable nature. One day the fish will be on a feeding binge and you can't seem to do anything wrong. The next day, using the same lure in the same place at the same time, you won't get a hit.

When bass are off feed however, they can be teased, cajoled, or angered into striking. Repeated casts to suspected lies with a noisy, hyperactive lure is one way to play upon this nature. Switching to a rubber worm is another productive approach.

Just what a bigmouth thinks he's looking at when he sizes up a rubber worm is open to plenty of speculation. It's hard to believe than any self-respecting, otherwise intelligent fish could mistake one for a legitimate meal. The absolutely worst-producing rubber worm I've ever used looked exactly like an honest-to-gosh worm, but bass want them, good-looking or no, and want them badly. Knowing this, imaginative anglers have turned a simple thing like a rubber worm into a very complex lure.

They come in short designs and long designs. Some of them are soft, others are hard, some float, some don't. Their tails are narrow, their tails are wide, and they come in all the colors of the rainbow, including polka dots.

Speaking from personal experience, I've had the most success with 6- to 8-inch worms of the softest rubber available, colored black or insect green, with wormlike, not fanciful, features cast in the rubber.

The floating kind have proven best in warm waters and at night. Sinkers work best during the day. And you can take it from there.

Working any kind of rubber worm is a matter of patience. Cast, let it sit, then move it across the bottom, through the weeds, or over the surface at a slow pace. When a bass picks a worm up, let him have it. Unlike more conventional lures, bass like to chew on these for a while.

Although plugs and worms make up the bulk of the hardware in a bass angler's tacklebox, junebug spoons like the Sprite and lead-headed jigs with spinners on wire spreaders like the Bushwacker also catch their share of fish. Extra attraction is often added to these spinnerbaits in the form of a strip of natural or colored pork-rind.

Any artificials you choose will perform most satisfactorily if they have some weedless feature. They'll give you greater latitude to work that water where fish are most likely to lie.

Natural baits for bass include just about any critter you might find in or near the water: crayfish, leeches, minnows, frogs, even small snakes and mice. Active live baits (frogs and minnows) can be still-fished with or without a float. Those that remain essentially static on a hook (leeches and crayfish) should be worked like a rubber worm.

Bass have hard mouths and ingest a bait deeply. The best hooks are short-pointed with a high barb and long shank. Choose sizes from number 2 to 4/0, depending on your bait size and the average size of the bass you're after.

Most bass lakes are tough to fish from shore, or by wading, so a boat and motor is a big asset. If you're into bassing big, you might want a specially built "bassboat" that boasts features like swivel chairs, foot-controlled electric motors and behemoth outboards that push these craft from hot spot to hot spot at speeds up to 60 miles an hour.

Bigmouth bass are largely inactive in water under 62 degrees. When the temperature climbs above that level, they can be found feeding around any natural obstruction that affords both food and protection: bridge pilings, rock bars, aquatic vegetation, and flooded brush to name a few.

Bedding, the time of mating, occurs in the spring—March in Florida, May in New York, early June in Maine. When legal seasons permit, it's this time when the biggest bass are usually caught.

The technique involves first finding a bed. This will be a scooped-out craterlike hole in shallow water, usually quite easy to spot since males keep the nest clean of silt and dirt, giving it a brighter appearance than the surrounding bottom.

Once a bed is located, the angler backs off and casts into the nest, usually with a rubber worm or minnow.

At first, the bass is interested only in moving the bait away from the nest. He might pick it up and carry it away three or four times. Finally, he gets angry and ingests the offender. Set your hook, and you're onto some action.

SMALLMOUTH BASS

The smallmouth claims its own circle of adherents, most of whom insist their favorite fish is the sportiest in the nation.

Using light spinning tackle and noisy propeller plug, Bob Rosko landed this fine smallmouth bass while working the shoreline of Pennsylvania's Susquehanna River with his dad.

They do have their point; a smallmouth is an extremely selective feeder when compared to his bigmouthed cousin. Where a bigmouth will slash at any potential meal when he's hungry, smallmouth are far more prone to pick and choose, and anglers have to be more attuned to their food preferences.

Pound-for-pound, I think the smallmouth is a far better fighter too. The largest smallmouth I ever took was a 4-pounder, and his flared, red gills as he tap-danced across the Hudson River are still as vivid today as they were ten years ago. I can't remember an equally memorable battle with any largemouth in his weight class.

The smallmouth is small by bass standards; that 4-pounder was exceptional for an eastern fish. In some of the famous southern smallmouth lakes in the TVA chain, 6- to 8-pounders are caught, but are by no means common.

This bass makes up for his size however, in his sheer activity on a hook. When you tie into one they shudder, shiver, dash, and can be counted on for plenty of aerial acrobatics at the end of each run.

In general, smallmouth favor cool clear water and prefer to hide out around rocks in rivers or lakes, rather than lush stands of vegetation.

They're common inhabitants of many eastern trout streams and the boulder-bottomed ponds of our northern states.

Rather than trying to bull their way to protection and break you off, a smallmouth's escape technique is to try to throw your hook back at you. His selective feeding habits preclude the use of large lures and dictate light lines. This all points the way to tackle on the light end of the spectrum, which also affords the fish a chance to do his fighting best.

Medium-light- to light-action rods, 6 to 7 feet in length are my favorites. Most of your fishing will be done either from a boat or on a large stream, so a short-swinging rod isn't necessary. The longer rods also help keep a taut line when the fish clears the water. Reels should be standard freshwater weights, 4 to 7 ounces, and there's no need for line heavier than 6-pound test. On eastern streams where angling pressure is heavy, the invisible qualities of 3- and 4-pound test are often desirable.

Look for lake-dwelling smallmouth around sharp underwater dropoffs, gravel bars, and islands with steep shores during the day. At this time these fish are most susceptible to trolling with plugs and spoons, just off the bottom. Smallmouth seldom feed at depths greater than 20 feet.

In the evening, these fish will often move into the shallows of a lake in search of minnows, crayfish, and frogs. At this time, they can be fished from shore, using shallow-running spoons and plugs, rubber worms, and occasionally, topwater gear.

River-dwelling smallmouth hole up in slack-water lies out of the main current—pockets behind rocks; deep, slow holes; and backwaters. There should however, be some current present. Dead water will be a poor producer.

The hellgrammite is a larva that ultimately develops into the dobson fly. It's an excellent bass bait—in fact, it'll be taken by most any species it drifts by.

When they're on feed, usually morning and evening, you'll find them at the foot of bubbling riffles and shallow bars where they pick up aquatic insects and minnows.

Smallmouth in rivers seem to prefer smaller lures than those in lakes; tiny plugs, jigs, spinners, and spoons. Like the fish in lakes however, they'll respond to hardware fished deep during the day and shallow during feeding periods.

Live baitfishing is productive for smallmouth, and the favored technique is drifting in a lake or bottom-bouncing in a river. These fish like to take food on the move.

A sampling of appropriate baits include minnows, soft-shelled crayfish, hellgrammites, and worms.

Don't overlook the possibility of spin-fishing with a fly. Some of the best river-smallmouth fishing I've ever had has been with a bubble float and bit of fluff. Choose large flies tied on a number 4 to number 8 hook. Some of the patterns to turn to include woolly worms, bivisibles, wulff patterns, and small, deer-hair bass bugs.

STRIPED BASS

No, you're not in the wrong section. Striped bass inhabit freshwater too. Part of the story is that they're anadromous—they spawn in freshwater. But more important to the freshwater fisherman is the landlocked striper— an oddball of the breed that spends all his life in freshwater.

Because of some weird and fortunate quirks of fate and nature, landlocked stripers became a reality in the 1940's. They established themselves in the Santee-Cooper lakes of South Carolina, spawned and prospered.

From that brood stock, transplants have been made throughout the South, and now, stripers are common catches in many natural lakes and man-made reservoirs there.

The fish average between 8 and 15 pounds, with 30 pounders not uncommon. Consequently, heavy tackle by fresh-water standards is the norm. Twelve-pound test line is about the lightest used, with 200 yards of it needed on a heavy-duty fresh-water reel. Rods are stiff and long. Though these fish are often trolled, enough casting situations arise to make an 8-foot rod something of an edge.

Artificial baits include large jigs, spoons, and topwater plugs—essentially the same stuff used in the sea, so you might check Milt's salty rundown.

Natural baits include large herring, shad, and pieces of cut fish impaled on a 2/0 to 6/0 hook.

Several techniques are employed, most of which require a boat. The most exciting is *jump fishing*, largely a fall and early winter pastime.

At this time, schools of stripers congregate to feed on surfacing baitfish. The brawl is usually given away by gulls and terns who gather to pick up the pieces. When these birds are sighted, anglers rush to the spot and begin casting into the school, usually with spectacular results.

Cut-bait fishing involves either drifting or still fishing, with the bait just off the bottom. This practice is most common in spring and early summer.

Deep-trolling with artificials probably accounts for the most stripers taken, since it works year round. However, the depths at which the fish often lie sometimes require conventional reels and lead-core line.

Next to jump-fishing, shore jigging rates as sporty striper angling. The technique is most often employed at the tailrace of a dam, but I've also used it with great success in the canal that joins the two Santee-Cooper lakes.

During the spawning run, stripers move upriver. They'll rest in eddies, and be stopped cold by a dam. By casting a jig into suspected lies, or the surging waters of a tailrace, you can often tease them into striking. More often than not, they hit that jig on the fall, so remember to keep a taut line and be sensitive to the lightest tap. A mouselike nip once caught me a 25 pounder!

CARP

Those of you who relish the delicate nuances of hairlining for trout or top-popping for bull bass are sure to shudder at the inclusion of this species. But don't get too snobbish; the lowly carp has quite a few things going for him.

Probably most significantly, a carp can live just about anyplace. This bothers some, and rightly so, since they often take up residence in water suitable to other gamefish—and squeeze them out. On the other side of the coin, they can live in and with pollution—a condition pitifully common around our big cities, and thereby provide kids and grown-ups alike with some sport close to home.

Secondly, a carp is a very able opponent on the business end of a spinning rod. They grow large fast, fight with dedication, and have surprising stamina.

Perhaps most endearing of all to those of us who often come home with an empty stringer, they're easy to catch, and where there's one of 'em there's lots of 'em.

You'll get the most fun out of carp if you go light. They're not a fish that tries to hang you up or throw the hook; they just get in there and

Carp are plentiful in most of our major river systems. On a spin-casting rig they're great sport and will fight harder than many species. Larry Kreh made this nice catch on the Potomac River in Maryland.

brawl, so a light-action rod, 4- to 5-ounce reel and 4-pound test line will be the most fun. If you're really serious about carp fishing, choose a soft rod. You'll be casting nothing but bait.

Of the baits that take these fish, most of them are unnatural. Corn is one carp-getter, oatmeal and cornmeal two others. Doughballs are a perennial favorite, and speaking from personal experience, the best bait of all. Mix flour and cold water until it's the consistency of putty. You can also add flavoring—vanilla, almond extract, or my favorite, blackberry brandy. (In my carp-fishing days, I liked to chew on doughballs!)

Carp have small, tough, fleshy mouths, and aren't particularly bright about the taste of metal, so use long-shanked number-6 to number-8 hooks with a short, sharp point. Carp are essentially bottom-feeders, so a slip-sinker or still-fishing rig will prove the most productive. Just cast into a likely looking spot, cradle your rod in a forked stick, and wait for a taker.

You can also chum for carp by putting a handful of oatmeal and a rock in an old, nylon stocking. Tie it off, and throw it in the general area of your hook.

There are times when carp will feed on top, most notably in ponds they share with goldfish. Sunday strollers occasionally throw bread out for the goldfish, and the carp quickly adapt to this free meal. With carp of this persuasion, you can bring along a loaf of fresh bread (stale bread won't sustain a cast), bury the hook in a quarter-slice, and cast your own bread upon the waters.

Carp will even take an artificial under these conditions: go to an up-holstery shop and buy some foam rubber. Cut it in the shape of a quarter-slice of bread with scissors and thread a stiff-wire harness, with treble hooks attached, through the foam.

Throw some pieces of real bread out for camouflage, and get ready for the action. Like dry-fly fishing for trout, or top-plugging for bass, you'll find this sophisticated, topwater technique the epitome of sport where carp are concerned.

CATFISH

Like carp, spinning for catfish is largely a baitfishing venture. They feed exclusively on the bottom and, except for the channel cat, prefer still to moving bait.

Tackle for catfish is determined by their size. Blue catfish often are caught in excess of 40 pounds. Channel cats sometimes go 15, and flathead cats 10. Bullheads, not really a catfish, but susceptable to the same angling methods, seldom exceed 3 pounds.

The spectrum of catfish rod and reels then, can go from the heavy-weights to the ultralights, and the hooks can run from 6/0's down to number 8's, but remember that these fish frequent snaggy habitats, so con-

Meet the catfish. Not pretty by any means, but great fun when taken on spinning tackle. Blue cats and channel catfish are among the most favored fresh water table fish. This heavyweight was landed in Tennessee.

Bullheads and this lone sunfish made for a pleasant morning's fishing with a spin-cast outfit. Both species are caught throughout the country and readily take a wide variety of natural baits.

sider equipment stout enough to snub them on a run or wrestle them from a pile of brush.

Catfish have bony mouths tough even in the fleshy parts. Use short-pointed, low-barbed hooks.

Catfish baits include worms, doughballs, cheese balls, cut fish, dead minnows, frogs, and meats like liver, beef, and chicken entrails. The riper these baits are, the better they seem to work. Catfish feed primarily by odors picked up by their "whiskers" (barbels), and are usually most active at night.

The grayling inhabits icy mountain streams and provides anglers using ultra-light spinning tackle with fine sport. It's found in many waters of the Northwest, but greatest success with it is experienced in Alaska and Canada.

GRAYLING

Grayling are a northern-dweller, found in the icy mountain streams and lakes of the Rocky Mountain West, Canada and Alaska.

Though their size isn't impressive (a 2-pounder is bragging size), the country they inhabit and their appearance is. A grayling's trademark is a saillike dorsal fin, speckled with iridescent blue and red, with pectoral-fin coloring to match.

Because the fish is small, with a delicate mouth, light tackle in the extreme is preferred. This lightweight tackle is of direct benefit to anglers too, most of whom find themselves huffing and puffing up the mountain trails that lead to grayling water.

Because of its compactness, I prefer a multisectioned 6½-foot trail rod for grayling, limber and light in action. Three- to 4-pound test mono is plenty in the line department, loaded on a 3- to 4-ounce reel. Although short ultralight rods might seem to fit best here, they don't. You might have to cast far into a lake to reach fish, and long rods do this best.

Natural baits for grayling include large nymphs, worms, and small minnows, though the latter two are relatively poor producers. Hardware works best when it's tiny— ⅛- to 1/16-ounce spinners and spoons.

Easily the best grayling baits are flies, and small ones at that. Number 12's are about the largest I fish, and number 14's are favored. Best patterns include black gnat, caddis, spruce grubworm, and green woolly worm.

Grayling characteristically hang out in schools, so when you tie into one, stick around. There will probably be other takers in the area. Favored hangouts for these fish in lakes are rocky dropoffs near shore and stream inlets and outlets. In streams, you'll be most likely to locate them in deep, slow-moving holes, especially when those holes lie at the foot of a bubbly riffle.

When grayling strike, they really hit hard, so when fishing with a taut line (as when retrieving a lure or a fly-and-bubble) keep your drag on the light side. They're fast to drop an imitation though, so if you're using dries, with their attendant slack line, you'll have to set your hook in a hurry.

PANFISH

Fish that fit into the panfish category include crappies, perch, and sunfish. Like carp and catfish, panfish are considered second-best as a gamefish, but in terms of man hours spent in their pursuit, they rate high in popularity indeed.

In most situations, panfish respond best to light or ultralight spinning tackle. Crappies and sunfish seldom exceed 9 inches, and yellow perch 12, so this light tackle amounts to an equalizer, as well as a means to handle the small baits they favor.

Crappies

Crappies are a breed that boasts two species—the white crappie and black crappie. Both are nearly identical in markings, size, and food preference. In terms of practical angling, their basic difference lies in habitat.

Yellow perch are popular because they're usually extremely plentiful and provide fast action on spinning tackle. Small minnows are a favorite bait for this tasty panfish.

White crappie prefer slightly turbid waters, blacks clear water. However, so many transplants and introductions have taken place that even this differentiation is disappearing, and both species often end up on the same stringer.

Minnows make up the bulk of a crappie's diet, and it's this natural bait, or an imitation of the same, that produces the most fish. Small spoons, spinners, a spinner-and-fly combination, or live minnows all work when trolled. Tiny yellow and white jigs are deadly once you locate concentrations of fish. Live minnows can be still-fished with a bobber and hooks as large as number 4. A crappie isn't particularly big, but his mouth is.

Particular hot spots for crappies are brushy shores, underwater logs, and sunken brush. The latter is so popular, in fact, that anglers often make their own fishing holes by sinking a mat of brush in the middle of a lake.

Once these brushpiles are located or manufactured, you can fish them by trolling around them, jigging above them, or using live minnows on a float.

Since crappie prefer water depths between 8 and 15 feet, live-bait fishermen will find the sliding-float rig useful for this species. Crappie are not bottom-feeders. Rather, they look for their food a few feet off the bottom.

Both species have the nickname of "papermouth" since they have very soft, tender mouths, so make it a rule to keep a light hand on your rod. Best fishing for both species is in midspring, when a combination of spawning and schooling often produces catches of many fish.

Perch

Perch, both yellow and white, are another panfish that enjoys quite a bit of popularity. They're common inhabitants of farm ponds and lakes nationwide and most often fall prey to natural bait (worms or minnows), still-fished or trolled.

Like the crappie, perch prefer to feed a few feet off the bottom. In water deeper than 6 feet, a sliding-float rig is best for baitfishing. Perch are essentially a school fish, and do plenty of roaming. Consequently, any area of a given lake will run hot and cold.

These schools are usually of the same-sized fish, so should you start to take perch in the 9- to 12-inch category stay with that school. If the fish run small, move on. Perch have a tendency to overpopulate, resulting in lakes glutted with stunted fish. When you catch nothing but 4- to 6-inch fish, better find another perch pond.

Although perch are primarily caught on natural bait, they will take a spinner-and-fly combination, small spoons, and tiny jigs. A jig and bait (maggots, grubworms, mealworms) is a favorite combination for fishing through ice.

When removing a perch from the hook, be careful. They've got as many spines as a porcupine.

Sunfish

Sunfish include four species of interest to the angler—the bluegill, pumpkinseed, redbreast, and redear. At least one of these breeds can be found in every state of the union.

Although sunfish seldom exceed a pound in weight, they're the hardest fighting of all the panfish, pitting their pancake-shaped bulk in a right-angle battle against the pull of a line.

Sunfish are most often found in weedy shallows, or in the shady protection of overhanging bankbrush or a tree limb. They inhabit ponds, lakes, and sluggish streams and feed most actively morning and evening.

Sunfish will take a variety of natural baits—worms, grubs, caterpillars, crickets, and, occasionally, small minnows. They feed a few feet off the bottom, so a float amounts to the best bait rig. They also take these baits when trolled slowly behind a supplementary spinner.

While sunfish will occasionally strike a small lure, their real love in terms of artificials is for flies—wets, dries, and especially floating rubber-legged spiders and small poppers. These poppers are particular fun since they sometimes turn up a bass.

Colors on artificials should be bright—reds, yellows, and oranges. Sunfish have a small mouth, so hooks shouldn't be larger than number 8 to number 10.

In the north, sunfish can be caught through the ice on jig and bait much like the perch.

Bluegills are favorites of youngsters throughout the country and will readily take a worm fished just beneath the surface on a float. A Virginia pond produced this beauty.

THE PIKES; MUSKELLUNGE

Muskies are the largest members of the pike family, attaining weights in excess of 60 pounds. Such giants aren't common however; boated fish run more in the neighborhood of 12 to 25 pounds.

The musky is one of North America's most difficult gamefish to catch. Experienced guides consider a day successful if they get a follow-up, the fishing good if they elicit a strike, and they become ecstatic when a musky is boated.

Although occasional fish are caught from shore, a boat is a big edge, as much because of the mobility it provides as its ability to keep ahead of a following fish.

Muskies like to lie in wait for a meal at the edge of weedbeds, off points of land, and in shallows on the edge of steep dropoffs. They're seldom caught in water deeper than 15 feet, and often are initially located by a swirl, created when they make a pass at a baitfish. Once a muskie's lair is spotted, you've got part of the battle won. Unless they're caught, displaced by a larger fish, or hooked, lost, and frightened away, muskies will remain in the same lie for an entire season.

Once a musky is located or suspected, casting begins. Short casts are favored, since bait control is essential. It's generally agreed that the faster, more agitated the presentation, the better your chances of tempting a fish to strike.

If you're lucky, you'll get some reaction, but often it isn't a strike. The fish will follow your lure, but not take a swipe at it. When this happens, it's imperative to keep your lure in the water and moving until the fish either strikes or loses interest. You can do this by trolling with your boat, by making figure-eights with your lure right next to the gunwale, or by taking a tour around the boat, leading your lure like a dog on a leash. Once these fish are interested in a meal, the presence of a boat or a fisherman doesn't seem to bother them a bit.

If you know a fish is in a lie, but he refuses to be interested, don't give up. Muskies can be teased into striking, and typical musky catches come attached to claims of 30, 40, even 50 casts before the fish took the bait.

Don't overlook the possibility of changing the position of your boat for a slightly different presentation, and of course, changing lures.

If your luck is running good and you get a strike, set the hook several times in quick succession. A musky will often chomp down on a lure so hard that it's immobile in his jaws, and nothing moves—including your unset hooks—until he releases his grip. They also have extremely hard mouths.

When you want to keep a musky, you'll have to kill him before bringing

This 38-pound muskellunge was landed from the waters of upper New York State by an angler working the weedbeds with heavy spinning tackle and a red- and-white wobbler. Muskies are extremely strong fish and will test an angler and his spinning tackle to the limit.

him aboard. Row on row of needle teeth, plus the habit of snapping and thrashing, make them dangerous companions in a small boat.

Tackle for this fish should be heavy; stiff rods, 20-pound plus mono, and heavy-duty reels with at least a 150-yard capacity. A fast-retrieve feature is also desirable.

Your casts won't be long, but they'll be many, so perfect balance of rod, reel and lure is essential. A steel leader or mono shock-cord of at least 40-pound test is also advisable.

Although some fish are caught using 10- to 12-inch suckers float-fished on 3/0 to 5/0 hooks, most musky angling is a matter of artificials. Underwater shallow-running plugs from 3- to 5-ounces are the favored lure, with yellow and black the most popular colors.

Most experienced musky anglers agree weather and season play an important part in the odds for or against success. September and October amount to the best months. Cloudy or hazy days are better than bright sunshine, a rising barometer is a good omen, and wind riffle or chop is better than a slick calm.

NORTHERN PIKE

The northern pike is one of my personal favorites as a gamefish. They're big —20 pounders aren't unusual—they're hard fighters, and they're possessed of an appetite and attitude that can only be described as wolfish.

These fish inhabit lakes and some rivers in our northernmost states and continue their range throughout Canada. Like the musky, they prefer relatively shallow water near shores, islands, and points, where they lie in protective cover, waiting for a meal to pass by.

Medium to medium-heavy tackle is needed to handle most pike. My favorite rig is a 6½-foot medium-stiff action rod, and an 8-ounce heavy-duty fresh-water reel loaded with 15-pound test mono. This stout tackle is often the only way to wrestle a large pike out of the weeds and brush where he usually hides. Steel leaders are also a necessity.

Northern pike are favorites throughout the entire range of many northern states. They'll take a wide variety of lures, and usually take up residence in or around weedbeds. This pair were taken on red-and-white wobblers from the waters of Lake Huron.

Baitfishing is a productive technique for northerns, with large minnows ranking tops as bait. Perch, suckers, and carp all work. When no live bait is available, the belly of a large perch or small pike, cut into a long, slender strip, also works wonders.

Fishing these with a float gets its share of strikes, but I prefer a sinking bait. Rig up with a 2/0 to 4/0 short-pointed, low-barbed hook, and cast a minnow into potentially productive waters. You shouldn't need a weight since the bait should be big enough to cast on its own.

Once the bait sinks, begin a slow retrieve, checkered with frequent pauses. When you feel a strike, give the fish a free line until he stops running, then set the hook.

Lures are also productive, either trolled, or cast from boat or shore. Work the edge of weedbeds, stands of flooded brush, sunken logs, and lily pads. The lure that's proven itself tops for pike is the red-and-white wobbler. Choose sizes between 3 and 5 inches long.

Another artificial that's proven its worth by me is the floating minnow with a dished lip for diving. Because of its buoyant nature, this lure can be made to barely skim the top of weedbeds—a trick impossible with sinking lures.

A further advantage to this lure lies in the pike's habit of following a retrieve right up to a boat or shore. With a sinking lure, there's not too much you can do but let it lie there. A floater on the other hand, can be made to vibrate, dance, and create all kinds of disturbance, often tempting a strike.

Pike are prone to feed in the daylight hours. Activity usually peaks out around 11 A.M. and 3 P.M. At these times, I've found a slow, measured retrieve most appealing. However, when the pike are off feed, you can often play on their predaceous nature by retrieving at top speed or trolling around a lake at half-throttle.

When removing hooks from a pike's mouth, you'll need some sort of pliers. Their needle-sharp teeth can make mincemeat out of a hand.

PICKEREL

These fish are the smallest of the pike family, but little feller or no, their behavior is identical to their big brothers—they're a water wolf.

Pickerel are found throughout the East and South, and there are three types native to America—the grass and redfin pickerel seldom grow larger than 12 inches long and consequently are the least desirable as a sport fish. The chain pickerel grows larger, averaging between 2 and 4 pounds, and consequently this species is the principal quarry of the spin-fisherman.

Tackle for pickerel should be light; they're not large enough to put heavy gear to the test, and although they've been known to strike a lure nearly as large as they, pickerel do show a preference for smallish hardware.

Light to ultralight rods and reels, loaded with 3- to 6-pound test will deliver both the right lures and the most fun. Although a pickerel has hellish teeth, steel leaders on this light line sometimes create casting problems. Use either the lightest, shortest leader you can find, tie up to an 8- to 10-pound test mono shock-cord, or make a habit of breaking off and retieing after each strike.

The best live bait for pickerel is a minnow, fished with a float. Frogs occasionally take fish, but rate second-best. Other common baits—nymphs, worms, grasshoppers and the like—seldom interest a pickerel.

The lure that takes top honors is a ¼- to ⅛-ounce wobbling spoon, colored red and white. This fish prefers to hide out in dense stands of aquatic growth, so a weedless hook on any lure will produce the most strikes. Slow-moving, flashy spinners produce well, as do fly-weight banana plugs, though both types get gummed up easily by weeds.

Prospect for pickerel anywhere you find aquatic growth. They'll lie motionless in this stuff, facing a patch of open water. When a baitfish swims by, they rocket out, snare their meal, then return to the same spot to lie and wait again.

If you're sharp-eyed, you can often see them where they hide, and cast directly to them. Pickerel aren't especially shy, and can be approached to within 12 feet.

During the winter months many spin-fishermen use tiny jigs or wobblers and fish through the ice for pickerel. In summertime they're often found close to shore among the weeds, where they'll take a wide variety of spinning lures, and especially live minnows. A Connecticut pond produced these in mid-winter.

Remember that pickerel don't like to chase a meal across a wide patch of open water. In practical fishing terms, this means small pockets of open water in the middle of a snarl of weeds hold good potential for a strike. So do slashes of open water between weeds and shore, and slack eddies in lush, sluggish rivers. Work any weedbed by casting parallel to its perimeter, rather than at right angles to it. In really thick weeds, don't overlook the possibility of using a streamer or bucktail with a light pinch of shot. I've caught many a chainside by using my rod like a cane pole, guiding a mickey finn or coachman streamer through an otherwise impenetrable tangle.

SALMON; COHO

The coho salmon is currently the hottest thing that swims. This fish, anadromous and native to the Pacific coast, is really the silver salmon and was introduced to Lake Michigan in the mid-'60's. He adapted to his exclusively fresh-water environment, and since then, has been providing upper Midwest anglers with exciting sport that often approaches the proportions of madness.

During the height of coho runs, sporting goods stores are stripped clean of tackle in a day. When schools are located, you can practically walk on water—stepping from boat to boat of course. Dedicated anglers have mortgaged their homes and spent their life savings to buy coho boats, capable of handling the rough weather common to the Great Lakes.

And it's not all that surprising. Coho grow to 20 pounds and up. They're spectacular fighters, stripping off 50 yards of line in the twinkling of an eye and often capping their runs by turning to the air. They can be caught year 'round too, so it's not too hard to understand how residents near a lake once thought doomed are so susceptible to this coho craze.

Coho are taken from water anywhere from 1 to 180 feet deep. The determining factor in where the fish will lie is temperature; they like it from 50 to 55 degrees.

When the fish are deep (usually the summer months), only conventional trolling rigs with wire or lead-core line will get to them. However spring, and especially fall (the time of spawning) finds them close to the top. At this time, they're well within the reach of the spin-fisherman.

The sheer size of the fish dictates heavy to medium-heavy tackle: 7- to 8-foot rods, 15- to 20-pound test line, and 8- to 10-ounce reels. This rig is used both for trolling, and when schools are located by feeding birds, to cast into the rolling fish. During the fall spawning run, coho concentrate at the mouths of rivers, ready to make their migrations. At this time they're ready game for the shorecaster.

These fine coho salmon were taken from the waters of Lake Michigan—within sight of Chicago's skyscrapers. Flashers ahead of subsurface swimming plugs sent into the depths with trolling sinkers proved the right combination for the heavy spinning tackle that had to be used as a result of the heavy terminal tackle.

Artificials are the most popular baits, with silver plugs and spoons, 3 to 5 inches in length the best producers. Other colors that find favor among fish and fisherman alike are steelblue, red-and-white, and around spawning time, fluorescent reds and oranges.

It's generally agreed that the lure you use isn't the telling factor in success though. What is important is (1) locating the fish and (2) fishing at the proper depth. Both these rules are interrelated.

Since temperature is so important to a coho, some idea of the depth at which their optimum water occurs is necessary. Bring a fishing thermometer with you.

Fish locaters amount to another real asset—not so much to locate the coho (during nonspawning times, the fish are quite scattered), but to locate the bait he feeds on—usually alewives or herring. When both bait-fish and proper temperature occur at the same depth, you're in business.

Quite possibly, this might be too far down to reach by conventional spin-trolling methods. Try rigging a heavy weight on a three-way swivel, and a lure on a 3-foot mono leader. Another way to get down deep without special line is to use a trolling plane.

These gadgets are affixed between line and lure, and plane downward, carrying you deep without too much weight. When a fish strikes, the plane straightens out, putting up little resistance and allowing you to fight the fish to the top without having to overcome any extra drag. One brand name that comes to mind is Pink Lady.

Trolling or casting for coho is a rather fast proposition when compared to other freshwater fish. You'll get the most strikes at four to eight knots.

Baitfishing for coho is another possibility, though it's seldom as successful as trolling. The technique is to locate baitfish, then lower a sinker and bait (sucker, shrimp, alewife) to that level. Anchor or drift, and give your offering some action by jigging. Large white or blue jigs are also used in conjunction with this approach, often coupled with bait.

Coho have received the most recognition as a Great Lakes fish, but their success there has prompted other fish and game departments to try experimental stocking in other states. If they adapt to other waters with the gusto exhibited in the past, the coho will surely rate as one of the nation's most popular gamefish.

SALMON; KING (ALSO CHINOOK)

Like the coho, King salmon have also been successfully introduced to the Great Lakes, and the techniques for catching them are essentially the same as those for the coho. Kings however, are larger fish, so even heavier tackle is the rule. They're also characteristically found at levels even deeper than the coho, so they're often beyond the reach of the spin-fisherman.

On the northern Pacific coast however, upriver migrations of this anadromous fish put him well within the reach of spinning tackle, and salmon in excess of 40 pounds are often taken.

Like the steelhead, a fish caught by similar techniques, salmon fishing is a progressive thing. Near the coast, it's a mid-to-late spring pastime, and in the mountain streams of Idaho and Washington, an early summer pursuit.

Heavy tackle is the rule, with 7½- to 8½-foot medium-heavy to heavy rods the favored sticks. Line weights go to 30 pounds, and reels are heavy-duty, with large capacities.

Bottom-bouncing terminal tackle, rigged on a three-way swivel is the usual angling method, with bait (shrimp or salmon roe) favored when the water's cloudy. Under clearwater conditions, lures are most often used. These lures are small when compared to the fish that strike them; ¼ ounce to ½ ounce are the most common weights, with silver, gold, and, fluorescent spinners the most popular colors and style.

Near the coast where rivers are wide, salmon are taken on the move or at rest, and from a variety of water. Favorite stalking grounds there are long, slow runs, the downstream side of gravel bars, and deep holes. As the rivers break up into tributaries, salmon seem to get more single-minded, and only can be persuaded to strike while resting on their way upriver.

Unlike the steelhead, who prefer shallow lies, salmon are prone to do their resting in deep, dark holes carved in the switchback of a small stream or at the foot of a falls. Even in these small streams, heavy tackle is the rule. You'll need plenty of beef to wrestle them away from snags and brush, and more often than not, the fish will win.

Realize too, that many streams favored by salmon are closed to fishing to allow undisturbed spawning. So check state regulations before you wet a line.

If you check the regulations in person you'll also be able to learn something about your chances for success. In the West, migratory fish are counted as they vault fish-ladders to clear dams, providing an accurate tally of just how many fish are in a given section of river, and the degree to which the run is underway.

In the Great Lakes, both species of salmon run upriver too, and angling methods approximate those used in the Northwest.

SHAD

Shad are anadromous fish, found on both coasts. They enter fresh-water streams and rivers during the spring, their run peaking out in Florida in March and Connecticut in May.

There are two species of shad—the American and hickory shad. Both are susceptible to essentially the same angling techniques.

Medium-light to light tackle is best; 6- to 7-foot limber rods, and 6- to 8-pound test line. This light tackle not only makes the most out of a very sporty fighter, it's also best-suited to the tiny lures these fish favor.

Shad techniques include shorecasting and trolling, and both approaches use essentially the same hardware: ¼- to ⅛-ounce spoons, spinners or jigs in silver or gold. Probably the most popular lure for these fish is a blend of spoon and jig called a *shad dart*. Occasionally, extra dressing is added to this hardware in the form of red, yellow, or white bucktail.

The trick to catching shad lies in a deep, erratic retrieve. These fish insist on picking a lure right off the bottom. Consequently, slow trolling is a must, and the addition of some extra weight in the form of a keel or rubber-cored sinker often spells the difference between success and failure. Another twist to rigging for shad lies in the use of two lures, one usually a spoon that rides slightly off the bottom, the other a heavy dart that scrapes bottom. The spoon is tied to a dropper or three-way swivel, and quite often, two fish can be taken at once.

Shorecasters find most success with a cast quartered across the current,

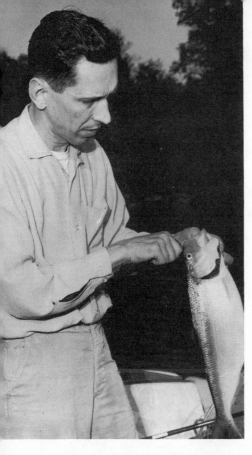

Shad readily strike a small shad dart and will give you great sport on light spinning tackle. They're caught in many California rivers by anglers who troll slowly. East coast anglers enjoy fine spring sport too, but small lures are an absolute must.

and an erratic, jigginglike retrieve that has their hardware hopscotching across the bottom. This technique also works well from an anchored boat.

Shad run in schools, so hooking one fish usually means there are more in the neighborhood. Favored places to prospect include the foot of shallow sand or gravel bars, the meeting of two currents, and best of all, the tailraces of dams.

There, these fish gang up in phenomenal numbers, and shad anglers along with them.

THE TROUTS

When I think "trout," images of pink-fleshed, brightly colored naturals pop into my head; wary residents of cold, clear waters, sensitive to the slightest bank vibration or slosh of a wading angler. But being something of a pragmatist, that image is gradually eased aside to share the spotlight with yet another fish, the hatchery trout.

It's a fact of fishing life that of all our fresh-water gamefish, the trout is most subject to extensive put-and-take fishing. A combination of marginal

A great deal of the trout fishing in the East is put-and-take. Fish stocked in the spring are quickly caught by huge crowds such as the one pictured here on opening day on a typical stream near a metropolitan area.

waters and public demand makes stocking the only practical way many urban-dwelling and southern anglers can ever hope to have these fish on a line.

It's a further fact of life that those in the pursuit of hatchery trout hardly will benefit by the reams of careful, calculated advice ground out yearly by outdoor writers, dedicated to helping their angling readership overcome the genius of native fish.

Plainly put, hatchery trout are rather dumb. They're easy to catch and should be caught, for left alone, most would die. But, they do respond best to techniques not usually associated with more conventional trout fishing.

In terms of tackle, anything will do. I can remember spending one opening day next to an old gent who was fishing with a surf-casting spin rig, bobber and worm. He caught his limit.

Of course, landing a 9-inch trout on 20-pound test line could hardly be called exciting, so to make the most of these fish, go light. A slender 6½-foot rod, 4-ounce reel, and 4-pound test mono is a passable combination.

Hatchery trout are most prone to take bait, since all their past food essentially falls into this category, Worms will always work. Other popular baits include corn, salmon eggs, cheeseballs, and cut liver.

Terminal tackle should include number 8 to number 12 bait-holder hooks, with perhaps a pinch of tiny shot. It's important to keep your bait as light as possible; these fish are used to a meal that floats down on them from above or hangs in the water. Fish pellets seldom make it to the bottom, so hatchery trout aren't keyed to look for a meal there. For this reason, float fishing at 2- to 3-foot depths is quite successful. So is a painfully slow retrieve that keeps your bait up off the bottom.

Presentation is nothing more than getting a bait in front of them—if they see it, they'll take it. However, finding the fish sometimes takes a little savvy.

Look for them at inlets and outlets of stocked lakes. A channel in a lake that also has a flow of current is another good place. In streams, any deep holes, the foot of waterfalls, tunnels and culverts all amount to hot spots. These places are good because they're a lot like the conditions an artificially raised fish is used to; the long cement ponds of a hatchery. When trout are removed from this familiar environment, they search out a similar spot in their new home.

Occasionally, stocked ponds and streams are listed as off-limits to bait-fishermen. Hatchery trout will take artificials, but make them small and move them slow. One-eighth-ounce wide-bladed spinners are good, and so are fly-weight banana plugs. The brighter they are the better they'll work, since most fish will strike from curiosity.

Don't overlook spin-fly fishing. The trick is to move your fly slow, and keep it well up off the bottom. A bubble float is the best way to achieve this effect.

The first two weeks of the season will find most hatchery trout either caught or dead. Occasionally, there's a second stocking where public interest in trout fishing runs high. After that two-week period, the few surviving stockers begin to get smart. They start to go native and become increasingly more difficult to catch. At this time, start to apply some of the more sophisticated techniques employed to fool native fish.

Brook Trout

Brook trout are most often found in shady, spring-fed streams and creeks. They have a natural liking for small water and a low tolerance for warm temperatures. In our northernmost states, brookies are also found in cold, deep lakes, often sharing those waters with lake trout, a species to which they're closely related.

Because the brookie is a smallish fish (2 pounds is bragging size), and his home a place of close brush and narrow banks, short, light, or ultra-light rods and 3- to 4-ounce reels are a good choice of tackle. All trout, brookies included, are wary and selective by nature, so the gossamer, low-visibility lines used in conjunction with light spinning tackle will always be a factor in an angler's favor.

The basic secret to snaring a brookie lies in understanding his means of protection. Rather than being overly shy or skittish, a brookie holes up in some apparently impregnable fortress—an undercut bank, a thatch of

The brook trout is a favorite of spin-fishermen and perhaps one of the easiest of the trouts to catch. Especially active during the spring, it will readily strike most any small spinners, wobblers, tiny plugs, and especially garden worms and live minnows.

drooping willows, or a deep, black hole—and waits patiently for a meal
to come to him. He's not a stalker like a brown or rainbow, so you have
to stalk him.

A brookie's lair can be approached rather closely. You can't disturb his
hiding place by wading through or joggling brush, and you can't make
your presence plainly known, say, by casting a shadow near him. But you
should be able to get close enough for extremely accurate placement of
bait or lure and thereby penetrate his defense.

For the baitfisherman, nothing beats garden hackle. A number 10 bait-
holder hook, hiding in a 4-inch worm will make a sucker out of the most
sophisticated fish. These trout prefer a slow, deliberate presentation and
look for most of their food a few inches off bottom. The addition of a
light piece of lead might help satisfy both requirements should the current
be swift.

Drift a bait into their lair from above, using the current to carry you.
On small, clear streams, be careful not to roil the water or disturb the
bank. The best way to drift a bait to a brookie is to open your bail and
feed out line manually. Don't let lots of slack develop or you won't feel
a bite.

Read the current so it carries your bait past a suspected lie. Brookies will
hide out in slack water adjacent to a feeding lane, then dash out to pick
off food, so plan on a strike during the drift, not the retrieve.

Baitfishing a deep hole requires that you get right on bottom, so add
weight until you pick up the rap of rocks. In cloudy or roily water, the
addition of a supplementary spinner often results in more strikes, since the
fish can more easily spot your bait.

Although worms are the most popular brookie bait, they're by no means
the only food this fish will take. Mayfly and stonefly nymphs make up a
large part of his diet. In warmer months, crickets and grasshoppers are
also good. Brookies aren't great minnow-eaters, so they account for a
less desirable bait. One rather weird meal that's caught many a squaretail
is the fin from another brook trout. However, the use of gamefish, or parts
of gamefish for bait, is illegal in some states.

Because brookies aren't fond of a minnow diet (with the exception of
lunkers), lure-fishing isn't as productive as bait or flies. Lures do catch a
lot of these fish though, probably because so many anglers prefer to use
them.

If lures are your choice, pick small ¼- to ⅛-ounce wobblers and
spinners with plenty of flash. Work them slow and close to bottom. Ultralight wobbling spoons, fished with a small rubber-core sinker a few feet
ahead of the lure, have proven their worth by me. As with bait, remember
that you've got to place your lure close to where a brookie lives. It's
difficult to drift a lure into place, but consider casting across current and
letting it swing by cutbanks, snags, and other hiding spots.

Brookies are especially fond of flies, and a fly-and-bubble can be maneuvered into potential lies much like bait.

Brown Trout

The brown trout is an exotic, imported to this country from Europe in the late 1800's. The brown is quite tolerant of both temperature fluctuations and turbidity and consequently has become a common resident in waters nationwide.

Brown trout don't fare particularly well in the small streams favored by the brookie. Rather, they're a fish of larger rivers and lakes. They also differ from the brookie in that they have a hideaway, but use this place mainly for resting during inactive periods. When they go on feed, they'll move out into a stream, favoring the foot of riffles and bars and the shallow ends of pools for their feeding areas. In lakes, they'll cruise the shallows.

Browns are wary to the extreme. Consequently, under clear-water conditions, it's important to use a light, low-visibility line and tackle capable of relatively long casts.

While they are selective feeders, browns show a real liking for a minnow, consequently they're a prime target for the lure fisherman.

I've found it to be a general rule that the harder a brown is pressured, the less likely he is to take a large lure. On New York's Beaverkill, I've had most success with tiny spinners and wobblers in the ⅛- to 1/16-ounce class. Conversely, when fishing the burly waters of the West, most notably the Madison, I get my best results by using number-4 and number-5 wide-bladed spinners and ½-ounce wobbling spoons.

In all waters however, a cast across stream has produced the most strikes: it's followed by a looped retrieve that covers the fanned-out gravel at the tail of a pool or dances through the runs and eddies at the foot of a bar.

Remember it's quite important that these fish don't know you're around. Never expect a strike from any area of water where you can see the bottom. It's a sure bet that fish lying there can see you.

During inactive periods, browns retreat to their hideaway. At this time, they can occasionally be persuaded to strike. Morning and evening then, the times when fish are most likely to be feeding, are the best times to fish midriver dining areas. During the day, try concentrating your casts close to banks.

When fish are feeding, several brownies can be taken from essentially the same spot. During inactive periods, you're up against a hit-or-miss proposition, so cover plenty of water.

Brown trout in lakes don't exhibit quite the wariness stream fish do. They can be caught by trolling or shorecasting with plugs, spoons, and spinners.

The brown trout is considered by many to be the most difficult trout to fool into striking. A tough adversary on light tackle, it's a challenge to the serious spinner who fishes the big rivers and lakes where browns grow to large sizes.

Trout are active even in cold water, so
that in early spring, with snow still on
the ground, many Oregon and Washington steelhead anglers are out in earnest,
trying their hand to coax strikes from the
rainbow trout that had ventured to sea
and have now returned.

Daytime is usually the best time to troll in deep water. Morning and evening shorecasting or trolling in water 4 to 8 feet deep is productive. Fish move into these shallows to feed, knowing they'll be rich in forage food. Fishing shallows with a fly and bobber at these times is often quite productive too.

Because brown trout are relatively intelligent, many of these fish grow to trophy proportions. They didn't get that way by being foolhardy, so the real lunkers are especially difficult to catch. One of their favorite tricks is near-exclusive nocturnal feeding, so fishing after dark is one way you might latch on to a memorable brown.

Another way to fool them is to fish spring's roily water. At this time even the best-educated fish stands a chance of making a mistake. The reason is threefold; cloudy, turbulent water masks your presence. High water dislodges fish from accustomed, often unapproachable hiding spots, and puts them off guard. Finally, their diet becomes less varied; worms lace the water and become their principle food—a bait wonderfully suited to the spin-fisherman.

This is the time for big nightcrawlers. Because the water's cloudy and your quarry big, use heavier mono than is accepted as standard—up to 10-pound test. Bounce-bottom, covering deep runs, channels, the foot of riffles, and the head of holes.

Don't overlook clear-water tributaries to muddy rivers. All trout will search these places out for a breath of fresh air, often lying right on the dividing line between clear and muddy water. Roily tributaries flowing into clear lakes are good for the opposite reason; fish know those cloudy waters will carry a lot of food.

Again, natural bait will be the best way to go. The water won't be clear enough for lures, and flies haven't yet become a major factor in a brown trout's diet.

Cutthroat Trout

The cutt is a westerner and favors cold, clean waters well above sea-level. He's equally at home in streams and lakes and, like most trout, grows largest in the latter.

Because the water he inhabits is invariably gin-clear, light line, and the tackle needed to handle it, is the rule.

This light tackle provides another edge in that it's best-suited to handling a cutt's favorite menu—flies. Cutthroat will take a wide variety of nymphs, wets, and, when actively feeding on top, dries. Should you see swirls however, make sure the fish are taking floating adults and not emerging nymphs just under the surface. This activity, called *nymphing*, has driven more than one unknowing angler up a wall.

Sil Strung landed these fine cutthroat trout while fishing a high mountain lake in Montana. The cutthroat is a beautiful trout and a tough fighter. It will strike a wide variety of lures and natural baits. Like most other trout, it's especially active during cool weather.

Next on a cutt's list of food preferences is bait, with garden hackle at the top of the list. Like the brookie, he likes both bait and hardware presented slow and deep.

A cutthroat will certainly take a swipe at a lure, and most anglers prefer to take them this way. The best-producing hardware is small, with lots of flash at slow speeds. Trolling a small banana or minnow-shaped plug also takes its share of fish.

Lake Trout

For the majority of the season, lake-trout fishing is a matter of deep-trolling with conventional reels, heavy rods and lead-core or wire line. However, two times a year the lakers become fair game for the spin-fisherman.

The first two weeks immediately following ice-out are easily the best. This is *turnover time*, a period when all the waters in a lake are close to or at the same temperature. The elimination of thermal stratification finds lakers entering shallow, shoreside haunts in search of food.

Since the fish are big, lures should be, too; ⅝ ounce is a fairly standard size by me. Rods, too, should be capable of long casts. Though these fish are in relatively shallow water by lake-trout standards, they seldom come in as close to shore as other species.

Deep-diving plugs and wobbling spoons will produce the best results. Lakers seem to prefer a fast, deep retrieve. I've also had some degree of luck casting a jig for these fish; letting the lure sink to the bottom, jigging, letting it hit bottom again, and so on.

Colors lakers on the prowl seem to favor are silver or white with splashes of fluorescent red. In terms of live bait, lake trout will take 4- to 6-inch herring, alewives, or suckers.

These baits are most productive when trolled in conjunction with a series of spinning blades called *cowbells*.

Although the potential whoppers you might tie into would seem to dictate heavy rods, reels, and line, I prefer to use a long, limber rod loaded with lots of 4- to 6-pound test. With this combination, a large lure and a soft cast, I've got tremendous reach. There's also the matter of feel. I've tried light surf gear on lakers and don't seem to be able to feel their characteristically gentle strike.

If you opt for a rig like this however, plan on losing a lot of lures. Lake trout like to forage around jumbles of rocks, and snags are common.

The other time lakers venture into the shallows occurs in the late fall, just before ice begins to form. The fish have just spawned, and they're quite hungry. The techniques that take them remain the same as those after ice-out, but for some strange reason, I've never had quite the luck at this time of the year that I've enjoyed in the spring.

One factor that might account for this is that I'd rather cast from shore than jockey a boat, and fall lakers don't appear to come quite so close to shore as those in the spring. This obviously points in the direction of the guy who likes to troll.

Rainbow Trout

The rainbow completes the trio of our three most popular trouts, the other two being brooks and browns. Where brookies are shy and sullen, and browns bullish, intelligent, and predatory, rainbows are the devil-may-care gadabout, shooting into a sparkling rapid to seize a bait, then pirouetting across the water in an attempt to give it back.

Rainbows are a spectacular fish; they never go about things halfway.

This fine catch of rainbow trout was made on ultra-light spinning tackle at Eldred Fishing Preserve in New York State. In many metropolitan areas fishing pressure is so great that anglers elect to fish at the pay-as-you-fish preserves where they are able to catch fine trout and avoid the crowds found at most public waters.

When browns or brooks are feeding on top, they dimple the water. Rainbows smack it. Hook a brown or a brook on a lure, and your first sensation is that the lure simply stopped. Have a rainbow take it, and your rod feels like it's going to tear loose from your hand.

This active nature goes even deeper than pure reaction. Rainbows prefer fast water. Where brooks and browns will lie in a slack, bows will often be found feeding right in the foam. They seldom take a bait unless it's on the move and can be teased into striking by successive presentations.

Thus, the basic secret to outsmarting a bow is hard casting and persistence. Once you've placed your offering before the other trouts, you're done. They take it or they don't. But a bow can be convinced.

This can be accomplished in a number of ways. One is simply working a suspected lie until you get a strike (if you miss the strike, the fish will be put down—they're not *that* dumb). Another is to work a lie from several different positions. Still another is to frequently switch lures.

What kind of lures? Quite honestly, with rainbows I have no favorites. Other trouts have indicated a preference pattern, but rainbows and I have established only the broadest limits.

First, they prefer spoons and spinners to plugs or jigs. Second, they like their hardware on the small side—⅜ ounce is about as large as I'll go, even when in water that's known for big fish. When fish average smaller, I go smaller. Finally, they prefer a fast retrieve and like to take that lure when it's fished upstream.

Rainbows have never proven particularly susceptible to the wiles of the baitfisherman. I have taken them while fishing naturals, but on those days, browns and bows always predominate in my creel. If you want to fish bait however, remember to keep it on the move. Bows don't look to the bottom for their feed, so a weighted bait is less desirable than one allowed a natural drift, though you might consider a wisp of lead to help compensate for line drag. Worms will probably prove the most productive, with nymphs taking second place. I've never done well with minnows on stream rainbows.

Flies make up a very important part of a rainbow's diet, but his proclivity for fast water makes a bubble and fly tough to use. In the swift stuff it's almost impossible to feel a hit. Occasionally, bows will be working a dry-fly hatch in slick water, and there they're susceptible to a spinning rig and fly. But at other times, feathers are best left to the guy with a fly rod.

Rainbows are also found in lakes. In the West and Great Lakes, they grow quite large, reaching the 40-pound bulk of the famed Kamloops rainbow.

Spinning techniques for rainbows in lakes differ greatly from those in streams. For one, they'll take a still bait, so bottom fishing with a floated worm is a consistently productive approach.

Like browns, bows in lakes prowl the shallows during feeding periods, and at this time they're prone to strike for the shorecaster or troller. They don't like a fast presentation though, so wide-bladed spinners and extra-active plugs are most successful. They'll also strike a much larger lure than their river counterparts.

Lakes are also great places for a bubble and fly. Nymphs, dries, and wets produce well, but top honors go to imitations of fresh-water shrimp. When this crustacean is present, he usually accounts for the bulk of a lake-dwelling rainbow's diet.

Steelhead Trout

Taxonomically, there's no difference between a steelhead and rainbow trout; practically, there's quite a difference.

Steelhead are migratory. In the Pacific Northwest, they live in the sea and journey hundreds of miles up fresh-water rivers to spawn. They also follow the same pattern in the Great Lakes.

There's also the matter of size; since these fish don't spawn until they reach sizable proportions, few steelheads are caught under 6 pounds, and many of them exceed 10 pounds.

They're also quite different in their feeding patterns, and the spinning techniques to which they respond.

Steelhead seldom eat on their way upstream. Many anglers feel that they strike from anger or curiosity and not hunger. Consequently, steelhead terminal-tackle is rather fanciful when compared to more conventional trout gear.

Basic tackle in the West includes a 7- to 8-foot medium to stiff-action rod, a heavy-duty 8- to 10-ounce reel, and at least 200 yards of 15-pound test. This relatively heavy gear is as much used to handle the swift rivers as the fish. In tributaries of the Great Lakes where waters run slower, medium to medium-heavy tackle is the rule.

The basic western terminal rig consists of a three-way swivel tied to your line. A heavy 3-foot mono leader is attached to the second eye, and 1 to 3 ounces of lead to the third. Steelheading is essentially a bottom-bouncing pastime, and a lot of weight is needed to get there in the West. Without the swivel rig, that heavy lead would make feeling a bite difficult.

On some of the slower rivers around the Great Lakes, a small rubber-core sinker on a single line is enough to get the job done.

There are two yearly steelhead runs; one in the spring and one in the fall. The spring run involves high, cloudy water, and at this time, bait is favored.

The most popular bait is cured salmon or steelhead roe (eggs). This is formed around a number-6 to number-10 treble hook, then covered with a mesh bag to keep it from floating away. A string of fanciful, buoyant fluorescent spinners and bobbers are threaded on the mono leader, then the leader is tied to the baited treble.

Other popular baits include fresh shrimp, Vaseline-covered sponges (this imitates egg clusters), and one to three salmon eggs fished on a single hook.

The fall run finds low, clear water, and at this time, lures are preferred. In the West, the technique again involves the use of a three-way swivel, since the rivers are still relatively fast, and getting close to the bottom is essential.

Wobbling spoons and deep-running plugs up to ⅝ ounce are used, and, again, fluorescent colors are favored.

When steelhead move upriver, they frequently rest in holes. It's during these resting periods that fish are most prone to strike, so learning to identify lies is essential.

As a rule, they won't be deep, dark holes of swirling water. Steelhead are more likely to select a slow-moving slick, 3- to 4-feet deep, or the downriver side of a shallow bar.

Place your cast across and slightly up the current. Keep a taut line, your rod tip high to prevent line drag, and don't retrieve until your rig has swung full downstream. Steelhead are ultimate nibblers, so you'll have some fingertip education to go through, as well as your share of snags.

When you think you feel a bite, strike hard and fast. Steelies won't hold onto a bait for long.

Remember that there will always be fish moving into and out of a hole as they run upriver, so it's senseless to do a lot of riverbank wandering. Find a good lie and stick with it.

WALLEYE

The walleyed pike isn't a pike at all—he's the biggest member of the perch family. Walleye also enjoy a reputation as the bread-and-butter fish of the Midwest, an apt description since their flesh is superb.

Except for rare occasions, walleye are exclusively bottom-feeders, so tackle that gets down there holds an important place in the scheme of walleye fishing.

Though walleye only average 1 to 2 pounds and aren't particularly spectacular fighters, I prefer medium-action rods and 8- to 10-pound test line. It's not a matter of beating the fish, but rather one of setting the hook. I've found walleye to be very delicate biters, and they have a hard mouth. Light lines and rod shafts are just too elastic for a swift, sharp, and sure strike.

When it comes to terminal tackle, number-4 to number-8 hooks, threaded through the lip of a minnow is the all-around walleye catcher. Rig them in conjunction with a slip sinker on 2 to 2½ feet of leader. Worms rate as second best and produce the most hits when blown.

Walleye frequent rivers, but the great majority of these fish are caught in lakes. Still-fishing at anchor or extremely slow trolling in a boat are usually the most productive methods.

Some knowledge of the lake bottom goes a long way toward filling your stringer. These fish school up in 20 to 30 feet of water over rocky bars and submerged islands, and knowing where these features occur will give you a big edge.

Walleye will hit a slow-moving lure so long as it's deep, but the most successful technique in the hardware department is jigging.

A school is located either by exploratory trolling or an electronic fish-

Milt Rosko lifts a fine walleye landed by daughter Linda from a wide mouthed landing net. This beauty was landed while trolling a live minnow down on the bottom at Lake Bemedji in Minnesota. The walleye· is not only a popular scrapper, but also an excellent table fish.

finder, then the anchor is dropped. By jigging just off the bottom, whole limits can be taken without moving an inch.

Yellow and white are the favored colors, and extra enticement can be added to the hook in the form of a minnow. Walleye are largely nocturnal feeders, so the period from sundown to total darkness is usually best.

Walleye bite quite gently and take some time to ingest a bait, so don't jump the gun when you feel a nibble. They also have rather hard and very toothy mouths. Strike hard and use a heavy mono leader or retie often.

4

SELECTING
SALT-WATER
SPINNING
TACKLE

I well recall having served a casting apprenticeship along the seacoast with a vintage multiplying reel—a reel on which after years of practice you mastered thumbing properly and could eventually control the line sufficiently to call yourself an accomplished caster. The reel was loaded with 9-thread Cuttyhunk linen line, which itself was difficult to control. The rod was a stiffish piece of split bamboo.

After years of having handled a conventional outfit, as to this day an outfit with a multiplying reel is called, I was somewhat apprehensive when one evening I repaired to the seacoast armed with a spinning outfit. The solid monofilament line slipped off the side of the reel's fixed spool during the cast, and a bail on a revolving head neatly wound the line back on the spool. The rod appeared much the same as a conventional surf rod, except that the tip was more limber and was built with ring guides having a much larger diameter than those I had become accustomed to using.

I had spent some time practicing in a neighborhood park frequented by youngsters playing baseball, but when I stood high on a rock, with waves crashing about my feet, I wondered if this newfangled spinning outfit would land a striped bass if I were fortunate enough to hook one.

SPINNING IS EASY

I found that casting came naturally and easily. While I thought at first it would seem strange, such was not the case. Indeed, I found I could cast a rigged eel with ease, and to a distance as great, if not greater, than what I'd been accustomed to doing with a conventional outfit. There were advantages too—an absence of the backlashes I occasionally experienced with a multiplying reel.

Several hours into the night and enjoying my new spinning outfit immensely, I received a wild strike right at the rocks from a striped bass that tried every trick in the book to rid itself of my rigged eel and to gain its freedom as it worked around the jetty front.

Holding the rod high in the air I could feel my heart pounding. I wanted this striper more than any I'd ever hooked. The reel's drag worked smoothly, relinquishing line under each determined rush of the bass, and the reel picked up line fast, thanks to its fast retrieve ratio.

Soon I had the beauty close to the rocks and when a wave brought it within reach I lifted my small hand gaff into a striped beauty of 21 pounds! I had landed my first spinning-tackle striped bass. At the time I felt it quite an accomplishment, particularly considering the circumstances: a big fish, hooked at night from a rock jetty covered with slippery moss, and with waves showering spray across me each time they crashed down onto the rocks. Today, many years later I still enjoy this exciting fishing, and I still consider every striper I land on spinning tackle an accomplishment.

SPINNING DIFFFERS TODAY

But today I look at spinning in salt water differently because I have since found spinning to be extremely versatile and well-suited to a wide variety of fishing applications.

My travels in the intervening years have taken me to all three of our coasts, the Atlantic, Pacific, and Gulf, as well as to many foreign ports of call. I've always carried spinning tackle with me and enjoyed using it on a variety of species almost beyond count, from bonefish on the shallow flats of the Florida Keys to albacore over a hundred miles offshore in the Pacific and cobia in the shadows of the oil rigs scattered along the Gulf Coast. Some of the fish I caught were big, others small. Some were game-fish, others bottom-feeders. I enjoyed catching them all on spinning tackle, and in this segment of our book I'd like to tell you how to enhance your enjoyment of spinning in salt water for the wide variety of species and varied types of fishing available.

Spinning is just as popular in salt water as it is in fresh. Here Johnny Abplanalp tries his luck on a tidal flat populated with bonefish and barracuda at Walker's Cay, northernmost island of the Bahamas.

SELECTION OF TACKLE A MAJOR CONSIDERATION

It's difficult in any book to cover everything about a specific subject, particularly one as broad as spinning, for it is employed throughout the entire world on a variety of species almost beyond count. For our purposes I'll cover spinning as it applies to the greatest majority of fishermen. While ultralight spinning tackle does find occasional use in salt water, as does very heavy spinning gear for big fish, these are the extremes, and for our purposes I think it's most important to discuss the tackle most of us regularly use to catch the widest variety of salt-water fish under normal conditions and using widely accepted methods.

But before you learn how to catch fish you must first equip yourself with spinning tackle suited to the species you're going to seek and the methods you're going to employ to catch them.

This isn't difficult to do, but it requires some thought, for if you equip yourself improperly you'll find spin-fishing awkward and difficult, and indeed it may handicap you to such an extent that you simply won't enjoy fishing with it.

Balance of Paramount Importance

The key to the selection of spinning tackle is balance. The rod, reel, and line must balance one to the other, so that as they are used together they function as a single unit to deliver a cast with ease and then to work a bait or lure and finally to hook and ultimately land a tough adversary.

Unfortunately, as a result of the competition among fishing-tackle manufacturers, there are so many rods, reels, and lines available on the market today that at best it's quite confusing to someone who is beginning. As a bit of background as to how this situation has occurred, let me explain that twenty-five years ago there were many small companies manufacturing rods and reels. Each had but a handful of good models, and for all practical purposes each balanced outfit did an excellent job. But then each manufacturer started adding more reels and more rods. With competition keen, large manufacturers bought out the small ones, and today we have a situation where some companies actually market 25 to 35 different models of spinning reels! Frankly, there's no need in the world to have this great number of models, ranging from economy to super deluxe models. All told, the great number of models, the greatest majority of which are almost identical, and some even having interchangeable parts, simply confuse the angling public and in many cases the tackle dealer and manufacturer as well.

With respect to rods it's even worse. There are hundreds of models, many just for the sake of having lots of models in their catalogs. Oftentimes the rod blank is identical, excepting its color, windings, and hardware. Sometimes the same basic blank is made shorter with no regard to action, but simply to fill what someone feels is a need. Indeed, even from one brand to another there are cases of the rod blanks being made by one company, and the component parts simply being assembled by others. So it's important that you take your time and within your budget select an outfit that's well suited to the fishing you plan to do.

I must say that I feel the angling public would benefit if most of the major manufacturers were to eliminate fully half of their line of rods and reels and concentrate their efforts on producing quality products, for in salt water, spinning tackle takes a lot of abuse, and much of that which is made available to the angling public today simply does not stand up to the corrosive action of salt water and the punishment meted out by tough gamefish.

Three Basic Spinning Outfits

I have a tackle room literally loaded with enough fishing tackle to stock a small tackleshop. I've accumulated this over a period of many years.

Surprisingly, there's a great deal of it that I seldom use. It's tackle that I've tried on a whim—a rod with a revolutionary new action that failed to meet my expectations and a reel that just didn't have the stamina I require of it in traveling and fishing about the country. In all my travels I find that I seem to settle on three basic spinning outfits that I carry with me wherever I go, and they do a fine job of seeing me through a wide variety of angling situations. Indeed, I'd go so far as saying that an angler equipped with these three basic outfits that I'm about to tell you about will do well wherever he goes. Granted, there will be some local conditions that may call for a slightly different outfit, but in the main the three basic outfits will see you through.

Selection of Salt-Water Rods

Before discussing the three basic outfits I find so useful along the seacoast, I'd like to highlight some things to look for in general when selecting the rods for the basic outfits.

A good rod for a specific situation should be sufficiently light, so as to enjoy maximum sport, yet it must have power to do the job it is expected to do, and this applies whether you're wading a flat for bonefish or jigging for grouper that may weigh 50 pounds or more.

The action of a rod can best be described as the manner in which the

Most salt water spinning rods have a screw-locking reel seat that firmly holds the reel in place, as does the rod pictured here; it was used to catch this fine mixed bag of spotted weakfish and striped bass while fishing in Chesapeake Bay off Saxis, Virginia.

rod responds to the power requirements of the type of fishing you'll be using it for. A good rod action for one type of fishing doesn't mean that the rod's action is good for all types of fishing.

Often anglers are confused and speak of action when they should be speaking of power. For a rod's power comes into play with its capability to handle certain line tests without breaking, the capability to fish and land a fish without undue hardship, and in spin-casting, the capacity to cast lures in a specific weight range, whether it be a tiny quarter-ounce bucktail jig, or a bulky, heavy-rigged eel. While there are some rods that have a combination of power and action that can do many things well, the greater the extremes they're called upon to handle, the more difficult it becomes.

Varied Labeling Confusing

When you walk into a tackleshop you'll find spinning rods bearing labels designating a wide variety of actions. The labels will read fast-taper, along with a variety of fast-tapers including medium-fast, long, and extra-fast, parabolic, progressive taper, speed-taper and quick-taper, to name but a few. Generally speaking, the progressive or slow-taper rod shaft has an even distribution of the rod's taper throughout the shaft and bends throughout the entire length of the rod. The fast-taper rods usually have a light tip-section, tapering quickly to a heavier butt-section.

Some rods have a soft rod shaft, while others tend to be uncomfortably stiff. There's no way I can tell you here specifically which rod label to buy, because even within the same labeling of a manufacturer you'll often find great differences in rods when comparing two similar models. However, you should shy away from the soft-tipped, wishy-washy rods that tend to have what I call a wobbly action. There are more salt-water spinning rods manufactured that are of poor quality than of good quality on the market as I write this. Many have been designed on a drawing board, and not out in the field, and as a consequence they are lacking in the attributes of a good rod when it comes to power and action. Still, these rods continue to be marketed and sold to the newcomer and will continue to be until the public becomes knowledgeable enough to distinguish the good from the bad. Part of the problem lies in the fact that there are fewer manufacturers each year, and those that survive market their products through extensive use of advertising on a sometimes uninformed, gullible public. Shop for a rod with care, and preferably in a tackle shop where you can be guided by the experience of the owner, rather than in the discount stores where the clerks often know absolutely nothing about fishing equipment.

Fiberglass Most Popular

For the spin-fisherman, the choice of rod tip materials centers around fiberglass, with a very limited, almost infinitesimal number made of other materials such as split bamboo, Calcutta or a variety of metals. Fiberglass is a top-quality material that stands up extremely well as a rod-shaft material. But, as with other materials, there are many types of fiberglass and many ways in which it is formed into a rod shaft. Some rods are made of glass cloth, while others from thousands of individual fiberglass fibers that run parallel the full length of the rod. Some of the rods are solid, but most are hollow. When comparing the weights of a rod, you can weigh fiberglass shafts that appear almost identical from the outside, and one will weigh fully twice as much as the other. Weight in this case is not a desirable characteristic, for usually the heavier rod is built using the same techniques developed when fiberglass first came into vogue many years ago. These rods are hollow and have very thick walls. The rod shafts built of modern, high-density fiberglass, with shafts of wide diameter and extremely thin walls, are the rods that I've found most to my liking. They're light in weight, have much better action, and more power on average than the rods built and still marketed today using antiquated methods.

Look for Quality Components

Salt-water spinning tackle has got to be rugged, and this applies both to rods and reels. Because of this you've got to be more concerned in your selection of tackle than might be the fresh-water angler. For he doesn't, on average, have to contend with fish as big and strong and doesn't have the corrosive onslaughts of salt water to contend with.

Flex Guides Favored

When you select a spinning rod you'll find that by far the greatest majority of them are equipped with what are popularly known as ring guides. These are rings of wire held to a bridge of wire and in some cases reinforced. For years guides of this type have been standard, but I find them of poor quality for the type of fishing I do. They tend to corrode quickly, and when transported or bounced about on a boat on a rough sea or when working from a bridge or jetty, the rings will frequently pop out of a guide, rendering it useless and often spoiling a day's fishing. Still other popular guides include agate guides within a metal or plastic ring, which I also find totally useless for salt-water spin-fishing. Then too, you'll find fancy gold-plated guides on some rods, and these too are worthless, unless you want to hang the rod in a den and admire its beauty.

Tungsten carbide rings are used on some rods, and while they're fine for freshwater rods, I don't like them on salt-water models, as I find they break easily when dropped or accidentally struck on a boat gunwale or rock.

I favor, and have on most of the rods I use, flexible guides. These are made by several manufacturers and marketed under a number of names. The one thing they have in common is that they're formed from a single piece of wire, with no bridges or soldering whatsoever. They're formed of stainless-steel, heavy-gauge wire, and usually heavily chromed. They're extremely strong: they flex when the rod flexes and can withstand many times the normal abuse a guide receives while fishing in salt water. It's virtually impossible to destroy one. I've seen a person accidentally deform one by stepping on it, then simply reshape it and continue fishing.

However, these guides are not readily available on most rods, and you'll have to look around until you find them. Almost without exception custom-rod builders use them, as they too recognize the quality. If you can't find a rod to your liking that has them, I'd suggest that as soon as the ring guides either wear or are damaged, that you replace them with the flexible or flex-foot type.

On a spinning rod the guide nearest the reel has the largest diameter, for it is the collecting guide, literally collecting the line as it slips off the side of the reel spool and funneling it through the other guides and eventually out through the tiptop. The number of guides on a rod will vary, depending on its action and the overall size of the rod. On average, you'll find medium and lightweight rods with six or seven guides and the larger boat and surf models with upward of eight or nine guides.

Rod Windings

The guides are attached to the rod with rod winding nylon, although some manufacturers use extremely fine nylon monofilament for winding. On quality rods there should be a wrapping of nylon beneath the guide, and then windings on each foot to hold the guide securely to the rod.

The finish on the windings should be substantial. Some companies use epoxy, while others use miracle plastic finishes and polyurethane varnish. The important thing is that the windings have sufficient coating to prevent the salt water from deteriorating them. On economy-class rods there is often so little varnish that the windings will deteriorate quickly.

Screw-Locking Reel Seats

The reel seat on the rods you select should be sturdily constructed, and of the screw-locking variety, preferably with double screw rings which will help hold your reel secure. Many good reel seats are made of anodized aluminum, while others are chrome-plated. As a rule the lighter rods, and especially the one-piece models, employ the aluminum seats, while the chromed models are a combination reel seat and ferrule, used to join the tip section of the rod with the butt section. If it's a combination reel seat and ferrule, it should be of the self-aligning variety and have a locking screw to hold the tip section securely to the butt section.

Rod butts come in a variety of sizes. On the lighter rods you'll usually find the butt is simply specie cork slipped over the fiberglass shaft of the rod. On some medium weight and surf rods hickory butts are used, while others employ fiberglass butts, and still other manufacturers use aluminum tubing. On lightweight one-handed rods, designed to be cast while holding the rod with but one hand, the butt usually ranges from 12 inches overall, including the reel seat, on up to 18 to 24 inches overall for medium-weight two handed boat-casting rods, and sometimes slightly longer for surf models, depending on the length of the rod and the size of butt that proves most comfortable for casting. You should grasp the rod as though you were going to cast and determine if the length of the butt in relation to the reel placement feels comfortable. Too long or too short a butt can make casting and fighting a fish uncomfortable.

Most butts have a small rubber button of some sort at the end, which helps keep you from bruising your stomach while fighting a fish, and it keeps the butt material from chipping.

Two-Piece Versus One-Piece

It is generally felt that a one-piece rod is superior in power and action to a two-piece model. Years ago this was true, for most rods employed a metal ferrule to join the two pieces, usually in the middle, and this not only weakened the rod somewhat, but detracted from the action as well. But today many manufacturers employ rods that are joined by fitting together without metal ferrules. These glass-to-glass sections are made independently and finely engineered so the tip section fits snugly over the end of the butt section, resulting in a joint that has no flat spots, and no problem of sticking when you wish to separate them. Manufacturers have various methods of fitting the two pieces, but glass-to-glass ferruling is for the most part superior to metal ferrules.

In the final analysis, if transporting the rod is no problem, stick with one-piece rods. But if you travel a great deal, then select the two-piece rods. You'll find them entirely satisfactory and in many cases virtually identical in action to the one-piece models.

Selecting Salt-Water Reels

Anyone who has fished or lived along the seacoast knows of the corrosive action salt water exerts on metal. Because of this it's most important that you purchase spinning reels designed expressly for salt-water use. To use some fresh-water models along the sea coast is pure folly, as the corrosive action of salt will reduce them to uselessness in short order.

INSPECT CAREFULLY BEFORE YOU BUY

I'll try to highlight the most important things to look for in purchasing spinning reels, but keep in mind that careful inspection of the reel and the counsel of a reputable tackle dealer are most important. All types of fishing tackle are constantly changing, and spinning reels are no exception. So as you read this there will no doubt be improved models that will prove superior to those that have been around for years. Keep in mind that elaborate advertising and discount-store pricing doesn't make a good spinning reel.

Modern engineering has resulted in many fine corrosion-resistant reels serving the salt-water fraternity. But they're really not as salt-water-proof as their manufacturers would like you to believe. But most have come a long way, and wise use of stainless steel, heavy chrome, marine bronze, duraluminum, and such synthetics as nylon and teflon have resulted in reels that hold up well along the seacoast.

BAIL WINDS LINE ONTO SPOOL

Open-faced spinning reels have a fixed spool, and the line is wound back onto the spool by a bail affixed to a revolving head. The bail mechanism is perhaps one of the most critical mechanisms on the reel. For each time you cast, the bail must be opened, and then as you retrieve, a turn of the handle closes the bail and permits line to be wound back onto the spool. The reel should have a sturdy bail and a strong spring that can be depended upon to firmly close the bail and hold it closed. The reel will also have a line guide or line roller, and here it's important to note that a roller is far superior to a line guide. For when line is drawn across a line guide there is a substantial amount of friction, which causes line wear. With a roller the line glides smoothly, minimizing wear and the possibility of line failure when fighting a big fish for a long period. Line rollers should be carefully inspected with a magnifying glass if you find your line is wearing, particularly if they're made of tungsten carbide, for often this material can be imperfect, and the slightest burr will chew up a line badly. While not available on many reels made today, the smoothest line roller I ever used was made of agate.

MANUAL PICKUP

Because of the problems that often arise with bail mechanisms and line rollers, many anglers convert their reels and use a manual pickup instead.

As its name implies, you manually pick up the line with your finger, instead of having a bail do it. As you begin your retrieve, the roller of the manual pickup arm catches the line and the line rolls smoothly on an oversized roller that glides along smoothly on ball bearings. I use manual pickups on most of my big salt-water reels, and find that most of the better fishermen I know much prefer the manual to the bail. Actually, once you get used to it you'll find it's more convenient using the manual pickup than a bail, simply because your finger reacts automatically; there's never a bail to bother opening.

Drag Extremely Important

The salt-water spin-fisherman must choose a reel with a drag that is absolutely smooth. Surprisingly, many spinning reels on the market today do not have smooth drags. In many cases a substantial amount of pressure is required to get the drag to begin slipping, after which the line flows from it rather smoothly. But even then there are many drags where there is a

Under a long run, your drag should relinquish line smoothly. Here Lefty Kreh applies additional pressure by cupping the reel spool as he pumps a big grouper from the depths in the tropics.

jerky relinquishing of line, which can often cause a line break when a big fish is making a long, fast run.

Many dealers will permit you to inspect a reel drag, as it only takes a few moments. The drag should never generate heat because of friction, so make certain that no two hard surfaces ever touch. There should be a hard plate of metal and then a drag washer and so on—never metal against metal, as this causes heat when a fish is making a speed run, and often results in expansion of the metals and ultimate freezing of the drag.

Drag washers are made from a wide variety of materials, ranging from felt to asbestos brake-lining material. But to make the drag really smooth many companies use teflon, either as washers or as part of the drag-adjusting device itself, so as to allow fine adjustment that permits line to slip from the reel smoothly at all times.

Under a long, sustained run, the drag should relinquish line steadily and smoothly. You must always remember, however, that as a fish takes line there is less line on the spool, requiring more pounds of pull to take line from the reel. Thus, if a gamefish runs off 100 or more yards of line you will feel what appears to be a tightening of the drag. The drag is not actually tightening, but there is less line on the reel. To compensate for this, many veteran spin-fishermen will ease off on the drag's tension when there's a lot of line off the reel, again tightening the drag somewhat as line is regained during the fight.

Make certain you loosen your drag-adjustment knob, backing it off completely, when the reel is not in use. This keeps the drag washers from being completely depressed under a tight drag, which ultimately will decrease their effectiveness.

STRONG ANTIREVERSE ESSENTIAL

Each spinning reel has an antireverse lever, which when set prevents the reel handle and revolving head from turning backward, as a fish takes line. With a strong fish and very heavy drag setting, a tremendous amount of pressure is brought to bear against the antireverse mechanism. Because of this it's extremely important that it be strong. However, I can say from personal experience that many reels on the market have extremely weak antireverse mechanisms, for I've had many fail me at critical points when fighting a big fish for a prolonged period of time. Just about the only way you can tell it is going to hold up is by first examining it to see that it's sturdily constructed and hope for the best on the fishing grounds.

RETRIEVE RATIO IMPORTANT

It's important that you purchase salt-water spinning reels having a fast-retrieve ratio. Many reels have 3½ to 1 ratios, and these are a bit on the

slow side, for often a fast retrieve is essential in working a lure fast for
speedy salt-water adversaries. Many of the reels I use have a 4 to 1 retrieve
ratio, which means each time I turn the reel handle once the revolving head
of the reel turns four times, winding line onto the reel rapidly. Some of
my big spinning mills have a 5 to 1 retrieve ratio, which I find especially
useful for deep jigging, especially for tropical species.

Internal Mechanisms Vary

The exteriors of most spinning reels are quite similar. But inside you'll
find very few the same. Each manufacturer develops a gear system that he
feels will do the best job for his reel. Only an engineer is qualified in most
cases to judge which of the many gear and bearing systems is best. Suffice
to say that the internal workings of the reel determine just how it will
preform.

As you retrieve by turning the reel handle, you're activating the gears,
which do several things. They turn the revolving head. But they also lay
the line on the spool. To simply work it back and forth would be useless,
as the line would tend to dig in under pressure. So the gears must perform
the function of winding the line onto the spool, while laying it on in such
a way that it doesn't build up either in the center or along the edges of the
spool, and to lay it smoothly, back and forth, so that even under tremendous
pressure the line will not dig into the line beneath it. It must do this
smoothly and here the ball bearings play an important role, enabling you
to retrieve with a minimum of physical effort.

Exterior Finishes Important Too

Perhaps by now we've impressed you that everything about a salt-water
spinning reel is important. Well, it is, right down to the exterior finish of
the reel and especially the reel spool. Most spinning reels have a durable,
corrosion-resistant exterior finish, with heavily chromed working parts. It
should have a large, comfortable handle, easy to grip, since you'll be handling it a great deal, using it to retrieve and sometimes to fight fish for a
half-hour or more.

Watch Spools

The spinning reel you select should have a spool which is easily removed. The spool should have a satin-smooth finish, as the line slips off the
side of the spool, and the slightest flaw will cause line wear. Be especially
careful always to inspect the outboard lip of the spool from time to time
as you use it. Banging it against a rock can cause a slight nick, which will
ruin a line in short order.

The spool should be sturdily constructed also, for tremendous pressures are built up by monofilament line, especially when a big fish takes a great deal of line, and the line is then packed back on the reel under pressure. Poorly constructed spools will expand, and literally blow up under the pressure.

I always carry several extra spools of line in my tackle kit for each spinning reel I own. In this way I can switch in a matter of seconds to a lighter or heavier line. The extra spools filled with line are especially appreciated when I lose some line. Casting with too little line on the spool is difficult.

Monofilament Lines Vary

Nylon monofilament lines, which are a solid, extruded line, are by far the most popular with salt-water spin-fishermen. While on the surface all monofilament lines look similar, out on the water there's a world of difference between quality and economy-grade monofilament.

Still, the urge to buy a line costing half as much as a superior line is great, but in the final analysis it's a false economy, as on the water economy-grade lines just don't do the job for you.

Quality monofilament lines are uniform in their test throughout the entire length of the line, with no variance of heavy, strong spots and light, weak spots. Quality mono is, on average, of finer diameter per pound-test than cheaper lines. Good monofilament is not wiry by nature, but soft and supple, and easily managed on the reel. It has a satin-smooth finish, resulting in a minimum of water resistance.

WHAT SIZES ARE BEST?

It's difficult to say just what sizes of monofilament are best for you, simply because fishing conditions and species vary from one section of seacoast to another. Over years of trying a wide variety of tests with many different outfits, I've tried to standardize the line tests that I use, as I find it simplifies my fishing and increases my casting efficiency.

As a cast in point, a light rod may have the ability to handle 6-, 8-, or 10-pound test lines. With the 6 you can cast a given lure much farther than while casting the same lure with 10-pound test. But with the 6-pound test you can't work a fish as forcefully as you can with the 10-pound line. As a result, in situations such as this, I compromise, and settle on 8-pound test with the light outfit, and while I sacrifice a slight bit of castability, I pick up a little extra strength, which proves advantageous in many situations.

The same may be said for the medium-weight outfits, in which the range is wide enough to accommodate lines from 10- through 20-pound test. I'll usually spool 15-pound test on these outfits most of the time, but will keep several spools stocked with the 10, 12, 17, and 20, for specific situations that require it.

Moving into heavy surf or boat-spinning tackle, where the outfit is capable of handling lines in the 12- through 30-pound class, I do much the same thing, usually settling on 17-pound test, which I like for heavy work, as it's extremely strong, particularly when you use the proper knots, and you can spool a great deal of it on the bigger salt-water reels. In isolated, specialized fishing situations I've used 25-pound test monofilament, but offhand I don't ever recall having gone as high as 30-pound test, although I know of some anglers who have even gone as high as 40-pound test, when used with extremely heavy spinning tackle and the largest salt-water spinning reels made.

Fill Spool Properly

One of the most important considerations in spinning is properly filling your reel spool with line. If you just crank it onto the reel, permitting it to come off the line spool with the spool rotating, you in effect put a twist into the line, eventually resulting in a totally unwieldy spool of line that is difficult to cast and virtually unmanageable.

The proper way to spool the line is to permit it to slip off the spool on which you purchased the line and to be wound onto the spool of the spinning reel, so as to have no twist whatsoever. Or, if you wish, you can remove your spool and place it on a line-winding machine, or simply use a hand drill and wind the line directly from the spool on which you receive it to the spinning reel's spool. A simple rule of thumb is if the spool is stationary, then the spool from which the line is being removed must be stationary. If the reel spool is in a line-winder and revolving, then the spool from which the line is being removed must be revolving too.

A number of companies sell prewound spools, which enables you to purchase spools completely filled with the line test of your choice, thus saving you the time of spooling it yourself. These spools may be exchanged when you purchase additional line. Additionally, there are also companies who market their lines on heavy-duty plastic spools which fit onto a spool adapter on your spinning reel and which may be discarded once the line has become too short or worn.

Don't Overfill or Underfill Spool

Too much or too little line on a spinning reel can cause you a great deal of havoc on the fishing grounds. An ideally filled spool should have the line come to approximately ⅛ inch of the edge of the spool, no more, no less.

Too much line will tend to result in several coils coming off at one time, causing a mass of monofilament the likes of which may take you ten minutes to untangle, if you can untangle it at all. Too little line, say a ½ inch from the edge of the reel spool, minimizes casting distance, simply because the line is drawn across the edge of the spool in such a restrictive angle as to prevent its smooth flow from the reel and consequently reduce the distance you can cast.

The Three Outfits

In thus far describing the rods, reels, and lines used for salt-water spinning I've discussed important things to look for in the selection of the three basic spinning outfits I mentioned earlier. Now I will cover those outfits, but ask that you bear in mind that I choose these as being versatile and suited to a wide variety of coastal fishing applications throughout the country and abroad. There are many variations to these basic outfits and many kinds of fishing peculiar to a certain area that may call for slightly different tackle. But I do feel that using this equipment as a base you will be guided through as wide a variety of fishing situations as possible with a maximum of effectiveness and enjoyment.

LIGHT ONE-HANDED SPINNING

The one-handed spinning outfit is without question the backbone of spinning throughout the United States, and this includes many types of salt-water fishing as well. The rods I use range from 6½ to 7 feet in length, and while looking much like a fresh-water rod, they have considerable backbone, substantially more than those models designed for trout or bass fishing. The butt is designed to enable you to cast with one hand, although many salt-water anglers when using this type of rod cup the end of the butt with their left hand when casting right-handed, which puts more power into the cast, a necessity at times when casting into the wind with a light lure.

To be effective the reel must be selected to balance with the rod. Too light a reel will give you the feeling of the rod being too heavy while casting, whereas too large or heavy a reel will give you the feeling that the rod is too light. The ideal reel that I've found for this rod is a salt-water version of what have become standard fresh-water models, except fitted with salt-water spools having a capacity of approximately 200 yards of 10-pound test monofilament line.

By carrying several extra spools of line I can have 6-, 8-, and 10-pound test lines with me and handle a wide variety of lure weights, from ⅛-ounce bucktail jigs to ⅝-ounce plugs and even 1- or 2-ounce sinkers with the 10-pound test line while bottom fishing. I can use it for light chumming and for pier and bridge sport, too.

This light, one-handed spinning outfit has served me well while wading the flats for bonefish in the Keys and Bahamas and working along the shallow beaches of the Gulf for seatrout and redfish. It's great when after pompano, blue runners, ladyfish and Spanish mackerel, and I've caught some nice snook and small tarpon on it too.

Along the Atlantic coast an outfit such as this is fine for light pier-fishing for croakers, spot, summer and winter flounder, weakfish, and porgies. Many anglers use it for school stripers, small bluefish, herring, and shad, enjoying maximum light-tackle sport.

It's the perfect outfit when fishing inshore shallows of the Pacific for starry flounder, corbina, rockfish, small barracuda, bonito, and the many species that congregate around the kelp beds, such as sand bass, mackerel, and kelp bass. Anglers who set their sights on the small white croaker, spotfin croaker, and the many surf perches often use the one-handed spinning outfit when conditions permit light tackle, for then they enjoy maximum sport with these tasty and often plentiful bottom-feeders.

MEDIUM TWO-HANDED SPINNING

The medium-weight spinning outfit might well be termed the most versatile of salt-water rigs, simply because it may be used effectively for a wide range of fishing conditions, ranging from light to heavy fishing, with reasonable effectiveness.

The medium-weight two-handed spinning rods I use range from 7 feet to 8½ feet in overall length. Most are of two-piece construction; some joined with glass to glass ferruling, with two sections of equal length, while others are joined at the butt, with the male ferrule fitting into the female ferrule which is also part of the reel seat.

The length of the butts range from 18 to 24 inches, which is considerably longer than with the one-handed rods, for here two hands are used while casting, hence the importance of length for leverage. The tips of all these rods are substantial and can handle lures ranging from ¾ through 2 ounces without difficulty, and often I'll call upon them to cast still heavier lures, which they'll handle without too much trouble.

On rods in this category I mount an intermediate-size salt-water spinning reel. Most reels in this class have a capacity of approximately 200 yards of 17-pound test monofilament line. Because the rods are rated and can handle lines from 10- to 20-pound test I also carry several extra spools. Where very long casts with medium-weight lures are essential I may use a spool of 10-pound test, which will have in excess of 350 yards of line on it. If I'm deep-jigging and casting is of no consequence and I just want lots of strength to pull big fish away from the coral I may load a spool with the 20-pound test, even though I'll have only about 175 yards of line on the reel.

This group of anglers found medium weight, two-handed spinning outfits ideal for fishing for big snook with live pinfish bait on the southwest Florida coast near Marco Island. Where swift tides and big fish are the rule, tackle must be balanced to meet the situation.

I've used my medium-weight, two-handed spinning outfits most everywhere I've fished with fine results. On the Pacific coast I've chummed albacore and small bluefin tuna employing them while baiting with live anchovies. Inshore along the kelp beds a wide variety of species have fallen to this powerful outfit, including bonito, barracuda, white sea bass and yellowtail. Some were landed while using live anchovies, while others walloped metal squids and jigs. Up in San Francisco Bay, right beneath the Golden Gate Bridge I used bucktail jigs to wallop big stripers in the swift currents around the south tower, and just offshore from that fog-shrouded bridge I landed king and silver salmon using plastic bait-tail jigs worked down 30 to 40 feet beneath the surface.

It's been a workhorse outfit for me on the Atlantic coast too. I use it almost exclusively for jetty fishing, having landed many stripers that topped the 40-pound mark on it, as well as jumbo bluefish, weakfish, and summer flounders. Off Hatteras and the Barrier Islands of Virginia I've called on it to land channel bass that approached the 50-pound mark. I've cast, chummed, trolled, and bottom-fished with it for practically every species caught in the Atlantic. It's that versatile an outfit.

Along the Gulf coast I've hit some beautiful cobia while working the oil rigs off Louisiana and also scored with them while tied up to shrimp trawlers off Mississippi. Chumming with shrimp, trash fish, and squid we attracted hordes of king mackerel, little tuna, and big jack crevalle within range, and the medium-weight spinning stick really took a lot of punishment, coming through in grand fashion. It's a favorite of bridge and pier casters throughout the South, simply because it's rugged enough to lift fish weighing several pounds with little difficulty.

HEAVY TWO-HANDED SPINNING AND SURF

Where long casts are required, or big gamefish encountered, the salt-water spin-fisherman must have a heavy, two-handed spinning or surf rod at his disposal. While I classify within this category both heavy boat outfits and surf outfits, as a general rule if you're doing heavy fishing from a boat you'll be employing a stiffish-action rod in the 7- to 8½-foot range, while along the surf will be a comparable, tough outfit measuring a bit longer, say in the range of 9 to 11 feet. These are rugged rods. In the case of the surf rig they can handle casting 3- or 4-ounce jigs or rigged eels of the same weight. They may be called upon to handle a 5-ounce sinker and big slab of mullet bait, and they'll need the power to subdue fish that often will top the 30-pound mark. When you pick one of these rods up you know you've got a rod in your hand, for they're not soft, but tend towards the stiff side. But they do a remarkable job, and you'll find them far superior to many of the so-called surf or heavy-boat rods on the market that have soft-tip actions and which simply cannot deliver long casts or heavy lures, nor bring big, strong fish through the surf.

The heavy boat-rod isn't used for small fish, but is used by the spinning enthusiast who wishes to troll for sailfish, or to live-bait fish for big king mackerel or wahoo, as well as the huge cobia and tough amberjack that reside around the oil rigs in the Gulf. Fellows fishing from the bridges in the Keys at night use the big rigs for hundred-pound-plus tarpon and big sharks too.

The reels used on the heavy spinning rods must be able to withstand the punishment meted out by tough gamefish. They're among the biggest of salt-water spinning reels, holding 400 yards of 20-pound test line, with some of the reels holding even more. Here too, however, most veteran boat or surf fishermen carry spools with several size lines, ranging from 12- to a high of 30-pound test. Sometimes the 12-pound line may be brought into play with a casting shocker-head, to cast a heavy lure into the teeth of a strong wind, while the 30 may be what is required to haul a big amberjack

Heavy surf tackle is a must when fishing a rough surf. The outfit used by Johnny Oney held his line high above the surf where he could properly work his Dasher propeller plug. Dick Kotis handles the gaff on a school striper, to get the fish out of a rough New Jersey surf.

from beneath the supporting piles of an offshore oil-drilling rig, or to pull a big white sea bass or husky yellowtail away from the heavy growth of the kelp beds.

I've noted that in the past couple of years many surf rods of extreme lengths, upwards of 14 and 15 feet. Don't be mislead into thinking you can make long casts with these long rods. I personally feel these rods are designed to catch fishermen. For I know many top-notch tournament casters, and these men readily admit, as do I, that they simply cannot handle a rod of that length. For all-around useful power, stick with the rods up to a tops of 11, perhaps 12 feet at the outside. Most of the time I stick with a 9- or 10-foot rod; I simply can't handle the big sticks. They just cut down on your effectiveness just where you need it.

The big 9- to 11-foot surf rods are favored by anglers fishing from the beaches and rocky coastline of Washington and Oregon for king and

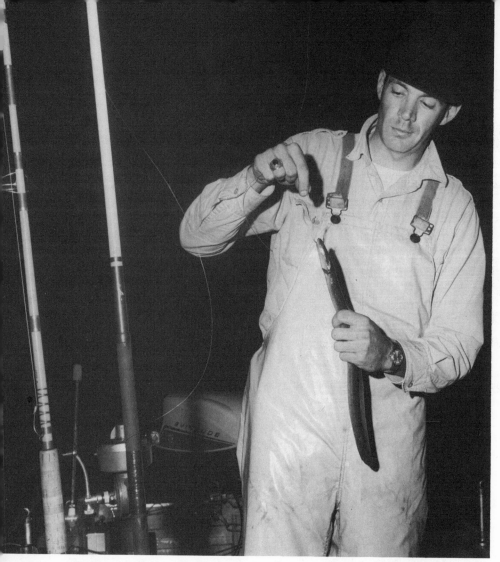

When you're using big baits, such as this live eel being hooked by Al Anderson for the big striped bass of Narragansett, Rhode Island, you need the heavy duty surf spinning outfits like those pictured.

silver salmon, and many also score when casting from shore along the Pacific for migrating striped bass.

Along the Atlantic coast I've used these big sticks for stripers off Cape Cod's beaches, bluefish off Rhode Island, and while casting a bait far seaward off Jersey beaches for a variety of bottom-feeders such as weakfish, summer flounders, and kingfish. Down in Virginia and North Carolina it has always been my standard on their beautiful beaches, where channel bass reign supreme but many other surf species run nearby.

Even Florida surfmen along the central and northern part of the state use the big rods, reaching far from the beach for blues, Spanish mackerel, and other species working along the beach. Just about the only section of coast where I've found no use for the big-surf spinning outfits was along the beaches of the Gulf of Mexico. There the beaches slope gently, and there's a moderate surf, and long casts and the heavy gear don't find much application, although I suspect there are times and specific spots where there would be a need for one of these big rigs.

Still another advantage of the big rigs, particularly in boat fishing, is that the wide-diameter spools of the reels, plus their 5 to 1 retrieve ratio, enable you to retrieve line very quickly. When deep-jigging this proves very helpful, for big pelagic species like a fast-moving lure, and with the big reels you can really move a jig. The big reels also help you regain line quickly when you've hooked school bluefin tuna while chumming, or any other big fish that take several hundred yards of line in a single run.

Key Is Using Right Outfit at Right Time

While limiting yourself to the three basic outfits I've discussed here may be an oversimplification of spinning-tackle selection for salt-water fishing, it is a fine beginning and should lead you in the right direction should you be new to the sport. The key, however, to obtaining maximum sport and thoroughly enjoying the use of this equipment is using the right outfit at the right time. Using too light or too heavy gear isn't fun, nor is it fun using mismatched outfits. Take care in making your selections and seek the counsel of competent tackle dealers. An evening spent wisely before you make your purchase will result in many hours of pleasure on the water, simply because you'll be using the right outfit for the fishing you'll be doing.

Closed-Face Spin-Cast

If you're a fresh-water enthusiast and enjoy fishing protected coastal waters for flounders, seatrout, spot, croakers, porgies, and the many other small species found in these waters, you'll find that the closed-face spin-cast outfit discussed in the fresh-water section of this book will serve you well, too.

I started my children, Linda and Bob, with closed-face spinning reels when they were just a couple of years old and found they were the perfect outfit for children. All they did was push the button to permit line to settle to the bottom, then turn the handle to reel in. Nothing could be simpler for a youngster, and it saved lots of grief for me, as there were no tangles or difficulties for me to worry about.

Here Milt Rosko unhooks a porgy for his son, Bob. The closed face spinning outfit is ideal for youngsters fishing in salt water. When he was just four years old, Bob had no difficulty pushing the button to let line to the bottom, or simply turning the handle to retrieve it, without tangles.

The children learned to cast with them with ease, and as their skills developed, they moved to more sophisticated tackle with ease, until now they are capable of handling a wide variety of tackle with no difficulty.

A word of caution, however: these reels are made primarily for fresh-water use, and if you use them for coastal fishing, you'll have to thoroughly clean them each evening on your return home, for corrosion will set in quickly if you don't.

5

SALT-WATER
SPINNING
TECHNIQUES

BOAT CASTING

The shore-based spin-fisherman is limited to fish spots within walking range, and which are as close as he can cast his lure or bait. Not so with the angler who uses a boat as a casting platform. The boatman has total flexibility, and can move from spot to spot, whether around the point of a rocky promontory to cast for hungry gamefish lurking in the rocks, or to speed to an excited cluster of gulls screeching and diving into the water to feed on baitfish, as those same baitfish are unmercifully attacked by fish from below.

Spin-casting from a boat is an extremely exciting sport, because you're constantly active, moving from spot to spot, probing each spot thoroughly, and then moving on until you hit paydirt. Of all the various methods of using spinning tackle, casting from small boats has grown tremendously in popularity within the past few years on all coasts.

All types of tackle may be used for this exciting fishing, ranging from the very light spinning-gear that delicately presents a tiny bucktail jig to a bonefish tailing in water barely a foot deep on a clear Bahamian flat, to the sturdiest heavy spinning-tackle in your locker as you cast to surface-feeding cobia many miles from shore.

Stealthy Approach Important

Each fishing situation must be approached in a different manner. But a consideration of paramount importance is that whenever you approach an

163

area you plan to fish, whether a tidal flat, school of surface-feeding fish, or a marsh bank, you do so quietly. All too often, inexperienced anglers approach situations like these with their engines wide open, frequently spooking any fish in the area, and ultimately spoiling the good sport that could have developed had they used a stealthy approach.

The manner in which a boatman approaches a school of fish tells you immediately whether he is experienced or a neophyte. Veteran anglers move upcurrent or upwind from a spot they want to cast to and then put their engine in neutral and just drift to the spot with no disturbance whatsoever. When done properly, you can often drift right alongside or over a school of surface-feeding fish and not disturb them at all, with the hungry fish right beneath and all around you as they feed.

The quiet approach applies even when you don't see fish in an area. Bonefish approaching a flat from deep water can be spooked as they prepare to enter a flat, as can dolphin resting in the shadows of a weed line or seatrout working along a marsh bank as they search for a meal. You simply can never go wrong by being quiet.

BUCKTAIL JIG A FAVORITE EVERYWHERE

The caster has a wide variety of lures from which to choose. But of all the lures at his disposal one lure, the bucktail jig, stands alone as being the most popular, whether he casts for salmon in the fog-shrouded waters off San Francisco's Golden Gate, probes the depths of a reef off the Florida Keys, or casts to surfacing stripers on the broad expanse of the Chesapeake Bay.

The bucktail jig isn't a very impressive looking lure. It's simply molded of lead, with its head available in a wide variety of shapes and sizes. Molded within the lead head is the hook, ranging from a number 4 or smaller, on up to huge 9/0 models. The hook size usually balances with the head size; small 1/16-ounce models having the small hooks, and the heavy 4- and 5-ounce models being equipped with the large-sized barbs.

Generally speaking, the bucktail jig heads come in two basic styles. Some are torpedo, or bullet-shaped, and have an eye protruding from each side, while others are flat and oblong, or lima-bean-shaped. There are hundreds of models, ranging from the exotic that are painted with an air brush, to the very basic, which are simply dipped into a can of paint. Suffice to say the elaborate paint is more to catch fishermen than fish, so don't let this be a consideration when purchasing bucktail jigs.

The jigs are dressed primarily with skirts of bucktail, although some are dressed with feathers, as well as nylon filament, all of which work enticingly in the water.

Bucktail jigs are favorites of spin-fishermen everywhere. They come in a wide variety of shapes and sizes and are ideal for a wide variety of fishing applications, including casting, deep jigging, and trolling.

There are some jigs designed for a specific type of fishing. The delta-winged jig is a typical example, for its shape is well-designed for extremely shallow-water work, such as on the bonefish flats or when casting over a shallow weedbed for seatrout. Conventionally shaped jigs would tend to foul in the sand or weeds, whereas the delta-winged model works just above the bottom.

Many anglers in recent years have improved the fish-catching effectiveness of their bucktail jigs by adding a sparse dressing of mylar, a reflective silver or gold plastic, to their bucktail or feather skirts. They've found the reflective qualities of the mylar work wonders in the depths, causing the bucktail jig to sparkle much the same as a small baitfish struggling in the current.

I became a believer in mylar simply by having fished with a number of anglers who used it on their bucktails and they outfished me solidly on several occasions, whereupon I quickly added the sparkling plastic to most of my jigs.

You'll find bucktail jigs painted every color in the rainbow. I've tried many of the various colors, but usually come back to using either solid-white jigs with white bucktail-skirts, or solid yellow with a yellow skirt.

Milt Rosko hooked this big barracuda
gaffed by Whitfield Aulbury while working a bucktail jig over the reefs off Walker's Cay in the Bahamas. Cuda of this
size are fine sport on spinning tackle. The
rod belt worn by the author enables him
to fight a fish with ease.

Attractor Helps

To enhance the action of my bucktails I often add a strip of pork rind or fresh squid to the tail hook. I've also used plastic phosphorescent worms with good results. These attractors give the lure that bit of plus action that often makes the difference.

A VARIETY OF PLUGS USED BY CASTERS

Plugs are still another very effective lure of the caster. They come in many shapes and sizes and several key designs. The swimming-plug models, both surface and subsurface swimmers are by far the most popular all around models. Each manufacturer of a swimming plug makes his model a bit different but essentially the majority of swimming plugs work the same.

The plug is either long and thin or rather squat, depending on what it's made to resemble. Swimming plugs are equipped with either a metal or plastic lip. This lip causes the plug to swim from side to side as it is retrieved. On the plastic-lipped models the lip is not adjustable, but on plugs equipped with a metal lip it may be adjusted to cause the plug to work either right on the surface or to swim down into the depths.

By bending the lip upward the plug will dive deep and by bending the metal lip downward, the plug will stay on the surface or near it. Thus, by simply adjusting the plug's lip you can make it do exactly what you wish.

Swimming plugs are made from either plastic or wood and are available in salt-water models ranging from 3 to 12 inches in length. The tiny models resemble silversides, mullet, and pilchards, while the larger plugs are designed to look like herring, menhaden, mackerel, and other large forage species. There are many finishes available, and here too, the finish is painted to resemble a bait species on which gamefish feed.

Poppers Work on Surface

Popping plugs are extremely popular with casters, for they work on the surface, and the strike from a gamefish is always right within view. Popping plugs are shaped with a concave head and taper to the tail. Most are equipped with one or two treble hooks hanging from the underside of the plug and another treble in the tail.

They come in a wide range of sizes and finishes, and the small models are best handled on a light spinning-outfit when after weakfish, school stripers, snook, small dolphin, and other species in the 1- to 10-pound class. Larger popping plugs are the order of the day when you set your sights on big barracuda, bluefish, striped bass, king mackerel, and big jack crevalle.

The concave head of the popping plug causes water to be thrown ahead of it as it is retrieved across the surface. With a slow retrieve there is just a curling of water, but if you work your rod tip you cause the plug to pop and gurgle, which excites many gamefish. In the tropics I've even had snapper and grouper come up from the depths to crash a popper worked over their coral lair.

Propeller Plugs

As their name implies, propeller plugs are equipped with small metal propellers, usually one fore and one aft. As the plug is retrieved the props cause a great deal of commotion, which excites many gamefish. Made in both surface and deep-running models, the plugs slide through the water smoothly, and you've got to give them action by working your rod tip. By drawing your tip forward quickly you cause the plug to dart ahead and then falter, much like a wounded baitfish. It's action like this that draws hungry fish to the plug.

Darters

The head of a darter plug is cut out at an angle, so that as you retrieve it the plug darts from side to side with an erratic, unpredictable action. You've got to work your rod tip to keep the plug working properly, and the more tip action you give, the better the plug will react. They're available in both surface and diving models, each of which will bring strikes from any species that feed on small baitfish.

Many Other Varieties

The mirror-type plug is still another fine producer for the casting enthusiast. It's made of plastic and molded to the general shape of a fish. They come in surface, medium-running and deep-running models. The mirror plugs have very little action of their own, and you've got to work your rod tip to get results.

Then too, there are flap-tail plugs, which have a metal spinner-blade attached by a swivel to their tail. The flap-tail works on the surface and leaves a V wake similar to that made by mullet swimming just beneath the surface. When retrieved the metal flap-tail spins and flops on the surface, making a commotion that attracts fish.

Additionally, there are many other variations of the basic plugs I've mentioned here. But by sticking to these time-proven basic models you'll find you will be prepared for any casting calling for a plug. Additionally, many of these plugs work extremely well when trolled, as will be discussed in a later chapter.

METAL SQUIDS

Years ago casters used block-tin squids almost to a man. For the block tin could be easily molded and, when polished, had a soft luster not unlike that of many silver-sided baitfish on which gamefish feed. With the passage of years the block-tin squid has moved out of the forefront, replaced by several new metal lures made of stainless steel or molded of lead and then either nickel- or chrome-plated.

There are more than a thousand varieties of metal lures which the spin-fishermen may employ while casting for gamefish. For purposes of our discussion we'll call all of the metal lures squids, even though some of them are often described as jigs, including the diamond, tri-sided, Belmar, and butterfish types.

Essentially, these lures were designed to resemble a small baitfish. Those having keels, such as the block-tin squids, and other models with a keel, work from side to side as they are retrieved steadily. This swimming action, coupled with their soft luster, is what brings strikes.

Other models, such as the diamond jig and tri-sided jig, don't have much action if retrieved steadily. With these you've got to impart a jigging action with your rod tip, causing the jigs to dart towards the surface, and then falter, much like a struggling baitfish.

The models most casters concern themselves with today are the versatile ones that can be used either for casting, trolling, or jigging in the depths, and many of the hammered, stainless-steel models work extremely well. For the most salt-water situations with any of these metal lures you'll find 1- to 3-ounce models perfect.

The action of most metal squids may be enhanced by the addition of either a bucktail or feather skirt, and some anglers add a strip of pork rind to the tail hook, or even a plastic worm.

RIGGED EELS PRODUCE TOO

The rigged eel is still another favorite of casters who fish for striped bass and bluefish along the middle and north Atlantic coast. It is really a combination lure and natural bait, for you rig a common eel on a small metal squid designed expressly for rigging eels. The eel, which may vary in length from 6 to 18 inches, gets its action from the metal squid, as the squid swims from side to side as it is retrieved, and the trailing eel does the same. It looks just like a live eel swimming and works equally well when cast from a boat, trolled, or worked from a jetty or the beach.

TERMINAL RIGGING VARIES

The terminal rigging you employ with the various lures just discussed will vary, depending on the species you're after. If they're toothy critters, as is often the case with tropical species, then you'll be obliged to use a short wire-leader to keep them from biting through your monofilament.

Number 6 or 7 single-strand stainless steel is used by many spin-fisher-men, or 30-pound test nylon covered stainless steel cable. This may be attached to the terminal end of your line with a small barrel swivel, or if you wish you may double the end of your line and use an Albright knot to tie directly to the wire. Both systems work well, and it's more a matter of personal preference as to which you should use.

To facilitate changing lures, many boat casters use a small stainless-steel duo-lock snap. This is small and strong, and works very well with most lures. If, however, you feel a direct connection is better, then you can use either a haywire and barrel twist with the single-strand wire or a Homer Rhode loop knot if you're using nylon-covered cable.

FISH ON TOP PROVIDE GREATEST SPORT

Most casting enthusiasts are in complete accord that nothing quite beats finding a school of fish feeding on the surface and simply shutting down your motor and casting to them. This kind of fishing is filled with excitement, and has contributed to the increased popularity of using spinning tackle during recent years.

In jotting down my thoughts preparatory to writing this chapter, I noted the various situations when I found fish feeding on top while I was traveling about, often simply moving from spot to spot when the exciting situation presented itself. The list was so long that it wouldn't be practical to include all of the situations. Suffice to say, however, that whenever you're moving about in salt water you should be alert to the possibility that you'll encounter surface-feeding fish. Because of this you should always be prepared for the situation when it happens, for only then can you enjoy it to its fullest. Indeed, there simply isn't time to begin rigging up and rummaging through a kit to find an appropriate lure. Everything should be riffed and ready so that when fish show, you're ready—right now!

It Can Happen Anywhere

I've encountered striped bass feeding on top in the quiet confines of a coastal estuary not a dozen feet in width and encountered albacore wildly gorging themselves on the surface over 100 miles at sea off Baja California. So you see it can happen anywhere.

It is important to remember that many pelagic species and inshore gamefish are often simply not feeding. Fish are not constantly gorging themselves on food, but are most active several times during the day, during peak periods of feeding activity. This is why schools of baitfish swim casually on the surface, while schools of big fish tend to ignore them, swimming at intermediate levels or near the bottom.

Suddenly an urge to feed develops. Many factors contribute to just when fish will feed, but it is generally agreed that moon, tide and sun trigger major feeding periods. The Solunar Tables originated by John Alden Knight many years ago show when these peak feeding-periods take place. There are two major Solunar periods each day and two minor periods, during which time fish are most active.

This is not to say that fish are totally inactive during other than Solunar periods, but it does bear out that fish are generally more responsive during these periods, all factors being equal, especially in moderate weather.

This explains in part why an ocean that seems barren of fish will come alive with gamefish feeding voraciously. Thus it is to your benefit to be prepared for these periods, for at this time the fish will be especially responsive to any lures you cast their way. Sometimes they'll feed actively for an hour or more, but more often they'll fill themselves and then retreat into the depths, remaining inactive until the next feeding period.

Don't Move Too Close

Sea birds often feed much the same as fish, and many anglers claim that all wildlife feeding habits are triggered by the same natural phenomena that cause fish to feed. As a result, you'll often observe great numbers of sea gulls and terns actively feeding on the same schools of baitfish that hungry gamefish are attacking from below.

The fact that the big fish are feeding makes it less of a job for the birds, as they can leisurely pick up the helpless fry that are being attacked from below. But the activity of the birds should always be watched for, since they are visible when circling and diving from a great distance, whereas fish might not be visible until you draw close.

When you observe this kind of situation don't move too close, as often this will spook the fish. When this happens, the fish may retreat into the depths and simply not resume feeding, thus diluting your chances of scoring.

The problem of boat casters running into schools of feeding fish and spooking them immediately separates the experienced angler from the novice. This is a universal problem of excited neophytes, who invariably spoil the fishing not only for themselves but others as well, by excitedly running their boat right into the school of feeding fish.

Use Wind and Current for Approach

Whether you observe fish feeding in a coastal bay or river or on the open expanse of ocean, always hesitate a moment before approaching and plan your strategy. Determine the direction of the current and the direction of the wind, and plan your approach to use them to your advantage.

This is easily accomplished by simply taking your boat out of gear and permitting it to drift along. In a matter of a few seconds you'll find just which way your boat will drift. Then move up, so the wind or current will carry you towards the fish, but not directly on top of them. The ideal situation is to be carried along the edge of the major activity, within casting range, yet not so close as to disturb the feeding fish.

Above all, be patient, for it's better to use the wind and tide to your advantage and spend a few minutes permitting it to carry you to the fish and then to enjoy good fishing, rather than spook them.

Stripers and Blues Popular Inshore

Along the Atlantic coast striped bass and bluefish are very popular with inshore casters. Both of these species frequent the open ocean, but they'll often invade tidal estuaries looking for food, so you can expect to find them most anywhere. Often weakfish and seatrout will frequent the same areas, and it's not unusual to occasionally be rewarded with a mixed bag that includes several of these species.

All of these will feed on a variety of forage species, and at various times during the course of the season you'll find them chasing sand launce, spearing, menhaden, mackerel, herring, and mullet, which are the major forage. But it's not unusual to find a variety of other small fish in stripers, blues, weakfish, and seatrout. For when they are in a feeding frenzy they'll strike most any small fish.

When the fish are feeding on or near the surface they are usually so intent on feeding that they will strike a lure without hesitation. But sometimes a surface lure will be the one that draws strikes, while on other occasions you'll have to probe the depths to score. Keep in mind that for every fish you see breaking water on the surface there may be dozens more in the depths, feeding on the scattered baitfish.

The Golden Gate Bridge is known to most everyone, but few realize that the swift waters beneath it provide bonanza striped bass fishing. Boat casters employ bucktail jigs to coax strikes from fish feeding in the rips at the South Tower. On the Atlantic coast there's equally good sport in an almost identical situation beneath the Verrazano Narrows Bridge.

Use One Up and One Down

If there are a couple of anglers fishing from one boat, it's always wise to use a double-barreled approach to feeding fish. I like to see one fellow rigged with a surface lure, such as a popping plug, surface swimming plug, or propeller plug. The other caster should use a lure that will probe intermediate levels, such as a bucktail jig, hammered stainless-steel jig, or a metal squid.

Using this approach you quickly determine whether the fish are more receptive to a surface lure or one down deep.

In retrieving any lure it's important that you impart an enticing action to it. Don't fall into a bad habit of so many casters, who simply cast and reel, cast and reel. Work each cast, alternating the speed of your retrieve, or working the lure with your rod tip. Try long pulls of the rod tip, causing the lure to move ahead swiftly and then hesitate before pulling the lure again. If this doesn't work, use a short, snappy whipping action of the rod tip, which makes the lure look like an injured baitfish darting about frantically.

As you drift along casting to fish make sure to bracket your casts. Cast into, beyond, and along the perimeter of the school until you receive strikes. Once you find the right combination you can often take fish after fish with little difficulty, often right until the fish have filled themselves and stopped feeding.

The species we've mentioned often will feed on the surface in open water, but occasionally they'll herd a school of baitfish into a trap. They may accomplish this along a marsh bank or a point of land, rock jetty, or bridge abutment. Once cornered, the baitfish can't get away without having to pass by the larger fish, and this results in mayhem for as long as the fish feed.

Be alert to these kind of situations, and pay special attention to spots such as these, for stripers, blues, and weaks regularly feed using the approach of entrapment if they can possibly do it.

Off from the kelp beds found along shore in the Pacific you'll regularly encounter a great deal of activity with hungry gamefish chasing bait. Such tough Pacific advarsaries as yellowtail, bonito, barracuda, white sea bass, and many other species work along the kelp because they know anchovies and other small baitfish seek the sanctuary of the often densely packed kelp.

In situations like this I've often drifted along just off from the kelp, where gamefish were giving baitfish fits, and simply cast small bucktail jigs, diamond jigs, and wobblers in along the edge of the feeding fish and scored. Remember that often the fish will be working right along the edge of the kelp, so you can't overshoot your casts without fear of getting hung up in the kelp. When a fish is hooked you've immediately got to put a lot of pressure on it and work it away from the kelp, for if the fish makes it back into the mass of kelp, with leaves as big as a man, and stalks as thick as a man's leg, the chances are the fish will entangle your line in the vegetation and you'll just have to break the line.

Remember that some of the baitfish in the kelp are but 2 or 3 inches long, so use small as well as medium lures. Plugs too will bring strikes, in both surface, or subsurface models, but stick with models up to around an ounce in weight. You won't see too many anglers casting plugs around the kelp beds, but this is more a matter of habit. Those anglers who do experiment and use them often post nice scores.

Watch for Flotsam

Regardless of which ocean you fish in, you'll find that fish tend to congregate around any flotsam. It may be seaweed, a floating board, log, branch of a tree, or just a collection of floating debris brought together when the wind and tide clashed. Baitfish in an area naturally seek the weed and flotsam because it offers them some protection. Big fish realize this, and they often congregate around the flotsam, for they know a meal is usually close at hand.

Dolphin are especially noted for being found in such areas, and over the years I've almost always found these sterling fighters in the shadows of flotsam on the offshore grounds and invariably eager to take a cast lure. Because this fishing is generally in open water it affords excellent light-tackle opportunities.

The dolphin will strike plugs, metal squids, and jigs, but the bucktail jig is by far the most popular lure used to coax strikes. Once you receive a strike from a dolphin you should take your time fighting the fish and give your fishing partner an opportunity to cast to other dolphin that may be following the hooked fish. Dolphin have a habit of doing this and often you can take several fish from the same school simply by keeping one fish in the water at all times, which in turn keeps the others in the school close at hand.

Jack crevalle, amberjack, blackfin tuna, king and cero mackerel, and a host of other southern species can often be caught while casting around flotsam. When using subsurface lures make certain to hesitate after your cast, permitting the lure to settle several feet before beginning your retrieve. In this way you'll avoid getting hung in the weed and to a hungry fish it appears as though a small fish has left the shelter of the weed and it's after the lure in a flash.

LIGHTSHIPS, CHANNEL MARKERS, AND OIL RIGS

Casting enthusiasts will often encounter fish in the shadows of lightships at fixed anchorages offshore, around channel markers inshore, and buoys anchored far at sea. In the Gulf of Mexico there are gamefish beneath almost every oil rig, including bluefish, king mackerel, amberjack, dolphin at the far off rigs, barracuda, and the ever present hard-tailed jacks.

Both offshore and in close to the beach from the Middle Atlantic states south and then along the Gulf you'll find cobia also have a habit of taking up residence wherever there is a shadow, including channel markers, buoys, piers, and bulkheads. It pays to investigate all such spots, carefully presenting your lures to the fish in the shadows. Cobia are often very stubborn and may refuse your offering no matter how you work the lure. At such times I just move off to another spot and keep looking for the fish. Eventually you run into several that are cooperative and will respond to a bucktail jig. Many cobia fishermen enhance their jig by placing a strip of squid or mullet on the hook. Some even use a whole needlefish or other small fish and find this brings strikes from cobia more readily than the plain bucktail jig. Here too, you've often got to coax the fish into striking, working the lure erratically until it irritates or excites the cobia into taking the lure.

CHANNEL BASS GREAT TO CAST TO

Each spring off the Barrier Islands of Virginia, the Outer Banks of the Carolinas, and along much of the Gulf Coast huge schools of big channel bass move through inshore shallows where they present an excellent target for the caster. These fish often swim in schools that number hundreds of fish ranging from 20 to over 50 pounds. On a sunny day you can spot them as they cruise several feet beneath the surface, for their mass alone actually shows up as a darker coloration in the water.

When you spot these big channel bass on top you can almost always catch them. The trick as with most surface-feeding fish, is getting close

Big channel bass such as this heavyweight can often be spotted cruising just beneath the surface off Virginia's Barrier Islands and the Carolina Outer Banks. They readily take a cast Hopkins lure or metal squid.

enough without spooking the fish. These fish will strike subsurface swimming plugs, cast spoons, and metal squids, but they are most often fished for with a 2- or 3-ounce hammered stainless-steel jig with a single free-swinging hook. Here too it is important that you hesitate for several seconds before beginning your retrieve, permitting the lure to settle several feet into the water at the level at which the fish are swimming.

SNOOK PRESENT DIFFICULT TARGET

Some of the most difficult casting is for snook in the Everglades. There snook often take up residence beneath overhanging mangroves, charging out as a small fish or other food moves by their lair. To catch these fish, which often weigh 5 to 20 pounds, you've got to present your lure within inches of their cover or they'll totally ignore it.

I've seen a good caster that could drop a plug or bucktail within inches of the mangrove overhang score repeatedly, while an angler in the same boat who lacked accuracy and dropped his same lure a couple of feet out from the entangled roots went fishless.

SHALLOW FLATS CRITICAL

Still another type of exciting spin-casting from a small boat is while fishing the shallow flats of south Florida and the Bahamas. In Florida a variety of species including bonefish, the elusive permit, tarpon, jack crevalle, and barracuda, plus a number of other species invade shallow flats to feed. Some of these flats have but 6 inches of water on them as the tide floods, but nevertheless fish move up on them to search for shrimp, crabs, and seaworms, plus some of the small fish that inhabit the shallows.

This kind of fishing requires a stealthy approach, for any noise in the bottom of your boat will immediately spook the fish right off the flats. The spin-fisherman doesn't fish blind in this kind of a situation, but instead poles quietly across the flats in a shallow-draft boat, searching for the fish. Once a single fish, or even a school is spotted, the boat is poled into the best possible position to intercept the fish, and the angler then waits until the fish move within range to present his cast.

In fishing of this type, accuracy and a delicate presentation are important. You've got to use small lures for the most part, with delta-winged bucktail jigs the most popular choice for bonefish. These tiny jigs that weigh 1/16, ⅛ or ¼ ounce are held just off the bottom by their delta-wing shape and they're an extremely effective lure. Permit, barracuda, jacks, and other fish encountered on the flats will also take the tiny jigs.

The best approach is to present your jig several feet ahead and off to the side of the moving fish and then to employ a slow retrieve, gently working your rod tip so the jig flutters enticingly, much like a crab or shrimp working just off bottom. A good trick is to permit the jig to move to the soft, powdery sand on the flat, and then twitch your rod tip as you retrieve, causing a puff of sand that often attracts the attention of cruising bonefish or permit.

Barracuda and tarpon are most responsive to plugs. I've taken them on darters, poppers, and propeller plugs. With the sharp-toothed barracuda it's not difficult to hook them, but with tarpon you're lucky if you hook one fish out of every half-dozen that strike, as they have an extremely hard, bony jaw that is difficult to penetrate. But for exciting thrills on spinning tackle it's difficult to beat the aerial display of a tarpon hooked on light gear.

A good trick when working the flats is to have two rods rigged; one with a small bucktail jig tied directly to your monofilament line, and the other outfit rigged with a short length of wire leader and a plug. In that way you can use the jig for bonefish, permit, and jacks, and have the plug ready for any barracuda that happen by—and tarpon, too, for that matter.

Fishing the flats is a science that requires patience, skill, and knowledge of local waters. Clear water, pleasant warm weather, and a bright sun are prerequisites for good flats-fishing. A pair of quality Polaroid sunglasses are a must when fishing the flats, as they eliminate surface glare and enable you to look through the water and spot cruising fish.

A delicate approach, employing a light spinning outfit and tiny jig, live shrimp, or piece of conch is necessary when working the bonefish flats, for the water is but six to eighteen inches deep.

These tiny bucktail jigs weigh but 1/16 and ⅛ ounce and are used on the shallow bonefish flats. Note that some are delta-wing shaped, which keeps them up off the bottom when working the shallows. A light spinning outfit and light line are a must for handling any of these tiny lures.

PELAGIC SPECIES MOVE FAST

When schools of pelagic species are feeding the surface, they often move extremely fast, and at such times the only way casting opportunities are available is for one fellow to run the boat and move up on the surfaced school, while one or two anglers cast to the fish.

With school bluefin tuna, little tuna, blackfin tuna, oceanic bonito, Atlantic and Pacific bonito, and albacore, I've seen all of them chasing bait and moving so fast that you just couldn't shut down and drift and cast to them. The approach of easing up on the surface-feeding fish and casting to them while slowly underway has been the most successful approach I've found, and when you get a good team of helmsman and casters working together, you can often enjoying exciting sport with these extremely fast gamefish.

For all the tunas and bonitos, I've found the bucktail jig to be the number-one lure, with chromed jigs a close second. The trick here is to work the jigs extremely fast. Cast right into the thick of the wild maelstrom of surface activity, permit the lure to settle several feet, and then work your rod tip as vigorously as possible, whipping the lure through the water and reeling as fast as you possibly can. When you get tired retrieving you know you're doing it right!

MANY OTHER CASTING OPPORTUNITIES

I'm certain you can well appreciate that the boat caster has a lot of possible situations where he can enjoy his sport, whether in water barely a foot deep, to water a thousand or more fathoms in depth. But there are many more opportunities than I've covered here. You can work along most any beach, breakwater, or marsh bank and cast to the shoreline with bucktail jigs, plugs, spoons, or rigged eels and catch fish on all coasts—and literally dozens of different species. You'll find pollock often taking up station in a tide rip where they'll readily strike, and king mackerel, too. Silver and king salmon take up station at the mouths of the many rivers which empty into the broad expanse of the Pacific and are great targets for casters. Pacific and Atlantic mackerel are targets of the spin-caster, and while small, the caster who uses light tackle and tiny jigs or spoons can have many fun-filled hours catching them as his boat drifts across the ocean.

DEEP-JIGGING PRODUCES VARIETY

While not truly casting, deep-jigging is an extremely effective technique of the spin-fisherman, and one which has gained tremendous popularity along all coasts in recent years. Over a score of years ago I wrote my first magazine article about the effectiveness of the versatile bucktail jig, and they're just as effective today as they were then. Because of their unique design they can be used to probe depths beyond the range of other lures, hence their extreme effectiveness in deep water situations.

As its name implies, deep-jigging is a technique to probe the depths.

Al Pflueger, Jr., the well-known, south Florida light tackle angler has caught dozens of species while deep jigging. Here he's just landed a big grouper while spinning a reef in almost two hundred feet of water.

These depths may be 50 feet, or they may plummet a full 200 feet to where deep-water residents take up station to feed. I've employed the technique successfully while probing the swift waters off Montauk for bluefish and sent jigs to the 200-foot level off Walker's Cay in the Bahamas where huge groupers, snappers, and king mackerel assaulted them. The big bucktail jigs have brought me strikes in the Gulf of Mexico while probing the dark shadows beneath oil-drilling platforms too, and I've caught rockfish off Baja California in the depths off Ensenada, Mexico. You can use them most anywhere, and catch a greater variety of species than by using any other angling method.

Spinning is ideally suited to deep-jigging, simply because with a spinning reel you can retrieve line quickly, far more quickly than when using a small, multiplying casting reel. For the most part a fast retrieve is the key to deep-jigging, which you'll find is a very easy technique to master.

When I'm deep-jigging I usually employ a medium-weight spinning outfit, with the reel filled with 15-pound test monofilament and occasionally even 20-pound test. I double the last 2 or 3 feet of line using a Bimini knot, and then use an Albright special knot to attach either stainless-steel leader-wire or nylon-covered stainless-steel cable to the double line. Finally I employ either a haywire twist and barrel twist to secure the single-strand wire or a Homer Rhode loop knot to secure the nylon-covered stainless-steel cable.

As a general rule I stick with big, heavy jigs. I find they get down deep faster and are not carried by the current as readily as are lightweight jigs. On shallow reels, or over broken, irregular bottom up to 50 feet in depth, with a moderate amount of wind or current, jigs in the 1- to 2-ounce range are fine. Sometimes I'll even use lighter tackle and line when deep-jigging in the shallows.

But when I'm probing really deep water I often use bucktail jigs weighing a full 4 or 5 ounces. These jigs go right down, even if you're moving along swiftly because of current or wind.

Select Spot Carefully

Many species take up residence around wrecks, oil-drilling platforms, coral reefs, or subterranean mountains or rockpiles extending up from the bottom. Often the fish are congregated tightly around such spots, and in order to score you've got to get your jig within range of the fish or go fishless. Study charts and use a fathometer wherever possible to pinpoint the exact location of such spots. Then use the wind or current to carry you over the spot so you can work your jigs through the depths.

I always like to drift away from an underwater obstruction, rather than onto it, wherever possible. In this way when you receive a strike you're pulling the fish away from the coral or wreck, as is the boat as it drifts along. If you're drifting into such an obstruction the fish can often reach the sanctuary of the bottom and often will cut your line on a sharp marine growth. You'll also lose fewer jigs by getting them fouled as you drift onto a reef. There are times, however, when you don't have much choice and simply have to start upcurrent from a spot and drift over the entire area in order to score.

Alternate Retrieve

Once you've shut down your engine, just permit the jig to plummet to the bottom. As soon as you feel the telltale thump of the bottom telegraphed up your line, begin your retrieve immediately. The important thing is to vary your retrieve until you find the combination that brings strikes.

First try a smooth, fast retrieve, turning the reel handle as quickly as you can. Then try a whip retrieve, working your rod tip in long sweeps, which causes the jig to dart toward the surface, then falter and settle and dart toward the surface again. If that doesn't succeed, try short lifts of the rod tip as you reel.

Alternate your jigs. If a torpedo-shaped model doesn't work, try a lima-bean-shaped model. Add an attractor of some sort to the jig. Most of mine have a sparse dressing of mylar, but frequently I add a rubber worm or strip of pork rind to the hook.

I've found that the whip retrieve consistently outproduces all other types of retrieves while deep-jigging. A good rule of thumb is that when you get tired you know you're doing it right! You've got to work the jig so it appears as though it's a wounded baitfish struggling in the depths.

Find Level at Which Fish Are Striking

Some species will hang right on the peaks of reefs and rockpiles, and the only way you'll score is by receiving a strike within a few feet of the bottom. This is especially true of bottom-feeders, although some will move right up from the bottom to take a jig at intermediate levels. This is particularly true of the groupers, snappers, rockfish, and codfish, to name but a few.

Pelagic species tend to work at intermediate levels or near the surface. But sometimes they're down deep. So you've got to work your jig through the entire range, from bottom right up to the surface, until you find the level at which the fish are striking.

Once you find that level you can drop the jig to the approximate depth at which you feel the fish are and thus not waste a lot of time working your jig through depths that do not hold fish.

Chromed jigs such as the diamond, butterfish, tri-sided, and a host of other jigs may be employed using the same techniques used with bucktail jigs, and you'll be rewarded with fast action too.

There's no limit as to the number of species you'll take on jigs worked through the depths. Jiggers have landed sailfish on these versatile lures. Many of the game pelagic species will strike them with a relish, including the tunas, bonitos, and mackerels. Striped bass and bluefish in the depths of a rip will wallop bucktails, as will many bottom-feeders on all our coasts.

BE READY FOR ACTION

Spinning is made for casting, and from a boat it's a great, exciting way to catch fish. Keep your outfits rigged and ready whenever you set sail, for the opportunities present themselves fast and you want to be ready for them when the sky fills with screeching and diving sea gulls, and helpless fry leap into the air as hungry gamefish attack them from below. This is spin-casting at its glorious best.

BOTTOM-FISHING FROM BOAT AND SHORE

Of the many ways you can enjoy fishing with spinning tackle in salt water, bottom-fishing is without question the most contemplative. You simply cast your baited rig from shore, breadwater, jetty, pier, or boat, or in some cases just let the rig settle to the bottom and then sit back and relax as you wait for a finny bottom-feeder to find the tasty morsel. Bottom-fishing enables you to enjoy the beauty of nature surrounding you in a way few other fishing methods do. You watch the circling gulls as they search for a meal, the crashing breakers as they shower water across the rocky shore, or the exhilarating feeling of inhaling the salt air and enjoying the clear sky and clean water about you.

Bottom-fishing is a good beginning point for the newcomer to spin-fishing, for it is relatively uncomplicated and rather easy to master. This is because you are presenting a natural bait right down where the fish live, which appeals to their senses, and even if they're not actively searching for food, they will often succumb to your offering.

Suit Tackle to Fishing

You'll be able to use any spinning tackle for bottom-fishing, but it's important that you balance the tackle to the species being sought. It's just not practical using a one-handed spinning outfit when fishing in deep water where a heavy sinker is necessary to get the bait to the bottom, yet this outfit is entirely practical when your sights are set on small bottom-feeders that are in residence in the shallow reaches of a tidal bay or estuary.

A Variety of Bottom Rigs Available

There are literally hundreds of different bottom rigs, each peculiar to a particular area or type of fishing. While each differs slightly, a careful analysis of many of them will show marked similarities. For our purposes here I'll discuss those rigs which I feel will serve you well in the widest variety of situations. Indeed, I've used the rigs for a great many species on all our coasts and enjoyed fine results.

Basic Bottom-Rig Components

The essential components of a bottom rig consist for the most part of a hook, sinker, and swivel. The kind you use and just how they're put together will determine the kind of a rig it will be. While initially the choice of components may not seem important, the choice is extremely important, so always take care in making the correct selection.

HOOK STYLES

Initially hook styles might seem complicated, simply because there are so very many styles and sizes available. Some are made for fresh-water fishing exclusively, others to be used primarily with lures. Even so, there are still dozens of styles used by anglers fishing with natural baits. The Claw and Beak styles are universally favored, and in a pinch may be used for practically every type of bottom-fishing. Such types as Carlisle, Chestertown, Sproat, Kirby, and the O'Shaughnessy all have their applications when bottom-fishing.

An important consideration when selecting a hook for salt-water use is that it be as impervious to the corrosive effects of salt water as possible. Most hooks destined for use in salt water are either tinned or bronzed or plated with gold, nickel, or cadmium. These resist salt water for a nominal period of time, which is an important consideration, for a rusty hook is simply of no use whatsoever on the fishing grounds. For the most part salt-water hooks are made of wire substantially heavier than fresh-water hooks of the same size and style. This extra-strong feature of the salt-water styles is essential, for often you're encountering fish that are extremely strong, and they'd simply straighten a hook made of light wire.

Sizes of hooks are designated by a number system. Beginning with number 1, the sizes with each succeeding number become smaller, and just about the smallest size used in salt water is a number 9 or 10 Chestertown, which is popular for flounders. Hook sizes larger then number 1, carry a numerical designation followed by the letter O which designates ocean.

Thus we move from number 1 to number 1/0, and 2/0 on up, with each succeeding number followed by the letter O being a larger hook. For the most part the angler using spinning tackle in salt water will seldom have occasion to use a hook larger than size 9/0, and this will only be while using very large baits for big fish.

Most hooks used for bait fishing have a curved, offset point that is tapered needle-sharp for quick penetration. On the shanks of many hook styles there are often one or two barbs extending outward, which serve to help hold the bait in place. These bait-holder barbs are especially useful in holding seaworms in place and keep a worm from sliding down and balling up in the curve of the hook. The barbs serve to hold a delicate bait such as shrimp in place, along with other small or fragile bait.

SWIVELS IMPORTANT

There are a variety of swivels employed in making up a bottom rig. For the most part they do not serve as a swivel does while trolling, but instead are used to join line and leader, or to provide an eye from which a sinker is attached either via a snap or dropper loop.

The three-way swivel is far and away the most popular swivel style used by bottom fishermen. It is particularly useful in making up a single-hook rig, as the line is tied to one eye of the swivel, the leader and hook to another, and the sinker to the remaining eye.

Barrel swivels have two eyes, and are also useful when making up a single hook bottom rig, especially when an egg-shaped sinker is used and slides on the line. In a rig such as this the swivel is also used between line and leader.

Swiveling arms are useful for multihook rigs. A swiveling arm holds the hook out at right angles to the line, and swivels freely, thus preventing the leader and hook from becoming entangled in the line.

Still another swivel type, especially popular among surf-casters, is the fishfinder swivel. It has a smooth metal ring through which you run your primary line, and it has a 2-inch long piece of stiff wire built into a swivel barrel, with a snap beneath it, to which you attach your sinker.

The bottom-fisherman, regardless of where he fishes, would do well to include a selection of these swivels in his kit, in a variety of sizes, so as to be prepared to make up any type of rig he might desire on the fishing grounds.

SINKERS TAKE BAIT DOWN

Most sinkers are molded of lead and come in a variety of weights and shapes. While initially one may think any sinker will serve to get a bait to the desired depths, it must also be remembered that sinkers play still other roles: some hold a bait in place as the sinker readily buries itself in the bottom, while others are designed for drifting and slide along the bottom easily.

For general bottom-fishing the bank style is perhaps the most popular on all three coasts. It is pear-shaped, with an eye where you tie in located near where the stem of the pear would be. It is six-sided, running the length of the sinker.

Bank-style sinkers come in weights ranging from about a half ounce up to a pound and more. Because this book deals with spinning it simply becomes impractical to use the heavy sinker weights, which are used primarily with conventional tackle for bottom-fishing in very deep and swift water.

Once the angler armed even with heavy spinning-tackle is obliged to go beyond 8 ounces in weight to get to the bottom he'd be better off using a multiplying outfit.

The dipsey- or bass-casting style is popular with bottom-fishermen, and is sort of teardrop-shaped, with a small swivel molded into the top of it. Available in sizes from about ¼ ounce on up to 3 or 4 ounces, it's popular especially over rough bottom, where it will slide along with a minimum of fouling.

A variation is a round sinker, which is shaped like a ball, with a tiny brass ring in its top. Round sinkers range in weight from about 1 ounce up to 20 or more, the heavy weights naturally being of little use to the spinning enthusiast.

Throughout the South the egg-shaped sinker finds many devotees. It has a small hole running lengthwise through it, through which you can pass your line, thus permitting the sinker to slide on the line. It's popular with both casters and boat-fishermen, and comes in a wide range of weights, with the ½-ounce- through 4-ounce models most popular with spin-fishermen.

The rubber-cored sinker is still another useful sinker for bottom-fishermen and is especially popular on the Pacific coast. It is oblong in shape and has a rubber core running through its center. To attach it to your line you simply slip the line into a groove running the length of the sinker and twist the rubber ears extending from each end of the sinker, which holds it securely in place without damaging the line in any way.

The pyramid-style sinker is shaped much like a pyramid, and it holds extremely well in the bottom. It is especially favored by surfmen, pier and bridge casters, for it prevents the current or waves from washing it about, as would be the case with a smooth, round type sinker. Spin-fishermen find sizes in the 1- to 4-ounce range most practical.

There are many other sinker styles, each peculiar to a specific section of seacoast, but for the practical use of the angler equipped with spinning tackle you won't go wrong sticking with these basic styles.

MAKING UP THE BASIC BOTTOM RIG

A basic bottom rig that I've found very effective wherever I've fished is very easy to make up. The first step is to tie a small three-way swivel directly to the end of your line. If you're using light line, say, under 10-pound test, it's wise to use a couple of feet of line and make a Bimini knot to double the end of the line and then use a clinch knot to secure the swivel to the line. Next tie in four or five inches of monofilament line with a loop in the end, of lighter test than the line you're using. Through the loop you can slip the style of sinker you elect to use. The purpose of using the lighter line is to enable you to break off the sinker only should it become fouled on the bottom.

To the remaining eye of the swivel you can tie in your leader. If small bottom-feeders are your target a 12- to 18-inch leader of 10- or 15-pound test monofilament is adequate. If channel bass or striped bass are what you're after, then a 36-inch leader of 30-pound test monofilament will be in order. If toothy bottom-feeders, or even toothy gamefish such as bluefish or king mackerel, are in residence in the area you plan to fish, it's wise to use nylon-covered stainless-steel cable, for the fish won't be able to bite through it.

High-Low Rig

A high-low rig, as its name implies, fishes one hook high and another low, giving you two chances to score down on the bottom. One hook is usually fished right near the bottom on a swiveling arm, while the second hook is fished 18 to 24 inches off the bottom, sometimes higher. The swiveling arms to which your leaders are attached hold the leader away from the line and prevent it from tangling. Your sinker is attached to a sinker snap located right at the end of the rig, beneath the low hook.

Some anglers make up their own high-low rigs, but complete rigs may be purchased in many tackle shops along the seacoast, as can most of the rigs I'll discuss here. In areas where bottom-fishing for such plentiful bottom-feeders as red snapper, rockfish, whiting, and squirrel hake is popular, some anglers use high-low rigs having three or four hooks, ranging right from the bottom on up 4 or 5 feet off bottom. For the spinning enthusiast the two-hook rig is just perfect, as it won't put undue pressure on your outfit.

Egg-Sinker Rig

Throughout Florida, along the entire Gulf coast, and in the Bahamas and other tropical islands as well, the single hook fished on the bottom with a sliding egg-sinker is far and away the most popular bottom-rig in use.

It's easily made up by slipping an egg-shaped sinker—the model with a hole through the middle—directly onto your monofilament line. With the sinker on your line just tie a small barrel-swivel to the end of your line using a clinch knot. This permits the sinker to slide freely on the line.

Next tie in a piece of leader material. Small diameter for small fish, and upward of 30-pound test if heavyweights are around. Its length should range somewhere between 18 and 36 inches.

Finally tie in your hook, and you're set to bait up and cast out.

This rig, with a small sinker and a 1/0 hook, may be used with a live shrimp when after seatrout, or with a 6/0 hook and live pinfish as bait when fishing a pass for snook, redfish, and tarpon. It's a versatile rig that works extremely well.

Fishfinder Rig

The fishfiinder rig works on much the same principle as the egg-sinker rig. With it you slip a chrome-plated fishfinder swivel onto your line, after which you tie in a swivel and complete the rig much the same as an egg-sinker rig. To the snap of the fishfinder you attach your sinker and you're all set to go. This rig is especially popular with surf-casters, for a big fish such as a striped bass, channel bass, weakfish, or bluefish may pick up the bait and move off with it without feeling the weight of the sinker.

Spreader Rig

The spreader rig is made of a stiff piece of wire, measuring between 12 and 18 inches in length. It has an eye on either end, to which you attach your snelled hooks, and in the center of the spreader there is an eye to which you attach your line, and directly beneath where your line is tied there is a sinker snap, to which your weight is attached. The spreader acts to keep two hooks spread apart, yet permits both of them to rest right on the bottom. It's an especially popular rig with anglers who fish for winter flounder, puffer, spot, and whiting.

Multihook Rig

Some anglers prefer fishing two and even three hooks off a single leader, and I like to refer to this type of rig as a multihook-rig. Generally it is used in conjunction with a three way swivel. This results in the two or three hooks tied off the single leader dropper fashion all resting on the bottom. This rig is popular when after winter flounder, croaker, spot, and other small fish.

Single-Hook Rig

Along the Pacific coast, and with increasing regularity along the Gulf, anglers are simply tieing a hook directly to the end of their monofilament line and then attaching a rubber-cored sinker a couple of feet up from the hook. This rig works very well to get the bait down to the bottom, especially when fishing in shallow water or where there is little tidal flow. It's especially favored when fishing around the kelp beds, as there is no terminal hardware to become fouled. It works well when sand bass, kelp bass, halibut, and rockfish are hugging bottom.

Along the Gulf coast I've used it from the surf with a tiny piece of shrimp or mullet as bait, and caught a variety of fish, including seatrout, black drum, flounder, and sheepshead.

Many Baits May Be Used

The rigs I've discussed are designed to present your bait within range of bottom-feeders. Just what bait you'll present will depend on the species you're fishing for and the type of bait most often found in the area you plan to fish.

All too often anglers become creatures of habit and use a bait simply because historically other anglers fishing the same area for a particular species have used that bait. I've observed this situation in many areas I've fished, and I believe that sometimes anglers minimize their chances of scoring by simply holding to too distinct a pattern when they select baits. Remember that for the most part any fish that is hungry is out to satisfy its appetite. When it sees food, it will often simply inhale it, thus satisfying its hunger. Too often anglers think of bottom-feeders, and even gamefish, as approaching and carefully analyzing a bait before taking it. Such is not the case.

There are, however, several important considerations. Fish will most certainly distinguish between fresh and decayed or stale bait. Indeed, I've many times witnessed where a fresh bait repeatedly brought strikes, while a stale bait, exposed to the air or sun went strikeless. Thus, it behooves you to keep all your baits as fresh as possible. Most salt-water baits should be kept out of the sun, preferably in an ice chest—off the ice so they don't get soggy or water-logged—or covered with damp burlap if ice isn't available. This applies to baits such as any dead fish that you may use, squid, seaworms, clams, mussels, shrimp, crabs, and other baits.

Examine Stomach Contents

Over many years of catching fish on spinning tackle with natural baits I've developed a habit of examining the stomach contents of the fish I've caught. Doing so has told me precisely what the fish I've caught had been feeding on before they inhaled my bait. Indeed, often the food they had been eating came as a surprise. I've found baby lobsters in codfish, many shrimp in striped bass when I failed to realize that shrimp were so plentiful, and dozens of tiny clams in winter flounders.

I've also learned that many prime baits constitute a very small portion of the diet of the species they're often used for. Striped bass eat very few seaworms, perhaps less than 1 percent of their diet, yet they're an extremely popular bait. But mackerel, which constitute a major portion of the striper's diet in some areas, are infrequently used, either live or whole or chunked when dead. Here, again, the choice of bait has become a matter of habit, rather than being determined by careful analysis of what the fish is most apt to strike. Always remember you're certain to score more quickly when you present a bait that the fish are feeding on at that particular time.

Shrimp Rate First

If ever there was a universal bait that could be used with equal effectiveness for a wide variety of species on all coasts it would have to be shrimp. There are many species of these macruran crustaceans found in coastal waters, some measuring barely an inch in length while others are fully 9 inches long or larger. Hardly any bottom feeders or gamefish will pass them up, as they are a staple.

Shrimp are stocked by most bait dealers along the seacoast. In southern climes hook-size shrimp, those measuring 3 to 5 inches in length, are stocked by many bait dealers. In other areas fresh shrimp are available, while quick-frozen bait shrimp may be purchased most anywhere.

You can even obtain your own, using either a cast net, small seine, or fine-meshed dip net in many coastal estuaries.

If the shrimp is alive the hook may be run through the hard shell of the back of the head, which keeps it alive, and it will continue to swim and dart about, particularly if it's a big shrimp. With smaller shrimp just run the hook through the shrimp, concealing it as best you can, keeping just the point and barb exposed for quick penetration. With tiny baits you can thread several shrimp on the hook.

Shrimp are without a doubt the favorite bait of salt-water anglers everywhere. They attract a wide variety of species. In many areas live shrimp may be purchased for bait, but fresh or frozen shrimp also bring many strikes.

I've caught species beyond count on shrimp, while fishing the open reaches of the ocean and the quiet confines of coastal estuaries. Big fish such as grouper will take a shrimp on the bottom, a hundred or more feet below the surface, as will wily bonefish while scouring the bottom in only 1 foot of water.

Seatrout, striped bass, weakfish, flounders, sea bass, croakers, surf perch, porgies, rockfish, sand bass, and kelp bass are but a few of many species that will take a shrimp bait fished on the bottom from surf or boat.

MEAT OF BIVALVES BRINGS STRIKES

Bivalves such as clams, abalone, mussels, and oysters are favored by many bottom-feeders. Oftentimes you'll find soft-shelled clams in their entirety in the stomachs of fish you catch. This is also true of mussels. Along the surf after a storm you'll often see thousands of clams that have been uncovered, and the crashing action of the waves has often broken many of them open. This results in a huge spread of food being presented to hungry fish in the area, and they'll often congregate to gorge themselves on the clams.

As a bottom bait you'll find any of the bivalves can't be beat for tautog, porgies, sea bass, codfish, pollock, black drum, and croakers. When fishing for codfish and using a 6/0 or 7/0 hook it's altogether proper to use half or even a whole sea clam, but when after sea bass that may weigh but a pound a smaller bait, about the size of a dime, is more appropriate. If winter flounders are your target, then a tiny bait measuring but a ¼ inch in width by 1½ in length will do the trick. These small baits may be cut from any of the bivalves.

Because the meat of many bivalves is soft, many anglers shuck the meat from them the evening before they plan to go fishing. They soak the meat of the clams, mussels, or oysters in a heavy brine of coarse salt. This soaking hardens the meat and it stays on the hook much better than when fresh.

SQUID POPULAR ON ALL COASTS

Squid is another universally popular bottom bait. They're found in substantial quantities in the waters off all our coasts. They may be used whole, in strips, or diced into small pieces. Whole squid are a favorite bait of west coast anglers who fish for white sea bass and yellowtail. They're a fine bottom bait when cut into strips for halibut and summer flounders. Diced into pieces the size of a quarter, they're readily taken by most bottom-feeders, including sand bass, sea bass, and tautog.

At times squid may be obtained at the fishing grounds, especially at night when they'll come up under a bright light held over the water, at

The octopus-like squid is a popular bait on all three coasts. Sometimes small chunks are used as bait, but most often strips are cut from the squid, for when placed on the hook they flutter in an enticing manner.

which time they are easily snagged. But most anglers obtain their squid at coastal bait shops, where fresh frozen squid is readily available.

SEAWORMS DRAW STRIKES

Seaworms of many types are found in the sand and muck bottom along many areas of coastline. The best-known seaworms include the sandworm, bloodworm, tapeworm, and clam worm. While these works do not constitute a major portion of the diet of bottom-feeders, there are few bottom-feeders that will pass up a worm on a hook.

Some worms lend themselves to being used whole, while others are used in pieces. They are all perhaps the most delicate of all hook baits used in salt water, and care must be exercised in placing them on the hook so they are not easily torn from it. The bloodworm is a long, blood-filled worm which outwardly resembles the common earthworm. It's among the most durable of seaworms on a hook, and will bring strikes most anywhere in salt water, from virtually all bottom-feeders. When used for striped bass, weakfish, and other big bottom-feeders, anglers often use two or more worms, running the hook twice through the worm to hold it securely. In the case of sandworms, when anglers are seeking large fish, a single worm is often used. The large, 6- to 10-inch-long worm is impaled by running the hook through its mouth and brought out its body about a half-inch down from the head. When hooked in this manner the worm stays alive and actually swims, which makes it an attractive bait. Of course, if you're fishing for small bottom-feeders, such as porgies, croakers, winter flounders, starry flounders, surf perch, or sea bass, then small pieces of any of the seaworms are a very effective bait. Indeed, some seaworms, the tapeworm in particular, is such a brittle bait, that it is only practical to use it in small pieces.

In using any of the seaworms, especially when a hook of size number 2 or larger is used, it is wise to use a Claw hook having a bait-holder shank. The tiny barbs in the shank of the hook keep the worm from sliding down onto the bend of the hook, and it makes for a far neater bait.

FISH LIKE CRABS TOO

I don't know how many kinds of crabs there are in the oceans off our coasts, but there are many. For as I've traveled about I've seen many different varieties, and all of them, either whole or in part, prove extremely effective as bottom baits for a wide variety of species. The blue crab, fiddler crab, green crab, calico crab, rock crab, and many other crustaceans are the housekeepers of the floors of our oceans, and they're a treat seldom ignored by bottom-feeders. Indeed, over the years I've inspected the stomach contents of many fish I've caught while bottom-fishing, and often I've found crabs more frequently than I would have suspected. Striped bass gorge on them, as do tautog, sheepshead, black drum, channel bass, snook, and even the princely tarpon.

Naturally, the bait must be tailored to the species you're after. If your target is tautog weighing but a few pounds, then a crab the size of a half-dollar is ample. If 50- to 100-pound tarpon moving through a pass are what you're after, then a crab measuring 3 or 4 inches from point to point across its back is ideal.

Crabs shed their old shell as they grow. During various stages of their life they are called by various names. When about to shed their old shell, they are called shedders. Immediately after shedding, they are soft and cannot maneuver on their own, often being carried at the mercy of the tide. At such times they're called soft crabs. As their shell begins to harden they're called tin backs, and when firmly hardened most are just plain called hard crabs.

Hard crabs make satisfactory baits, but it is generally felt that the soft crab or the crab in a shedder state makes the best hook bait.

Crabs may be obtained while using a crab rake in the sand, picking them up from around dock pilings with a long-handled net, by drawing a seine through shallow estuaries to capture drifting soft crabs, or by searching among the rocks at low tide for crabs trapped as the tide recedes.

Because crabs easily fall from a hook, many anglers employ elastic string to secure the bait to the hook, or they use small common elastic bands to hold the bait securely on the hook.

ANY MARINE ANIMAL WILL PRODUCE

It would be difficult to list every single bait that will take bottom-feeders, for there are just so many. Conch of various types are found in many waters, and the tough meat found within the shell makes a fine bait. I've employed small pieces while fishing the shallow flats for bonefish, yet probed the depths around rocks and wrecks while using conch for codfish, pollock, and tautog. Simply stated, it's food, and when a fish is hungry it'll waste little time in taking it.

The sand bug, or sand flea, as it is called in some areas, is still another fine bait. This small crustacean, which seldom grows larger than a quarter, is found in the sand along the surf. It makes a fine bait for sheepshead, pompano, tautog, and a host of other species. Of the many baits that are easily obtained, I've observed that anglers seldom use the sand bugs, yet I have found them in the stomachs of many species that I have caught, most notably, striped bass, channel bass, and black drum.

SMALL FISH WIDELY USED

There are literally dozens of different forage species that may be effectively used as bottom baits for many species. Sardines and anchovies are favored by West coast anglers, while Gulf coast fisherman employ pilchards, balao, and mullet to coax strikes. East coast bottom-bouncers use salt-water minnows, spearing, sand launce, herring, and a host of other small fish.

When available, a small live baitfish often works best. Many anglers reason that a baitfish on a hook transmits distress signals through the water that attract other fish. But if live baitfish aren't available, then use them dead, but make certain they're fresh.

In placing a baitfish on a hook it's more important that you impale it on the hook properly than when you're using most other baits. With live baitfish, it's best that they be hooked either through the lips, eye sockets or gill collar, so that as the current moves against them, or as the bait is drifted across the bottom, it always faces the current and swims in a lifelike manner. With dead fish, place them on the hook so they lie flat and slide through the water. Keep in mind that a baitfish hooked through the back and drifted across the bottom will be spinning and dragging along in an unnatural manner.

Live baitfish are an excellent bait. Here an angler purchases live pilchards on a Florida pier. Other popular live baits include anchovies and sardines on the Pacific coast, mullet and killies on the Atlantic and pinfish on the Gulf coast.

Many anglers who consistently use baitfish when after bottom-feeders use a two-hook baitholder. As a rule the primary hook is a large Carlisle-style hook, which has a small O'Shaughnessy-style hook attached to the shank of the Carlisle near its eye. The small hook acts to hold the head of the baitfish, while the larger or primary hook is passed through the center or back section of the bait. In this way the baitfish is always held flat, and when a fish strikes it is most apt to get the primary hook in its mouth. This hook is especially popular with anglers who fish for summer flounders, but it works well when after other species and using any of the small forage species as bait.

CHUNK OF FISH WORK TOO

It's a matter of survival of the fittest in the ocean, with the larger fish eating the smaller. So it stands to reason that a fresh chunk of fish on your hook will draw many strikes from the fish you're seeking. Often I've run out of choice baits while on the fishing grounds, I have simply taken a small fish from the fishbox, cut it up, placed it on my hook, and continued to score.

Indeed, many anglers prefer a fresh piece of fish to other baits. Over many years my dad has always preferred a fresh strip of fluke belly as bait while after other fluke than to using a choice piece of squid as bait. For he found the fluke belly was a tougher bait that often resulted in more strikes than many other types of bait that he used. So immediately after

The salt water killie, commonly called a minnow in many areas, is a popular bait for a wide variety of bottom feeders, especially summer and southern flounders. It is best hooked through the lips, so it can swim about in a natural manner.

catching his first summer flounder, he cuts a couple of baits from it to continue fishing.

As a general rule, the oily species of fish are favored as hook baits. Mackerel, sardine, mullet, herring, spot, pilchards, menhaden, and butterfish are among the most popular baits. Depending on the fish you're after and the size of hook you're using, you may use a fillet sliced from the side of the fish or just a small strip or even a tiny piece just large enough to cover your hook.

KEY IS FINDING FISH

You can't catch fish when there aren't any in the spot you're fishing. While this may sound like something everyone would understand, it's really the reason many people don't catch fish. They're simply fishing in spots where there are no fish.

So your first consideration when bottom-fishing, whether it be from boat, the surf, jetties, piers, or bulkheads, is to select a spot where you feel fish will naturally tend to congregate to feed.

When you're out after tautog or sheepshead, you'll learn that they like rocky bottom, wrecks, or mussel-encrusted pilings around which to set up residence. By looking for these spots and concentrating your fishing there, you're bound to score.

Flounders generally like a smooth-sand or mud bottom, while sea bass

The yellowtail snapper is a favorite of southern Atlantic bottom fishermen. It resides near reefs or coral and on broken, irregular bottom. This beauty took a piece of conch, but they'll also take shrimp or small pieces of fish.

and porgies like mussel beds. Kelp bass, sand bass, Pacific barracuda, and halibut often will stick close to kelp beds, simply because small fish are plentiful there and it's easy for them to obtain a meal. The many species of Pacific rockfish will often look for rocky bottom 100 or more feet in depth.

In southern climes the groupers and snappers seek the waters around coral reefs, because here too they know a meal is close at hand. Where reefs aren't in an area, they'll choose the waters above a wreck, or the piles supporting an offshore oil-drilling platform.

So you see, there's no one spot to go fishing. It depends on the species you're after and the waters you plan to fish. Along the surf you'll have to look for deep cuts inside bars, and on jetties the rips and eddies caused by the current will often hold feeding fish. Seldom are any two spots identical.

But they are very similar, and you've got to study the water to determine the spots to fish. Often a difference of just 10 or 15 feet will make the difference between success and failure. I recall many times when porgy fishing that we'd be anchored over a particularly hot mussel-bed and were catching fish every time our baits reached bottom, while boats surrounding us went fishless, simply because they were off the hot spot.

HOOKING FISH COMES WITH EXPERIENCE

Some anglers think of bottom-fishing as simply lowering a baited hook to the bottom, receiving a strike, and hauling in the fish. Bottom-fishing is much more than that, and only once you've fished with a really sharp bottom-fisherman can you appreciate the skill that comes from experience.

Species such as tautog and sheepshead take a bait very swiftly, and if you don't react almost instantly, they'll strip the bait from your hook. But striking a summer flounder immediately would yank the bait right away from it. Thus it becomes important to learn just how a fish takes a bait and how you should react. This can't be learned from a book, because there are too many variables. Sometimes the current plays a role, which requires you to hesitate simply because the bait is drifting swiftly, and a fish grabs it, but takes a few seconds to mouth the bait. At other times a fish may suck on a bait, which is particularly true of winter flounders, and you've got to tease it by slowly lifting your rod tip, which will often cause the fish to take the bait.

Remember that many fish will move about searching for food. Sometimes on a flooding tide they'll take up station in a tide rip and feed for several hours, only to leave the area as the tide slackens to take up residence in a rip that will form as the tide ebbs. Some species will feed voraciously on a running tide and simply refuse all offerings when the tide is slack or near slack. As you develop skills and experience you will become aware of each situation in the particular area you fish and for the species you're after. With experience behind you it's often possible to select the prime tide and a particular spot, and in just a couple of hours of exciting sport have more action than anglers who may have spent an entire day on the water, but who had not studied the water and the species they were after.

SHORECASTING FROM SURF, JETTIES, BRIDGES AND PIERS

Spinning has done more for the angler fishing from shore than any single innovation in fishing history. For many years it took much painstaking effort

to master the art of casting with a multiplying reel. When spinning became popular, it enabled a newcomer to cast a lure several hundred feet into the surf with little difficulty. Lures that by their very light weight were difficult, if not impossible, to cast suddenly could be cast with little effort while using the fixed-spool mill. Anglers quickly found that surf, jetty, bridge, and pier fishing could be fun, and the ranks of anglers soon swelled. For here, for the most part, was one of the most economical ways of enjoying salt-water fishing. You simply selected the kind of fishing that appealed to you and tried your hand at it.

Strength Not Required

Often people observing beach-casters with their long surf rods get the impression that surf-casting is difficult and requires strength. Neither is true. It's relatively easy to learn to cast, as the accompanying photographs indicate, and it can be mastered by anglers of all ages, including women, many of whom enjoy many relaxed hours along the beachfront.

The tackle you employ while surf-fishing will vary from one spot to another. On the beaches of Cape Cod and the rocky shoreline of Montauk on Long Island and from the tumbling surf to the Barrier Islands of Virginia

Surf fishing is often a contemplative waiting game. These two casters patiently wait for strikes on the dark sand beaches near the mouth of San Francisco Bay.

and the Outer Banks of the Carolinas, the heavy surf-rod is most often used, for long casts are often required and the long rod also assists in keeping the line well above the crashing breakers. The same tackle finds use while fishing from the surf and rockpiles of the California, Washington, and Oregon coast.

But on the gently sloping beaches of the Gulf of Mexico many casters employ one-handed spinning tackle, because the surf is usually moderate and most often warm and wadeable. As a result the heavy surfing-tackle would prove less desirable. There are times, however, when heavyweights such as tarpon and redfish are encountered along the Gulf surf, and at such times the medium-weight spinning outfit is brought into play.

There's no set rule on what tackle to use in a specific area. Selection will depend on the type of conditions encountered and the lures and baits being used and the species sought.

Surf and Jetty Conditions Vary

Each group of spin-fishermen—the troller, chummer, boat-caster and bottom-fisherman—looks for a particular situation where fish will congregate. The surfman and jetty fisherman must also look for good spots, for

The first step in surf casting is to pick up
the line with your index finger and to
open the bail of the reel.

Sweep your rod behind you, and when
you reach this position, begin your sweep
upward and forward, pushing with your
right hand, and pulling downward with
your left. This will generate the power
that will take your lure far beyond the
breakers.

At this point maximum power is brought to bear, yet note that the line is still held firmly by your index finger. The rod should be brought forward smoothly over your shoulder.

Follow through is important. As you release the line with your index finger, let the rod follow the line as it sails through the air; this will give maximum distance to your cast.

often fish will hold in just one small area, while avoiding miles of adjoining beach. The same holds true on coastal jetties and breakwaters, as well as natural rocky shoreline.

Usually fish stay in a specific area for a reason. More often than not it's because food is plentiful there or is close at hand.

All beaches and jetties are not alike, so it behooves you to study the conformation of each area you plan to fish and plan your fishing accordingly. You can best determine the underwater configuration of a stretch of beach-front and the water around a jetty by visiting it at low tide, preferably on a clear, windless day when the water is clear and the sun high, so you can study it thoroughly. It may sound like a waste of time to some, but over the years I've done this a great many times, and it has proved invaluable, for I knew precisely where fish might take up station to feed on the flooding tide, and where they would not be as well.

Few stretches of beach are absolutely flat. Some spots drop away from the beach abruptly, while others have a gentle slope. In some spots you'll find a deeply cut hole between a beach and sandbar located several hundred feet from shore. At other spots you'll find a ridge of sand extending seaward from the beach, built up by swift currents running around a jetty front.

Wherever there are ridges, abrupt dropoffs and deep cuts you'll usually find fish congregating nearby. For as the tide floods, the swift currents often carry food into spots such as this. These spots are also a natural congregating place for small baitfish that larger fish feed upon.

Check Area at Low Tide

Investigation of the bottom is often possible at low tide, and at such times you'll often observe rocks and other debris on the bottom. When you find this type of debris there will often be a great deal of marine growth around it and mussels clinging to it. The bottom will often be populated with crabs, and the sand will hold sand bugs and clams. Shrimp are often plentiful in such a spot, as are small baitfish, making it a natural for larger fish when they're looking for a meal.

The churning action of the water, especially where waves build up off-shore and come crashing down on sandbars and then level out and continue in to crash again on the beach, is a natural. For in a spot such as this bottom food is constantly being exposed, which makes it easy for a hungry fish to find a meal. The strong current that accompanies a moving tide often causes the baitfish in residence to seek the protection of the shallows in near the beach.

In discussing bottom-fishing I've included the many types of rigs and natural baits that could be used to advantage from both boats and shore, including the surf, jetties, bridges, and piers. Within this section I will discuss primarily the use of lures from shore, but much of what I say with respect to lures will apply equally well to using natural baits while bottom-fishing from the surf, jetties, bridges and piers. For where you find fish that will strike lures you'll also find they will often take a natural bait as well.

A Wide Variety of Lures Available

Years ago shore-based casters were limited in the lures they could use. By and far the most popular lures were block-tin squids and heavy chrome-plated lead squids. These could be cast with ease with a multiplying reel, hence their widespread popularity. Big plugs and big-rigged eels and other heavy lures saw great use too.

With the advent of spinning and the ability to cast light-weight lures, the range of lures available grew to include smaller metal squids, many types of plugs, bucktail jigs, rigged eels, and a wide array of chromed and stainless-steel wobblers designed to imitate small baitfish. Many of these were so light in weight that it would have been difficult, if not impossible, to cast them with a multiplying surf outfit.

BASIC TERMINAL CONNECTION

Before discussing the various lures I use while fishing from shore, I'd like to cover a couple of the most popular methods employed by surfmen to attach their lures. First of all, to tie a lure directly to the end of your line minimizes its action in most cases. There are exceptions to this rule, but those lures which work well with a direct tie are in the minority, and even then will usually work better when there is a loop or some play between line and lure.

If I'm fishing in an area where most of the fish I'm apt to catch have no teeth, such as striped bass, channel bass or snook, I'm apt to use a nylon monofilament leader. In using a light line I'll often double the end of my line the equivalent of 1½ times the length of my rod. Thus, when using 12-pound test monofilament line I in effect have 24-pound test at the terminal end, with several turns around the reel spool, which gives me an extremely strong end-section and thus enables me to place a tremendous amount of pressure on the line when casting.

Another method in popular use is to attach 10 or 12 feet of shock tippet directly to the end of your casting line, by employing an Albright Special knot. Both systems work well and give you a shocker at the terminal end, which is not only useful while casting, but when landing fish as well.

Still, some fellows frown on the shocker and simply use a double-improved clinch knot, joining their line to a tiny swivel, to which they've tied a

2- or 3-foot length of leader material, usually about twice the strength of the line being used. The purpose of the heavier leader is to save those fish that might otherwise have their gills, fins or scales cut through the line.

WIRE FOR TOOTHY SPECIES

When bluefish, king mackerel, bonito, and barracuda come within range of the shore-based caster, along with other toothy adversaries, then a wire leader they cannot bite through is a must. Number 6 or 7 single-strand stainless-steel leader wire may be used, or 25-pound test nylon-covered stainless-steel cable.

A short, wire leader should be used for toothy species. This young angler fishing from the jetty at Indian River inlet in Delaware used fine stainless steel wire to keep the bluefish from biting through his line while fishing with a metal squid.

SNAP FAVORED BY MANY

To facilitate lure changing, many beach casters employ a snap of some sort, attached between their leader and lure. I've tried a great many snaps and settled on the stainless-steel duo-lock snap, which is made from a single piece of wire, is extremely strong, and, because of its small size and compactness, does not detract from the action of most lures, however small they may be.

I attach the snap directly to the leader using a clinch knot with monofilament leader, a Homer Rhode loop knot if I'm using nylon-covered stainless-steel cable leader material, and with a combination haywire and barrel twist if using single-strand stainless-steel leader.

There are at least a half-dozen or more other models of snaps on the market, but I'll not mention them here, as I feel the duo-lock snap is so far superior that I don't even include any of the others in my surf bag. The other snaps have applications for offshore and other fishing, but for beach fishing stick with duo-lock and you can never go wrong.

Note that I haven't mentioned using a snapswivel as a connector between leader and lure. I think the snapswivel detracts from a lure's action, and is also apparent to fish, particularly when used in clear water, so I don't recommend its use.

PLUGS A FAVORITE

Plugs are a favorite of shore-based casters, and spinning enthusiasts use models measuring as little as 2 inches on up to 8- and 9-inch-long monsters that they cast seaward to lure a wide variety of gamefish into striking. Plugs are designed for the most part to simulate a small baitfish and manufacturers in recent years have gone to great pains to create lures that are shaped and painted and swim much the same as a real fish.

The surface swimming-plug, often called a minnow plug, has gained tremendous popularity with spin-fishermen because while it is light in weight, it isn't too difficult to cast a fair distance. But what has made it so popular is its effectiveness with a wide variety of species and the exciting surface strike that one receives while using it.

The surface swimmers come in a wide variety of sizes and finishes. Some resemble tiny spearing and menhaden, while others are made to look like herring, mackerel, pilchards, mullet, and a host of other forage species found along the surf, around breakwaters, and in bays and rivers along the coast.

When using them you'll find that a slow, lazy retrieve often works best. When retrieved in this manner, the plug works from side to side in an enticing manner many species find irresistible. Oftentimes the gamefish will

Included here are the favorite lures used
by Atlantic coast surfmen in quest of
striped bass, bluefish, and weakfish. Included from top to bottom are a Hopkins
lure, Creek Chub popping plug, rigged
eel, Creek Chub Pikie subsurface swim-
mer, block tin squid with pork rind, Mirrolure deep diving plug, and Upperman
bucktail jig.

be working along the surf, looking for small fish right in close to the sand, and you'll be surprised when you receive strikes just 15 or 20 feet from where you're standing.

When the surface swimmers don't bring results, then there are the sub-surface models, which probe the intermediate levels and down near the bottom. They're identical to the surface models, except that in some cases they're weighted, or their lips designed to draw them into the depths. Here too, a lazy retrieve usually works best, although there will be times when a bit of speed may be necessary, so don't fall into a pattern of retrieving at but one speed.

POPPERS DRAW WILD STRIKES

Surfmen and jetty jockies also find popping plugs potent lures. They're especially effective when worked over spots where you know fish are in residence, but other lures fail to draw a strike. The poppers have a concave head, and when drawn across the surface of the water, they literally pop, sending a shower of water ahead of them as they are drawn through the water.

They may be retrieved slowly, at which time they gurgle and bubble along and make quite a surface disturbance. But the most effective way of fishing them is to work your rod tip with long sweeps or with short pops or mixing the two up. This erratic, enticing surface action drives fish wild, and it'll bring furious strikes from striped bass, bluefish, barracuda, amberjack, seatrout, and a host of other species.

MIRROR PLUGS LOOK LIKE FISH

Mirror plugs are meticulously designed to resemble small fish, and the eye to which you attach your snap is located on the top of the plug at its head. When drawn through the water these plugs have little action of their own, so you must impart action through use of your rod tip and alternating the speed of your retrieve.

They're available in surface, medium-running, and deep-running models, and are an extremely effective lure, particularly in situations where a rough surf rules out surface lures, or where a swift tidal flow makes it difficult to work other types of plugs through the depths. Used on all three coasts, they're especially popular throughout the South.

PROPELLER PLUGS GET NOD, TOO

As their name implies, propeller plugs are equipped with propellers, usually one fore and one aft, although some models have but a single propeller. Most of the plugs are cigar-shaped, and they come in either surface or deep-running models. Their main attraction lies in the commotion created as the props spin as they are retrieved. Sometimes a slow retrieve, with a lifting of the rod tip occasionally, turns the trick, while at other times a fast, steady retrieve is what it takes to draw strikes. I've scored with these plugs practically everywhere I've fished, including the beaches of Baja where I casted for Pacific barracuda and bonito.

Many Other Plug Types Used in Local Areas

Each section of coastline has a number of favorites that find great local acceptance. The flap-tail plug is extremely popular with Atlantic coast striper anglers, for as it is retrieved across the surface it closely resembles a wounded mullet leaving a wake. The darters are popular in snook country, especially the southwest Florida coast, where beach anglers score consistently, while heavily leaded deep-diving models find favor while probing the depths of passes leading into the Gulf, where they account for Spanish mackerel, jack crevalle, blue runners, snook, redfish, and many other species for beach-based anglers.

Metal Jigs In Many Varieties

The modern-day offshoot of the old block-tin squid come in a wide variety of truly fine lures. The Hopkins lure is far and away the finest of the relatively new models. It is made of hammered stainless-steel and has

The Cape Cod Canal has a constant parade of ship traffic passing through, but there are many fine catches made from its waters by anglers casting from the rocky riprap. Plugs, rigged eels and bucktail jigs all produce results at various stages of the tide.

a stainless-steel split ring, to which a feathered or bucktail-dressed stainless-steel hook is attached.

The body of the Hopkins resembles a knife handle in shape, although it has a unique taper that gives it a fine action. Its body is hammered, and, when retrieved, the lure has a soft, glistening luster that many fish find irresistible. Because of its shape and weight, the Hopkins casts extremely well, even when cast into the wind. It may be worked near the surface or permitted to settle into the swift waters of passes and deep cuts and brings strikes from many species.

There are many other fine new metal squids and wobblers that the beach-based angler can bring into play. Some are stamped from stainless steel, while others are molded of lead and then chrome- or nickel-plated. Most have a free-swinging single or treble hook, dressed with either bucktail or feathers. Many have a keel and have a swinging, side-to-side action as retrieved. There are literally hundreds of models available. Some are long and thin, designed to resemble a sand launce, while others are short and wide, much like a pilchard or mullet.

BUCKTAIL JIGS VERSATILE

Bucktail jigs are one of the most versatile lures in the arsenal of the beach-based angler. They may effectively be used from the surf to probe the deep pockets inside bars, from piers and bridges where they can be worked right to the edge of the structure, and from rockpiles. They are especially effective in inlets and passes for they settle well into the current, and can literally be bounced on the bottom in the strongest of currents. Quite the contrary, light-weight jigs can be used along river banks where there is a gentle slope out to a channel edge, where they often coax many species that lie in wait along this edge for unsuspecting prey.

Unlike deep-jiggers or spin-casters working from a boat, surfmen and other land-based anglers usually don't use heavy bucktail jigs. They stick primarily with the ½- and 1-ounce models, which handle well and are of a size comparable to the myriad bait species found along the shore. The exception are those anglers who fish from inlet jetties and bridges, where often they bring 3- and 4-ounce models into play to suit the particular situation, usually that of deep water and swift current.

A variation of the bucktail jig that has found popularity among spin-fishermen is a bait-tail jig. This is really the same head as is used on a bucktail jig, but instead of a bucktail or feather skirt a plastic bait-tail is slipped on, or a long rubber eel or worm. The long, shimmering plastic tail results in an extremely enticing action, and during the past several years this has grown in popularity in many areas, particularly among jetty, bridge, and inlet fishermen. Just the current working against the lure gives it an irresistible action.

Rigged Eel Classified Lure

While not truly a lure in the strict sense of the word, the common eel rigged on a small metal squid is for all practical purposes a lure. I include it in this listing of popular lures used by shore-based anglers because it is extremely effective on the Atlantic coast for striped bass and to a lesser extent bluefish. It finds limited use elsewhere, but is a difficult lure to beat with bass and blues.

Most rigged eels used by spin-fishermen range from 6 to 16 inches in length, and are rigged on a block-tin or lead squid that weighs about 1 ounce.

During the past several years there have been some excellent plastic eels mounted on small squids and they have produced fine results for surfmen and jetty jockies. They come in a wide variety of sizes and in several colors, including black, gray, red, amber, transparent, and blue. Some spin-fishermen swear by them, much preferring the plastic models to the real eels.

Lures Must Be Fished

Often I've sat along the surf and watched newcomers on the beach. You can always spot them, for they're casting as far seaward as they can, and they quickly reel their lure back in, casting again and retrieving again. Occasionally they catch a fish, but more often than not they get a lot of exercise instead. This is simply because many fish are not located far from the beach and the lures are being retrieved without any concern for current or water conditions and without imparting attractive action.

A troller can put a lure out and just troll along and eventually catch fish, because the movement of the boat keeps his lure working most of the time. But the surfman has to be constantly concerned that his lure is working properly. When a wave pushes against the line as you're retrieving, the lure is dragged quickly toward the beach, and as the wave crashes the lure often stops cold, and works feverishly as the water recedes. If you just cast and retrieve at a constant speed, you aren't the master of your lure, and its action will suffer accordingly.

The veteran surfman casts where he feels the fish will be feeding. Sometimes this will require a long cast, other times a short one. You should always fish out your casts. For often big fish will be resting right in the undertow or moving along it as they search for a meal. Over many years of fishing from the beach I have hooked hundreds of fish within 25 feet of where I was standing, and this applies equally to jetty and rockpile fishing too.

Patience is a virtue of all surf casters. This spinning enthusiast brings a surf stool to sit on and a sand spike for his outfit. He enjoys the fresh air as he waits for a strike away from the crowds.

Stripers know that baitfish will often seek the sanctuary of the shallow water between the sand and where the beach drops away. Often they'll move along it, looking for an unsuspecting baitfish, and be onto it in a flash. This is why it's important to work that lure right in until it reaches the sand. I've observed tarpon moving along a beach at Captiva Island on Florida's southwest coast. These were 100 pounds and more, and they were herding mullet in the shallows. Every now and then one would charge a nervous mullet. I saw the same thing happen with snook, and it's common for bluefish to do it too. Even summer flounder, popularly called fluke in many areas, will move into extremely shallow water along the surf, rest concealed on the bottom, and then pounce on any unsuspecting fish it sees in the shallows. On several occasions I caught fluke on small metal squids, having first observed excited baitfish leaping into the air right near the sand. Only once I had caught the flounders did I realize it was the flatfish that were the culprits, as all along I had thought they were small bass or blues. Had I not worked the metal squids right to the sand I wouldn't have had a bump, of that I am certain.

Currents Play Important Role

When anglers look at the broad expanse of ocean crashing onto the sand along the surf, they often fail to realize that strong currents exist, sometimes pushing the water in one direction along the beach, sometimes in the opposite, and sometimes not moving at all. These currents are caused by tidal flow and by wind and other factors. But they play an important role in where fish will take up station to feed. A flow of water inside a sandbar will flow either up or down the beach, flowing to the spot of least resistance, which is usually a break in a bar, where the volume of water will move seaward. It's at spots like this that many fish take up station to feed, for they know that crabs, seaworms, shrimp, tiny baitfish and other food will be carried to them by this current.

Often the fish will take a lie in the deep water, where the swift-moving water flowing over the shallows smooths out, for here it is easier for them than were they to be constantly fighting the swift current.

The wise surfman working a stretch of beach will carefully work all the beach, but he should give particular attention to the spots that are most apt to hold the fish. By concentrating your efforts where you feel the fish will be holding—facing up into the current waiting for food to be brought to them—you'll stand a good chance of scoring.

Salt-water species can be just as finicky as those found in our fresh waters, and sometimes they simply won't rise up from the bottom for food. Thus, it's important that you probe each level at which the fish might be feeding, using surface lures, those that probe intermediate levels, and others that can be effectively worked along the bottom. While along many

stretches of surf the water depth at which your lures will be working may be only 3 to 8 feet, a plug working at intermediate levels may be totally ignored, while a small bucktail jigged along the bottom may bring immediate strikes, or vice versa.

Dusk and Daybreak Favored

Time of day plays an important role in surf fishing. Many fish, particularly gamefish, are hesitant to move into the surf during the height of day, with the sun at its zenith. Surfmen all over regard daybreak and dusk as the optimum periods to fish, for it is at these times that many fish move into the wash to enjoy a meal and then retreat into the depths to rest.

I've experienced phenomenal fishing for about an hour in the morning, just as the sky turns pink, and again at dusk, when the sun has settled beneath the horizon. The fish would begin to feed and strike voraciously and just as suddenly would stop. Veteran surfmen and jetty jockies are aware of these patterns, and they take particular pains to be prepared, for they realize that the feeding time is limited, and they've got to score then or perhaps go fishless.

This is not to say that, particularly with bottom-feeders, you can't enjoy good fishing throughout the day, for you can. It's just that these two periods provide the finest action.

You'll find that dusk and daybreak are favorite fishing times along the surf. Surf species often congregate in key spots and frequently you'll find several surfmen there, too. Beach vehicles with four wheel drive, often called beach buggies, are used by many surfmen to move from spot to spot until the fish are located.

Some Are Nocturnal Feeders

Many species feed extensively at night, and while but a limited number of anglers work along the surf and jetties at night, there is some excellent sport to be enjoyed. Some of the finest catches of striped bass, bluefish, weakfish, seatrout, channel bass, snook, and several others species that I've ever made from beach and rockpile have been well after dark.

Night fishing is a rather specialized sport, however, in that you have to be certain of your tackle and gear, as you're working with it in darkness. But most important, you've got to know the waters you plan to fish, as visibility for the most part is rather limited.

I should note, however, that nighttime fishing as far as I'm concerned is among the most enjoyable spin-fishing that I regularly do. Often during the summer months there's a pleasant breeze off the ocean in the evening, and it's extremely relaxing for me to work a stretch of beach or rockpile. For the fish are usually more cooperative than during the day, and there are fewer anglers. Indeed, often I work for hours on end, seeing just an occasional fisherman now and then at spots that during hours of daylight are crowded.

Probe Carefully and Thoroughly

When I'm fishing an area, whether beach, rockpile, bridge, or pier, I seldom set up station at one spot and stay there for hours on end. I like to move, probing each spot I fish carefully and making certain I have fished it thoroughly before I move on to another area. Because of this I never carry a tackle kit when along the beach, but instead carry all my necessary tackle in a canvas shoulder bag. I've found military-surplus bags fine, as well as those models specifically designed for surf fishermen.

Thoroughly fishing a spot takes a bit of doing, for it requires at least two, or perhaps three lures—top, in-between and bottom—and varied speeds of retrieve. While I usually concentrate the bulk of my effort in short casts, I always make several good, long heaves, because there will be times when the fish are farther out.

Almost without exception, you'll find that most species will strike a lure retrieved erratically rather than one that is reeled at a constant speed. It takes a lot of concentration to constantly be working the lure, but it is the mark of a good fisherman. For it is far easier to fall into that pattern I mentioned earlier of just heaving out and reeling in, mechanically so to speak, which doesn't give most lures the exciting action that fish can't resist.

Passes and Inlets Require Different Techniques

On all our coasts there are many passes or inlets emptying bay, sound, or river waters into the sea. Some are so narrow and shallow that you can wade across them, while others are a mile or more in width. I've fished passes that I could cast across, yet were 50 feet and even deeper, the pass being eroded by huge quantities of water flowing through it as the tide ebbed and flooded.

Many passes in remote areas are flanked by sand beaches, while in heavily traveled areas there have often been breakwaters or jetties built to hold back the ravaging effect of the surf on the channels through the inlets, such as those which are so numerous in Maine, and also on the Pacific Northwest coast. Each pass or inlet must be studied independently, for no two are alike. They all present an exciting challenge to the shore-based angler, for these waters are virtually impossible to fish from a boat in many instances, thus making them a natural for the spin-fisherman who casts from sand or rockpile.

Natural Feeding Places

Inlets and passes funnel food from inshore regions into the big bays and sounds, which in some cases again funnel them out into the broad expanse of the Gulf or our oceans. Fish know this, and rather than probe a large area looking for a meal, they lazily take up station in the rips and eddies of coastal inlets, or right down on the bottom, where they'll seek the relatively quiet water ahead of or behind a rock, or where a dropoff provides a break to the current.

Here they fin, facing the current, waiting for the food carried at the mercy of the current. They swiftly move to engulf a shrimp, soft crab, minnow, seaworm or other food, and then return to their lie to wait and watch.

In these situations there are several approaches you can use, but your selection of lures will vary, because you've often got an extremely fast current ripping out the inlets, which will make many lures ineffective.

Because many fish take up station right down on the bottom, you'll need a lure that will get down fast. I've found bucktail jigs ideally suited to this type of fishing, and on many occasions I use a 2- or 3-ounce jig to probe the depths of an inlet, and frequently I hit paydirt with them.

To get the jig down where the fish are I cast up into the current, and then permit line to pay out, ensuring that the jig will go straight down. Once it touches bottom, I take the slack out of the line and permit the jig to literally bounce along the bottom as it is carried with the current. Each bounce is pulsated up the line, and you can feel a regular rhythm as it is carried along.

Most often the strike will come just as the jig lifts off the bottom at the end of the swing. I suspect that the fish watch it bouncing along and then, when they see it move off the bottom and change direction, they're after it in a flash, for fear it will get away.

Let It Work in Current

Occasionally I've stood at the seaward end of an inlet, either on the rocks or beach, and let the jig swing into the current, up off the bottom, where it was moved back and forth in the rips and eddies. With the jig at the mercy of the churning currents I've worked my rod tip, causing the jig to move ahead into the current, struggle a bit, and then be swept back. Fish find this irresistible, and I've received many strikes when the conventional bottom-bouncing technique failed to bring strikes.

I've also used surface lures at the seaward end, casting them out and across, and permitting the current to carry them far out, simply by letting line slip from the fixed spool-mill. With the lure several hundred feet seaward, I've let the current give it action, which caused the plug to resemble a baitfish struggling on the surface against the current. Sometimes I've walked back and forth, permitting the plug to work across 100 feet or more of fine rips, and fully fifteen or twenty minutes after having cast the plug received exciting surface strikes from fish moving into the rip.

Change as Currents Moderate

When the tide or current begins to moderate, a different approach is necessary, for then the fish which frequently hugged the bottom will begin to move about searching for food. This calls for a change of technique, and you'll find that metal squids, surface plugs, and medium runners will work well and bring results where on a swift tide their use most often would have proved fruitless.

In passes and inlets you'll find that fish will hold in certain spots while avoiding others. They may take up station behind or ahead of a cluster of rocks, or where there is a dropoff or shelf. In some shallow inlets with a low tide and clear water condition and little wind you can sometimes take an hour on the slack water and look down into the depths and see just what the bottom looks like from a boat or map the bottom conformation using a fathometer and put this information to good use while working from shore later.

The fish you'll catch from passes and inlets while using lures are almost beyond count, simply because most coastal species will frequent these spots to feed at regular intervals, because they know food will be carried to them. Along the middle and north Atlantic coast bluefish, weakfish, striped bass, and summer flounders will be the species most often walloping your lures, although mackerel, codfish, and pollock will move into northern inlets frequently and provide fine action, as will silver hake and, occasionally during the fall, Atlantic bonito and little tuna.

Southern anglers catch channel bass, tarpon, snook, jack crevalle, seatrout, Spanish mackerel, and big sharks from the waters of passes. Occasionally cruising king mackerel provide exciting fun, as do grouper, blue runners, bluefish, and other tropical species.

Southern California anglers find Pacific barracuda and Pacific bonito frequently working inlet waters, and, farther north, anglers casting from shore catch stripers, king salmon, and silver salmon where bays and rivers empty into the cold Pacific.

Jetty Fishing Differs

To hold back the ravages of the ocean and to keep it from eroding beaches on all our coasts, municipalities and the federal and state governments have built many breakwaters and jetties, which make ideal fishing platforms for shore-based anglers. The angler desiring to relax and fish with natural baits can catch a wide variety of bottom-feeders using the rigs and natural baits discussed in the previous section.

The spin-fisherman who likes to climb around these rock or concrete and steel breakwaters, probing the waters has many thrills awaiting him, for some of the most exciting shore fishing imaginable may be enjoyed from these man-made breakwaters, as well as from the natural rocky promontories along the Pacific northwest coast and the Rhode Island and Maine coastline.

I don't know what it is that makes me like jetty fishing so much. Perhaps it's knowing that sooner or later I am going to encounter a hungry gamefish feeding along the rocks. Then there's the excitment of waves crashing around you and white water full of life and the tang of salt air and, especially, the challenge of fishing these fishy haunts by moonlight or even in the dark of the moon.

Special Clothing Required

Because you'll be climbing around rocks and concrete that are often covered with slippery marine growth, it's wise to wear footwear that will ensure firm footing. I have ordinary golf soles cemented to the soles of my boots and waders, and the aluminum cleats in the golf soles hold securely even on the slipperiest of jetties. When I'm fishing in southern climes where boots would be uncomfortable I wear a pair of canvas-topped golf shoes and find them comfortable to walk in while on any jetties. Some anglers wear ice creepers on their boots, but I find these tough on the feet and prefer the golf soles.

On occasions you'll be sprayed and sometimes even be hit by waves breaking across the rocks, so a good light-weight suit of rain gear is a necessity. So is a miner's headlamp if you plan to do a lot of night fishing.

The headlamp leaves both hands free while climbing around the coastal rockpiles and while fighting tough gamefish.

Make certain you carry a rope with you, on which to string your catch. The rope is a handy place on which to string fish as you catch them, but most important it makes it easier to carry off your catch from the jetty, especially if you've landed a couple of heavyweights!

BRACKETING AN AREA A MUST

An extremely important consideration when fishing coastal jetties is that you bracket the entire jetty with casts. For there are literally dozens of spots on every jetty where gamefish may take up station to feed. Most often the fish are searching for food and feeding in close to the rocks, so when you work from coastal rockpiles and breakwaters you'll find that the best results will come when you use lots of short casts, probing every spot where a fish may be looking for a meal, rather than casting great distances seaward. Remember that shrimp, baitfish, and crabs are often seeking the sanctuary the rocks offer, and, in order to get at the food, the bigger fish have to come really close.

I recall hundreds of occasions when I've hooked big fish so close to the jetty that they've actually startled me. The fish actually charged plugs, rigged eels, metal squids, and bucktails just 10 to 15 feet from where I was standing!

I've observed tarpon over 100 pounds swimming within 10 feet of coastal jetties, watching for mullet or other forage species that were crowding the rocks. This same scene has been repeated with striped bass, weakfish, and bluefish, to name but a few. Jacks frequently herd baitfish into the rocks, as do snook and many other southern species.

WATCH MOVEMENTS OF WATER

Remember that tides and currents play an important role around coastal jetties. Some jetties are completely covered and unfishable on a flood tide, and you can only score by fishing them a couple of hours either side of the top of the tide. Other jetties have practically no water around them at low tide—in fact, even sand in front of the rocks—and bait and gamefish only move in around the rocks as the tide rises.

Of course, there are currents to contend with around jetties, too. Sometimes a current will move down parallel with the beach and virtually boil around a jetty front, forming a rip where gamefish will take up station to feed because soft crabs, shrimp, seaworms, and small baitfish are carried there by the current and held captive in the swift whirlpools around the jetty front.

Because of this situation, you'll find a particular jetty will provide good action on a particular corner of the rockpile at a particular stage of the tide.

In fact, on some jetties the pattern is so pronounced that I can walk to a particular rock and almost predict that at a particular stage of the tide I'll receive a strike within my first half dozen casts. Indeed, when jetty fishing, you'll find that many strikes will come on your first or second cast to a spot, simply because the fish are there and feeding, and they're after your lure the moment they see it.

Work Lure to Edge of Rocks

Earlier I mentioned how fish along the surf will work close to the beach, and the importance of working the lure right to the sand. This is doubly important when fishing from a rockpile. Yet so very many anglers hurriedly retrieve their lure so it won't foul in the rocks. By so doing, they minimize their chances of scoring, for the fish are either feeding in the rocks or observing the lure move toward the rocks, and this critical zone from 1 to 25 feet from the jetty is where many of your strikes will come, and that's where you want your lure to be working perfectly. So hold back on that urge to reel fast as your lure approaches the rocks.

When I'm working a jetty that has a lot of rocks which are tumbled into the water, I select a spot down close to the water and make several casts, one in toward the beach, the next straight in front of where I'm standing, and the third out toward the front of the jetty. Sometimes I'll also shoot a cast as parallel to the jetty as I can, so that my lure resembles a small fish working along the rocks.

Perserverance Pays Off

If I don't receive a strike I'll move out 15 or 20 feet and repeat the same procedure, continuing on out the jetty, and then working back in toward the beach on the other side. By working steadily and moving around you'll usually hit paydirt. If I haven't received a strike, and everything in the way of conditions looks good, I'll repeat the same procedure, changing to an entirely different lure, until I find the combination that works. If I've found that a particular lure or area is productive and I don't receive a strike when working one jetty, I'll simply move on to another. In areas such as Long Island and New Jersey, where there are many jetties, I'll often fish six or eight jetties on a single tide, and sometimes it's the last jetty that I hit that gives me bonanza fishing.

It has often been said that the camaraderie among pier casters is second to none. Along many coastal areas there are municipal piers from which you can fish free of charge.

Don't Overlook Bridges and Piers

Bridges and piers abound along the seacoast, and these are excellent platforms from which spin-fishermen make many fine catches. Natural baits may be fished from them using the rigs and techniques discussed in the earlier section devoted to bottom-fishing, but exciting sport awaits the angler who uses artificials from these structures.

Fish congregate around these structures simply because small baitfish tend to congregate around them, which makes it easy to obtain a meal.

Because you're fishing from a height that may range from 10 to 40 feet or more, a whole new series of techniques must be brought into play, for presenting a lure from this height is quite a bit different from doing so from the sand or rockpiles.

BUCKTAIL JIGS FAVORED

The bucktail jig lends itself well to fishing from high structures, as it can be worked at any level with ease and will work very well even in a swift current, such as is encountered around many bridges.

I always carry a selection of sizes with me to suit a variety of tidal flows, with the light-weight jigs favored when the tide's moving along lazily, and the heavy-weights when it's running as though through a millrace.

From a high pier the bucktail can be cast out and worked right to the

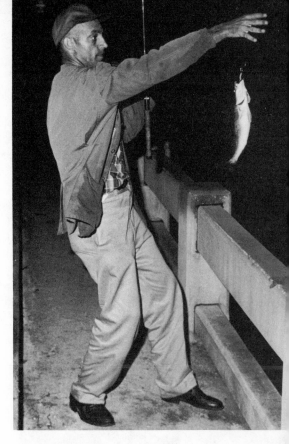

Bucktail jigs and plastic-tailed jigs are favorites of bridge casters who make many fine catches from coastal bridges after dark. Here Jack Randolph lands a fine seatrout while fishing from one of the thousands of spans across Florida's waterways.

edge of the structure, as can be done from bridges, docks, bulkheads, and any other high structure.

PLUGS BRING STRIKES TOO

I include several surface swimming-plugs and several deep-running models without a lip in my kit when I'm fishing from piers and bridges. I find the lipped models difficult to work properly from a height and the mirror-type plugs and other models with the connector eye on the top of the head most effective. For when worked from a height these models work much the same as bucktail jigs, enabling you to work them either near the surface or in the depths.

MOST SPECIES SELECT SPOTS TO WATCH

Most salt-water species that reside around bridges take up station and watch for food being carried along with the current. Over the years I've watched many fish feeding, and they simply faced into the current, finning lazily and watching. As a crab, seaworm, small fish, or other food drifted past with the current, they would be onto it in a flash and then quickly return to their station to watch and wait.

Around coastal bridges, docks, and some piers—especially where the current is swift—the fish will take a position immediately ahead of a bulkhead or piling where the current splits, for here there is a spot they can swim in with little difficulty. Directly behind the bulkheads or pilings— whether a foot or a dozen feet in width—the fish will take up position also.

Fish dislike resting and waiting in direct sunlight, so you'll usually see them facing into the current in the shadows of the bridge or pier. At night the fish will literally hug the shadow line, and if you have keen eyesight, you can spot them finning just inches beneath the surface in the shadows, watching for bait to come down with the tide in the area illuminated by bridge, pier, or dock lights.

I've observed snook, tarpon, striped bass, weakfish, seatrout, and many other species working this way. While you can often see the fish doing this, catching them is something else again.

During the winter months huge schools of whiting, often called silver hake or frost-fish, move under the lights of coastal piers in New Jersey, Long Island and Massachusetts, and casters make many fine catches using spinning tackle and baiting with strips of squid, or pieces of mackerel or herring.

Cast into Current

When fish are working along a bulkhead or shadow line you've got to present your plug or bucktail jig up and across the current for them, so that as you retrieve, the lure will be carried toward the fish, as you retrieve it. Don't worry about having the plug or jig come inches from the fish. This isn't necessary. What is necessary is that you get it within the angle of vision of the fish. Once it spots the lure it will waste little time making up its mind, for it will be swept along by the current and be out of range quickly if it doesn't act.

Sometimes a steady retrieve across the current works well, but at other times you've got to work the plug or bucktail jig with your rod tip, causing it to work erratically, much like a wounded baitfish struggling on the surface.

Use Figure-Eight

On the downcurrent side of a bridge, pier, or dock your lure will quickly be swept away from the water where fish are apt to be holding. In this situation I've found it best to use a heavy bucktail jig, and to point my rod tip straight down, and hold it close to the bridge, so that I can work the jig, using a figure-eight movement of my rod tip, which makes the jig look like a small fish or shrimp darting about erratically. If the jig is swept away from the eddies by the current you'll seldom get strikes. It's got to be worked almost straight up and down for you to score.

Work Close to Pilings

Around many bridges there are ice-breakers or catwalks supported by wooden or concrete pilings. Remember that around the underwater maze of piling fish often take up residence, whether there be one or two piles or dozens of them. Work your lure past each, and you'll often be rewarded with strikes.

Fish with Firm Drag

Because there are many barnacles and mussels clinging to the supporting piles of these structures, there's always a chance of losing a big fish, for the instant your line touches a sharp barnacle or mussel, the line will be severed. In an attempt to prevent this from happening I fish with a heavier line than I might ordinarily use from the surf or jetties, and use a heavier rod, with the drag on a very firm setting. The sturdy rod, heavy line, and firm drag-setting are usually sufficient to bring a strong gamefish to the surface. Once it's on top I try to hold the fish there, which often will cause it to move away from the obstructions and permit me to lead it to shore, or to guide it into a net lowered by a rope, or to lift a long-handled gaff, or gaff lowered by rope, into the fish.

Sometimes Casting Pays Off Too

While thus far I've spoken about casting artificials to the fish residing close to the pier or bridge, there are often occasions when schools of fish will be feeding well away from the pier or bridge from which you're fishing. This calls for long casts, and at such times metal squids and stainless-steel or chromed jigs are the lures that must be brought into play for with them you can get the necessary distance.

Pier casting in many areas is year-round sport, with anglers scoring around the clock. Often, after dark, many species will move in to feed on baitfish attracted by the lights. Sturdy spinning tackle is a must here, for most fish are reeled right up and over the railing.

There are also times when long casts may be used to probe the depths upcurrent from piers and bridges. I've frequently cast a bucktail jig far up into the current and then permitted it to settle to the bottom. As the current bounced it along the bottom back toward the bridge, I retrieved line, keeping slack out of the line and working the lure with my rod tip. Often as the lure lifts off the bottom as it nears the pilings or bulkhead, you'll receive a strike from a hungry scrapper that's been watching it bounce along.

Seldom will you receive strikes when you cast your lure downcurrent simply because most of the fish are facing up into the current. Unless downcurrent there is a spot where the fish might congregate you'll find that you'll be wasting your time. I've known a few spots, however, where there were pilings and the remains of an old bridge extending up from the bottom, and many fish would congregate. By working my lure downcurrent and then retrieving it erratically, the fish would spot it and I'd quickly receive a strike. Here again, as with most types of spin-fishing, it's a matter of knowing the waters you plan to fish, especially the bottom conformation and the spots that are most apt to hold fish.

BAIT UNDER BRIDGE LIGHTS

On many bridges there are lights down close to the water, and at night the light attracts huge schools of baitfish. Often the baitfish will congregate beneath the lights for hours on end with no action, when suddenly the spot will turn into a maelstrom of feeding fish and excited baitfish leaping into the air. On some fishing piers the management actually lowers lights close to the water with the express purpose of attracting baitfish at night, which they know will ultimately attract more respectable species.

OBEY LOCAL ORDINANCES

I think it's important to note here that local ordinances vary widely when it comes to fishing from bridges. Some municipalities prohibit fishing from bridges—and even from adjoining bulkheads, for that matter. But the trend along the seacoast has been towards wise utilization of these structures designed to move traffic, but which serve a fine purpose for the angler seeking economical recreation.

Indeed, throughout the South there are many bridges which have catwalks running alongside the railing, which are expressly for fishermen. Others have small fishing piers alongside the bridge, while in many areas condemned bridges have not been torn down, but instead left intact, for the express use of anglers.

TROLLING

Spinning tackle is basically designed for casting, and while it may be employed with fine results while trolling fresh water, and for light salt-water trolling, it is not the ideal tackle to use. This is especially true for offshore trolling for large game species, where conventional reels and regulation-class rods are designed specifically for big gamefishing. Even in many inshore fishing applications, where wire line, lead-core line, deep-planning devices, or heavy trolling-weights must be used, the conventional multiplying reel and conventional rod perform more satisfactorily.

I mention this, and feel it is important to do so, because over recent years many anglers have been misdirected into thinking that spinning tackle is so versatile that it may be used for any and all types of fishing. While I will agree it may be used for most any type of fishing, it is important to remember that other types of tackle, especially in big gamefishing, will do a better job.

I am fully aware that many anglers have landed the marlins, sailfish, tuna, and other great gamefish while employing spin gear, but in the main these accomplishments were by anglers skilled in the use of all types of tackle who simply set out to do something that did not conform with accepted offshore techniques.

Many party boats combine trolling to locate the fish, with chumming to hold them. This is the case with boats such as the Maverick, a West coast packet, about to leave during darkness for the famed albacore grounds many miles from shore.

Proper Swivel of Paramount Importance

As you stream line from a spinning reel while trolling, the line uncoils from the reel as you let it slip from the spool and then is recoiled as you reel it in, the bail carefully winding the line back onto the spool. Because of this it is extremely important that you use a swivel of excellent quality between your line and leader, or lure, so that line twist caused by a flopping bait or lure that tends to spin and twist as it is trolled is minimized.

After years of trying practically every type of swivel made, I've settled on ball-bearing swivels as having the finest, true swiveling action of any swivel made. This positive swiveling action eliminates line twist for the most part and keeps your monofilament line from being twisted into an unmanageable mess should you be trolling at a speed that results in a lure twisting. This all important swivel between line and leader pays for itself many times over, eliminating needless replacement of lines otherwise ruined by trolling.

Still another feature of the ball-bearing swivel is its strength to size ratio. Not only does it swivel well, but it is extremely strong for its size. You will find that for light trolling in bays, rivers, and estuaries the number 3 or 4 ball-bearing swivel with a coastlock snap is ideal. They test out at 30 and 40 pounds respectively and, for the angler equipped with spinning tackle, are just about the largest swivel-and-snap combination he should use. Remember, even with heavy spinning-tackle it's doubtful if you'll be using line testing over 20 pounds, thus it would be foolish to use large swivels testing 100 pounds or more.

Double Terminal End of Line

The terminal end of your line always is subjected to the greatest amount of punishment. This is especially true in trolling, and I've found it best always to double the last 10 feet of line while trolling offshore with spinning tackle and to double slightly less than 10 when inshore. This enables me, when landing a big fish especially, to get several turns of the double line onto the spool of the reel. Thus, at the critical time for netting or gaffing, your terminal end is double the strength of your regular line test. This proves advantageous in the event you have to exert a bit of extra pressure on a fish, to draw it within reach of the gaff or to keep it from getting into the rudder or propellers and from diving beneath the boat.

I've found a Bimini bend, also called a Bimini knot or twenty-times-around knot, ideal for doubling the terminal end of line. It's practically a 100-percent-line-strength knot, an important consideration, as other types of knots often weaken a line appreciably.

Once completing the Bimini knot I then use an improved clinch knot to tie the double line directly to the ball-bearing swivel. This too is a strong knot ideally suited to this purpose. Make certain you don't simply loop the swivel onto the loop of the double line, as this makes for a weak connection, and under great pressure the loop will cut through itself.

Leaders Vary

Attached to the coastlock snap on your ball-bearing swivel will be any one of several leader materials.

Monofilament makes a fine leader material, for it is practically invisible in the water. It's ideal when you're trolling for fish with no teeth, such as striped bass, channel bass, amberjack. I like to use a leader sufficiently short so that I can reel the fish within range of the net or gaff, without having to handle the leader. In a small outboard rig where you're close to the water, this means a 4- to 5-foot leader is more than adequate. A longer leader may be used when fishing from an offshore sportfisherman, and it is not unusual for trollers after sailfish, white and striped marlin, wahoo, yellowfin tuna, and other pelagic species for use a leader measuring 10 to 15 feet in length. Naturally, when you use leaders this long it becomes necessary to draw the fish within range of the gaff by grasping the leader and working it hand over hand until the fish is close at hand.

The strength of leader you use will be determined in great part by the outfit you're using and the fish being sought. When I'm trolling a tiny bucktail jig, using 8-pound-test monofilament and a light one-handed rod, with my sights set on weakfish in a marsh creek, I use perhaps 10-pound-test leader. Quite the contrary, if big amberjack are my target around an offshore oil-drilling platform, then I would use 30-pound-test monofilament leader, even if my spinning line was only 15- or 20-pound test. A leader receives more punishment than the line, for as you fight a fish the fish may turn as it swims away from you, and its tail and body will rub against the leader. Additionally, a fish may wrap up in the leader, or the leader curl beneath its gill cover, or even become entangled in the lure that you're using.

WIRE FOR TOOTHY FISH

When bluefish, king mackerel, barracuda, snappers, or groupers are your target it's wise to use either stainless-steel cable or single-strand stainless-steel wire as leader. For most trolling situations while using spinning tackle you'll find number 8 or 9 single-strand wire more than adequate, and either 30- or 45-pound-test nylon-covered stainless-steel cable fits the bill nicely. Very light tests are extremely fine and difficult to work with.

Snap May Be Used

There are a variety of ways in which you can attach your lure to the terminal end of the leader. Some anglers make a direct connection, employing any one of several kinds of loop, including the Homer Rhode end-loop or Improved end-loop with monofilament leaders or a haywire and barrel twist with stainless-steel wire or tiny sleeves with nylon-covered stainless-steel cable.

To facilitate changing lures many anglers find a small stainless-steel snap a great convenience. There are many such snaps on the market, and after having tried most of them I've settled on the duo-lock snap as the finest. It's made from but a single piece of strong stainless steel and does an excellent job. Because it is small and made from a single piece of wire, it does not detract from the action of a lure and is hardly noticeable. Here, too, the size of snap should balance with the lures you're using, for a very large snap with a very tiny lure would certainly spoil the lure's action.

Variety of Lures May Be Used

Many of the same lures used by the casting fraternity may be trolled with equally fine results, including subsurface swimming plugs, bucktail jigs, and the wide variety of block-tin, chromed, and stainless-steel jigs and squids. Rigged eels work extremely well when trolled, accounting for many fine stripers and blues.

Feathers a Standard

The trolling feather, with its chromed head and pearly eye, plus a full skirt of feathers trailing from the head, is a universally favored trolling lure. It will bring strikes from albacore far at sea in the Pacific, bluefish in close to the beach off Delaware, and dolphin along the edge of the Continental Shelf off Louisiana. It's a simple-looking lure, which when trolled through the water resembles any one of the myriad baitfish on which gamefish feed.

Trolling feathers come in a wide variety of head weights, and for most trolling situations where you'll be using spinning tackle I would think it best you stick with heads ranging in weight from ½ through perhaps 2 ounces. Trolling with heads of heavier weight would place too much of a burden on most spinning tackle.

Red and white, with white predominating, is the favored color combination of most trollers. But solid white, yellow, blue, black, green, and combinations of these, almost always with a trace of red, all bring strikes at one

Atlantic bonito will readily strike a trolling feather, as did this one hooked by the young angler while trolling at famed Barnegat Ridge from a party boat out of New Jersey. Bonito like a fast-moving lure and often the best results will be achieved by fishing the lures close up in the wake.

time or another. It's wise always to have several light-colored feathers in your kit, as well as several dark ones.

The feathers are usually purchased unrigged. The head has a small hole running through it, through which you run your leader material, after which you attach a strong hook to the terminal end of the leader and then pull the hook up tight, so that most of it is concealed within the feather skirt. I most often use a strong, forged O'Shaughnessy-style hook with trolling feathers and other lures. The size of hook should balance with the size of the feather and species you're seeking and will run from a 3/0 on up to a 7/0. Sizes larger than 7/0 would be impractical to use with most spinning tackle, for the tackle wouldn't be sufficiently powerful to rip the large hook into the tough jaw of a big fish. You'd stand a far better chance of hooking a lunker with light tackle by using a smaller hook, which will penetrate beyond the barb with relative ease.

SPOONS AND WOBBLERS

On the salt-water scene spoons and wobblers, which are regularly cast by fresh-water enthusiasts, are seldom cast in the salt, but are instead trolled. I suspect this is because salt-water anglers have heavier metal lures such as squids and jigs, which are easier to cast. Thus, they leave the spoons and wobblers for trolling, and as a trolling lure both of these provide many fine catches.

I define both spoons and wobblers as lures which are stamped from a flat piece of metal stock. It may be brass or stainless steel, and it is shaped somewhat to resemble a fish, generally with a slight taper at the head and a wide body tapered to a point near the tail of the lure. Spoons usually have a rigid hook held in place securely by a screw, whereas wobblers generally have a split ring in the tail and a free-swinging tail hook. Along the seacoast you'll find many people use the words "spoon" and "wobbler" interchangeably, which is understandable, since the action of these lures is similar.

Spoons and wobblers are usually chromed or nickel-plated or of stainless steel, so that as they are trolled their shining surfaces reflect, and the glitter attracts fish from the depths.

The size of the spoon is generally the same as the size of the hook on it. Spinning-tackle trolling sizes 3/0, 5/0, and 7/0 would cover most situations, with the smaller sizes ranging 3 to 4 inches in length, and the larger, 6 or 7 inches long.

The action of the spoons and wobblers may be enhanced by adding a feather or bucktail skirt. Some anglers add a strip of pork rind to the hook, and I've even seen fellows add a fluorescent plastic worm with good results.

Bone and Plastic Squids

Many years ago bone squids came into being. Fashioned of real animal bone, the squids had a shallow-curved keel and were shaped to have the general outline of a small fish. A hook was attached to the bone squid in much the same fashion as one is attached to a spoon.

These bone-white squids enjoyed popularity for years, and were made in the same sizes as spoons. It was quite natural for them to evolve and eventually to be made of plastic in its many colors and shapes. Today the troller has both bone and plastic squids in his tackle arsenal.

Most Any Lure Will Produce

The many lures of the caster, plus those discussed here as essentially trolling lures, are the ones most often used by the spin-fisherman who likes to probe the briny while trolling. There are many other lures which produce, including the famed cedar jig, surgical-tube lures, many soft-plastic lures designed to resemble baitfish and squid, plus a whole array of others. The key, however, is to select several basic lures and to become accomplished at using them. Once you have the confidence in the lures you're using, you'll score more regularly than haphazardly using every lure ever made.

Baits Rigged for Trolling

A wide variety of baits may be rigged for trolling, with mullet, balao, sardines, eels, needlefish among the most popular, although they don't find too great a popularity among spin-fishermen, as they are just too large a bait and instead find favor with anglers trolling with regulation-class tackle.

The strip bait, cut from either squid, pork rind, or the belly of a fish, is an effective bait of the troller, and may be used with fine results for practically every species that will take a trolled bait, whether a summer flounder down on the bottom or a speedy wahoo.

It's cut to a torpedo shape for the most part, ranging in length from 5 to 9 inches and rigged on a single hook with a loop of wire holding the head section of the bait. When trolled through the water, either as a skip bait on the surface, or down in the depths with the aid of a trolling sinker, the tail section of the bait flutters in an enticing manner that most fish find irresistible.

Trolling Sinker Sometimes Needed

If, while you're trolling, you note that your lures are sometimes skipping out of the water, it may be necessary to add a trolling sinker to your line to keep the lure from skipping about excessively. I always carry a selection of torpedo-shaped trolling weights with me, ranging from ½ ounce through 3 ounces, and these are often used, even when, just for a matter of making a change, I want the lure to work deeper. In inshore trolling this is often more important than when well off the beach, especially if fish are hugging bottom and you want to get your lures down to them.

Let the Lines Out

The game pelagic species found far offshore respond to a lure trolled at a much faster speed than do those species that frequent inshore coastal waters. The billfishes, wahoo, dolphin, king mackerel, albacore, yellowfin and bluefin tuna, and the many bonitos will strike a fast-moving lure more readily than a slow-moving one. The inshore species, among them bluefish, channel bass, striped bass, yellowtail, white sea bass, snook, tarpon, weakfish that may run from a low of 5 to perhaps upward of 100 pounds.

Let's begin with offshore species, as they're all fine gamefish that will certainly give you a noteworthy struggle should you be fortunate enough to hook one on spinning tackle. The heavy-duty spinning rig is made to order for this fishing, with a reel loaded with several hundred yards of 17- or 20-pound-test line and a rod that can take the punishment meted out by gamefish that may run from a low of 5 to perhaps upward of 100 pounds.

On all of our coasts these species reside in what is most often referred to as blue water, that pure, deep-blue ocean water usually encountered far from shore, and in some places at the edge of the Continental Shelf. At some spots, such as Walker's Cay and Chub Cay, as well as other isles of the Bahamas archipelago, the dropoff is within a couple of miles off shore, which is ideal for the light-tackle enthusiast, since he doesn't have a long boat ride before he gets into fishable water.

Basic Trolling Pattern

From most of the craft used for offshore trolling it's very easy to troll four lines astern. Two lines are usually fished straight off the stern and are called *flat lines*, while the two remaining lines are fished from the outriggers and are called *rigger lines*. The flat lines are usually fished up close, atop either the first or second wave tossed up in your wake, while the rigger lines are just outside of your wake, back around 100 to 125 feet. This gives your lures a good spread, and those species that are attracted to your boat's churning wake, such as the tunas and bonitos, will most often strike the flat line, while the more wary species, such as the king mackerel, billfish, dolphin, and wahoo will take out after the rigger baits or lures.

Vary Speed and Direction

You must always remember that whether trolling offshore or in close to the beach that you will have currents to contend with. Because of these

The oceanic bonito being unhooked here was landed with spinning tackle while trolling off Ocean City, Maryland. These fish will readily strike feathers, spoons, cedar jigs and bucktails. As with most bonitos and tunas, they prefer a fast-moving lure.

currents it is wise to vary your trolling speed and the direction in which you troll, until you find the right combination.

On the offshore grounds, where the water is often 100 or more fathoms deep, there are no landmarks, wrecks, or tide rips through which you can troll. It is basically open-water trolling, and a good spread of lures that are working properly is what will bring you the strikes.

There are, however, a number of things you should watch for. When fish are feeding on the surface there is often a great deal of gull activity, for the birds pick up scraps of fish left by the game species. Always be alert for working gulls and investigate the area. Even after the bird play subsides it is wise to crisscross the area, for your spread of lures may coax strikes from hungry gamesters that have retreated into the depths.

Still another indication of feeding fish is a noticeable light slick or film on the surface. This oily slick is caused by large concentrations of fish feeding down deep, and as they feed and sometimes regurgitate, the slick rises to the surface.

Watch for Flotsam

Floating debris is another thing to watch for when you're trolling offshore. Often dolphin, jacks, mackerel, billfish, and others will hang in the shadows of floating debris. They do this for a purpose, for they know small baitfish seek the small sanctuary offered by the flotsam, and if they hang around long enough they'll come by an easy meal.

The same holds true for weedlines. When you get the wind blowing in one direction, and the current in directly the opposite direction, you often get huge weedlines built up offshore and within the weeds are a wide variety of species. By simply trolling up and down the weedlines, you can often coax strike after strike. It's exciting fishing too, for if you're alert you can spot the fish lingering in the shadows beneath the weeds before they're tempted out to strike your lures or baits.

Try Jigging Lures

If you observe fish feeding on the surface or working beneath a weedline, and you can't get them to strike, try jigging your rod tip vigorously, especially with trolling feathers, bucktail jigs, cedar jigs, and metal squids. This causes the lure to dart ahead, then falter for an instant, and sometimes this erratic action will provoke a hungry fish into striking a lure it might otherwise ignore.

In the case of tunas and bonitos, once you hook one of these tough gamefish it is wise to quickly begin jigging the remaining lures in the water as you proceed to fight the hooked fish. These species are extremely curious, and often dozens of them will swarm around or near a hooked member of their clan. When they spot your lure being jigged vigorously, they'll often strike it immediately. Jigging may be accomplished with a variety of lures, but it works best with spoons, bucktail jigs, chromed jigs, and other lures that will quickly settle into the depths and flash erratically as they are jigged.

Often you can coax strikes from a dozen or more fish from a single school simply by keeping a hooked fish in the water and working your remaining lines, sometimes while trolling ahead ever so slowly even though a fish is hooked.This trick works extremely well with most schooling species such as the tunas and bonitos, but it works equally well with dolphin and other tough gamefish.

Inshore Trolling Requires Different Approach

Inshore along the beaches, around rocky breakwaters, and in the many bays, rivers, and estuaries along the coast, the trolling enthusiast who employs spinning tackle is confronted with situations that differ greatly from those he encountered while trolling many miles from shore.

For here you can search for spots frequented by gamefish and bottom-feeders and present your lures in such a manner as to coax strikes regularly. For inshore feeders are essentially creatures of habit. They'll find a tide rip that is to their liking, or a point of land, rocky breakwater, or bridge abutment, and they'll return almost on a daily basis at a given stage of the tide, to enjoy a leisurely meal. Once you determine the spots and the tide on which the fish feed, you can score regularly.

This shouldn't be construed to mean that inshore trolling is a snap. It isn't. It's just that you can study it more thoroughly at times and find the fish following a reasonable pattern in their feeding habits. It still takes a good presentation of the right lures to score.

Patterns Similar Most Everywhere

Over my years of traveling around the country I've enjoyed light-tackle trolling at practically every coastal community I've visited and have landed a score of different species using essentially the same rig.

While each area has its own pet lure, I found the chromed spoon to be a standard with trollers. As the trolling feather is number one with the off-shore fraternity, the spoon gets the nod with the inshore talent.

I've caught channel bass in Hatteras Inlet, North Carolina with spoons; big bluefish off Block Island, Rhode Island; snook in the mangrove islands that lace their way behind Marco Island, Florida; and big tarpon in Tampa Bay, Florida. On the Pacific, stripers walloped the spoons with a relish in the tide rips off Alcatraz Island in San Francisco Bay, while down in Enseñada, Mexico, it was difficult to keep the Pacific bonito away from the spoons trolled along the kelp beds. The list goes on and on.

It was simply a matter of using a 2-ounce trolling sinker—between line and leader—to hold the spoon just beneath the surface and to use a 6-foot length of number-8 stainless-steel leader and slowly troll the spoon about 100 feet behind the boat.

The ideal speed was when the spoon caused the rod tip to pulsate steadily. Once the lines are out it's a matter of carefully studying the area you're going to troll and to present your lures so they'll pass through a spot where fish are apt to be feeding.

Look for Tide Rips

Tide rips are usually located where the current rushes around a point of land, rocky promontory, bridge abutment, or where there is a marked change in bottom conformation, such as a shallow shelf abruptly dropping off into deeper water.

Spots such as this change from hour to hour during the rising or falling tide. What may be a churning maelstrom on an ebbing tide may be as quiet as a mill pond on slack water and perhaps have no rip whatsoever on the flooding tide.

So you've got to time your trolling activity to spots when conditions will be right at a particular stage of the tide, and then, as the tide and conditions change, move on to spots that develop into their own on different tides.

In the swirling waters of a tide rip, small baitfish are often trapped in the clashing currents, as are crabs, shrimp, squid, and other food, and both gamefish and bottom-feeders congregate there to feed.

When trolling into the current in a tide rip, you can be practically motionless and your lures will still work vigorously. To make headway, you may have to advance your throttles. But when working with the current, your speed will have to be still faster, because the current will be pushing your boat along, and your lures will be dragging behind listlessly unless you speed up to compensate for the current.

Whether trolling with, against, or across the current, it is wise to move in a zigzag, thus causing your lures to slide back and forth as they're working in the rip. To a fish, this looks like a helpless baitfish struggling in the current, and they're onto the lure in a flash.

When trolling a rip, it's extremely important that you be alert as to your position in the rip at all times. Then, if you hook a fish, try to return to the exact same spot and concentrate your efforts in that particular area, as that may be where the fish are schooled up and feeding.

Remember, at some spots, particularly at the point of islands or penin-

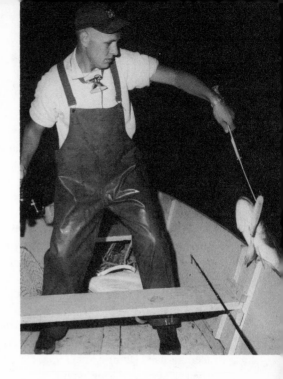

Big stripers often take up residence in tide rips, feeding on the wide variety of food carried to them by the current. It was in the famous rip at Sandy Hook, N. J., that Howard Beyer hooked this big striped bass on a subsurface swimming plug while trolling.

sulas, the rips may run seaward for as much as a couple of miles, yet the bulk of the fish may be confined to a relatively small area. I've found this to be true with tarpon, snook, channel bass, striped bass, bluefish, cobia, Pacific bonito, Pacific barracuda, and king and silver salmon.

Troll Around Kelp Beds

Along the Pacific coast there is a lot of fine sport to be enjoyed while trolling around the kelp beds. Many who have not fished the kelp beds of the Pacific think of them as being nothing more than seaweed. True, the kelp is seaweed, but unlike the soft, leafy type of seaweed that drifts freely on the Atlantic and Gulf coasts, the Pacific kelp is more like a tree that grows in the sea. It has stalks as thick as a man's leg, and its leaves are 5 feet and more in length and a full foot in width.

You've got to be constantly alert while trolling around the kelp in a small boat, because you can be fouling your lures constantly. Most successful trollers stay along the outer edges of the kelp, working their feathers and spoons on short lines, say 75 to 100 feet, which minimizes fouling.

This type of trolling is ideal for the spin-fisherman using medium-weight tackle, for there are a wide variety of species that reside in the kelp and provide fine sport. Most strikes will come to spoons, bucktail jigs, and small trolling feathers, with Pacific bonito, Pacific barracuda, mackerel, white sea bass, and yellowtail providing the action.

Back-Country Trolling Is Contemplative

Thus far I've talked about trolling far offshore and trolling for the many species that frequent inshore waters both in the open ocean and in bays. But some of the most contemplative trolling of all takes place in the thousands of tidal rivers and creeks along the coast. These are the slow-moving bodies of water where baitfish abound and a wide variety of game-fish congregate to feed.

As a general rule the fish that frequent these waters are small, and they provide great sport on light spinning-tackle and small lures. Throughout the northeast Atlantic, mackerel by the thousands invade the waters during the summer months, and the small-boat troller, armed with some shiny spoons, feathers, or bucktail jigs, can catch mackerel in the 1- to 3-pound class until arm-weary. It's not difficult fishing either. You just look for the gulls, and where you find an abundance of these working birds, you're almost certain to find mackerel feeding beneath them.

The important thing is not to turn right through the school of surface-feeding fish. Doing so will spook them, and they may not return to feed on the surface for a long while.

This kind of fishing is ideal for the entire family, as the mackerel are easy to catch and thus keep the interest of the youngsters. While the macks are the target, it's not unusual to be rewarded with strikes from harbor pollock, codfish, hake, and an occasional striped bass.

Tidal Creeks Produce

Striped bass, channel bass, and weakfish are three of the East coast's most popular gamefish. Often these three gladiators invade the upper reaches of tidal creeks to feed, gorging themselves on the abundant shrimp, crabs, minnows, and other baitfish that flourish in these waters.

When the tide is on the flood, these fish move in, and at such times, you can often troll these waters, providing you do so from a small outboard rig. Trolling permits you to cover a lot of area, and by using either small spoons, subsurface swimming plugs, mirror plugs, or bucktail jigs you can often connect. Keep in mind that the natural food will be seeking the protection of the marsh grass as the tide floods, so it's important that you troll as close to the grass as possible without fouling.

Throughout Florida and along many sections of the Gulf coast there are similar meandering estuaries, populated by snook, small tarpon, redfish, ladyfish, and seatrout. They're all a barrel of fun on light tackle. While many spin-fishermen prefer to cast for these species, it's important to note that by trolling you're usually able to cover far more water than casting, and because of this, you may locate schools of fish that would otherwise not be found.

On the surface many of these backwater areas look alike. But down on the bottom there is a conformation that may be misleading. Hundreds of feet of shallow, uninteresting bottom may fall away sharply at a bend in the river, and the fish may congregate right along the edge of a dropoff, out of the swift water, waiting for food to be carried to them by the current.

Troll Resting Areas

Practically every coastal river in the country is now spanned by several bridges. Fish congregate around the bridges because there is always an abundance of food available. They most often take up station just ahead or behind the abutments, for it is here that the current is minimal. Facing into the current they quickly dart out to take any food carried along by the flowing water.

By carefully trolling back and forth so your lures work across and behind the abutments, you'll frequently be rewarded with strikes, regardless of what coast you fish.

Cover Open Bottom Too

Many anglers fail to realize that some species travel a great deal during the course of a day. They may move from one tide rip to the edge of a dropoff that is to their liking. In the course of their travels they often frequent either natural channels or the man-made shipping and navigation channels. This is important, because frequently you can troll along the channel edges and enjoy fine sport. I've experienced good sport while trolling for big tarpon in Florida by simply blind trolling along the channel edges of the many rivers that dot the southwest Florida coast. The channel edges approaching New York harbor each season give up many excellent striped bass catches to trollers who work with plugs and spoons, slowly trolling them deep for bass that move with the tides as they search for a meal.

Clothespin Helps Keep Lines Apart

A little trick that I've found useful whether trolling offshore or in along the beaches, especially when it's windy, is to take a couple of clothespins and attach them to a short piece of line, which I in turn attach to the stern cleats of the boat. I then run the lines from the tip of the rod and snap them into the clothespin. Thus, instead of the lines being 7 or 8 feet in the air, they go right into the water at transom level. This keeps the lines deep and prevents the wind from blowing them about and possibly becoming tangled. It's good to remember and in addition to saving tangles it does keep your lures deep, which is important at times.

More Deep Than on Top

So very often I've spoken with trollers who are more concerned with fish feeding on the surface than those down in the depths. While admittedly trolling near schools of surface-feeding fish is very exciting, it's wise to remember that for every fish you see on top there are literally dozens in the depths.

You should be alert to this and strive to fish your lures at various levels. This can be accomplished with the aid of trolling sinkers, and by lengthening your line or slowing your speed until you get the lures to the desired depth.

With spinning tackle you'll be a bit handicapped for really deep trolling, especially with wire or lead-core line. But during recent years I fished with a number of Pacific coast anglers who used heavy spinning-tackle and cannonball-type sinkers, which were attached to a quick-release mechanism. As soon as a king or silver salmon struck, the quick-release mechanism released the sinker and permitted the angler to work unhandicapped by the heavy sinker. While this method is most popular with anglers using multi-plying reels and heavy rods, it may be used with a heavy spinning-outfit with satisfactory results.

The trollers who fish for king and silver salmon using these rigs ply the open waters of the Pacific, using anchovies or herring rigged for trolling. While artificials aren't too popular with trollers in the Pacific Northwest, those anglers who do use plugs, spoons, and wobblers make many fine salmon catches.

Screaming Reel Offers Delight

Each angler falls into a pattern of the kind of fishing he likes, and the troller is basically a searcher at heart. He likes to put out a spread of lures, set the antireverse on his spinning reel, and place it on a rod holder, and then proceed to work a good-looking beat of water, intent on probing every rip and eddy that may hold a hungry fish. His reward is sudden, and accompanied by a screaming ratchet of the spinning reel, signaling that he's succeeded in coaxing a strike.

Troll and Chum Combination

In the following section another highly successful technique employed by the spin-fisherman will be discussed. Chumming is an extremely effective method of attracting fish to your hook. But many anglers employ a double-barreled approach, trolling until fish are hooked, at which time chumming begins and hopefully attracts the fish right up close to the boat, where they can be caught in any one of several ways. Remember this combination approach. It's just another way of making for a more enjoyable day on the water, whether you troll many miles from land or delight in the quiet solitude offered by a coastal estuary hidden among the marsh grass.

CHUMMING

The technique of chumming can be defined as simply dropping pieces of food into the water, to be carried by the current or to settle into the depths to be found by hungry fish that in turn will follow the food to its source. At that time, you hope, they'll be attracted to a carefully presented natural bait or lure, and you'll be in business!

In salt water, chumming is most often done from a boat, but many knowledgeable spin-fishermen employ this technique from a variety of spots, including bridges and piers, breakwaters, rock jetties, and natural rocky promontories, as well as from sand beaches and marsh banks. It proves especially effective when fish are congregated in an area where you cannot present your bait or lure while casting, trolling or bottom-fishing, in that it draws the fish to you while either drifting, anchored, or fishing from a fixed position.

A Variety of Species Will Respond

At one time or another it is safe to say that every fish in the sea will respond to a properly developed spread of chum. Indeed, big-game anglers regularly chum for giant bluefin tuna that weigh upward of half a ton, dropping whole herring and mackerel overboard and attracting the behemoths within a rod's length of the boat.

For our purposes, however, we'll concern ourselves with the techniques for chumming species that fall within the province of the spinning enthusiast. Included in this range are some of the game pelagic species that roam the waters of the world, as well as small bottom-feeders that often weigh but a pound.

Attract, Don't Feed

The key to successful chumming is to attract the fish within range by using just a nominal amount of chum. Chumming too heavily causes the fish to set up a feeding station well back in the slick, and at such times they'll seldom venture within range of your baits or lures. On the other

hand, chumming too lightly will result in the fish lazily picking up pieces
of the food, yet they'll fail to respond because there is insufficient food to
arouse their interest.

Just how much is enough is something you determine through experience,
for a variety of factors enter into the picture, including the chum you're
using and the fish you're after, plus such variables as wind, water clarity,
and the speed of the current. Suffice to say, however, that you know immediately when you're doing everything right, for at that time the fish will
readily respond.

Any Natural Food May Be Used

Most any food from the sea that fish regularly feed on may be used as
chum, and there are even a number of foods such as rice, corn, and other
products that are occasionally brought into play along the coast with fine
results.

Fish in any one of several forms are by far the most popular chum used
along the seacoast. Small live fish, such as anchovies, are regularly used as
both chum and hook bait for a wide variety of species on the Pacific coast.
Along the Gulf, chunks of pilchards and mullet are a favored chum, while
Atlantic-coast anglers frequently grind menhaden, popularly called mossbunker, into a fish meal which makes an extremely effective chum.

In addition to fish, shrimp are a popular chum wherever they are readily
available. Along the Gulf and south Atlantic coast whole shrimp quickly
attract a variety of fish when they're used as chum, and most of these are
the same large shrimp you might serve on your dinner table. Along the
middle and north Atlantic coast, where tiny, inch-long grass shrimp are
plentiful, these too make an extremely effective chum for a wide variety
of species.

Crabs, crushed and ground clams, ground mussels, pieces of squid and
the common sand bug are all used as chum at one time or another. So are
the many seaworms, including the popular sandworm, bloodworm, and
tapeworm found in the sand along many of our beaches. These are often
cut into small pieces and readily attract many bottom-feeders and gamefish.

Suit Tackle to Species Being Sought

The beauty part about chumming is that because you're not trolling
where heavy pressure might be brought to bear on your tackle, nor using
heavy terminal-tackle while bottom-bouncing, you can generally employ
lighter tackle while chumming than while employing other techniques.
Here's where it's important that you carefully select a basic outfit well suited
to the species you'll be chumming for. If chumming for bonefish, or sea-

trout, then naturally a light-spinning outfit is best. Moving on to such species as bluefish, striped bass, and other gamefish of moderate size, a medium-weight rig unquestionably will do the best job for you. If, however, you decide to chum and use spinning tackle for albacore, school bluefin tuna, little tuna, king mackerel, and other tough adversaries, then the heavier spinning tackle discussed earlier must be used if you expect to enjoy the fishing to the fullest.

Always keep in mind that while the lightest possible tackle for a given situation results in maximum sport, by going too light in your tackle selection, you can handicap yourself and wind up with a standoff while fighting a fish, which takes a lot of the pleasure out of the fishing. The tackle ideally suited to chumming any particular species is that which is sufficiently light to give the fish a sporting chance, yet has enough power so you can land a fish within a reasonable period of time and also have sufficient backbone to keep a fish from getting under the boat or back to a coral sanctuary or entangled in a heavy growth of mangrove.

Little Terminal Tackle Required

There's very little terminal rigging required for many types of chumming. The simplest of all is just tieing an Eagle Claw style hook directly to the end of your line, baiting up and drifting or casting the bait back in the chum line. This method of rigging is especially popular when you're after species that do not have teeth, or whose teeth are not so sharp as to readily cut through the monofilament line. Rigging in this manner works extremely well for striped bass, Boston mackerel, weakfish and seatrout, snook, little tuna, school bluefin tuna, albacore, and bonefish.

But should your target be those adversaries endowed with a set of sharp dentures, such as king mackerel, bluefish, groupers, and snappers, or other sharp-toothed species, it becomes necessary to use a wire leader.

Wire Leaders Necessary at Times

Several choices are available in leader wire, as well as a couple of methods of rigging it. A popular way of rigging is to use a tiny barrel-swivel tied to the end of your monofilament line, to which you attach a short length of single-strand stainless-steel leader. Here too, the size of the wire you use, and its length, will be determined by the fish you're after. A foot of number 5 or 6 wire is fine when after yellowtail snapper that average but a couple of pounds apiece in weight, but when big king mackerel are your target, then 3 or 4 feet of number 8 or 9 is better suited. As to the reason for the extra length, keep in mind that many of these species will actually swallow the bait you present to them, hence the importance of the leader sufficiently long so they cannot bite through it after being hooked.

Single strand wire will occasionally twist and kink, breaking at the most inopportune times. Because of this, some anglers prefer using nylon-covered stainless-steel cable. This fine leader comes in a variety of strengths, with 20- through 75-pound-test being the general range used by salt-water spin-fishermen.

A favorite method of attaching your line to this type of leader is to employ either a surgeon's knot or an Albright knot. Both are strong connections, eliminating the need of a swivel between line and leader. These knots, incidentally, may also be used for joining single-strand stainless-steel or stainless-steel cable to your line.

The terminal connection when using single-strand leader is a combination haywire and barrel twist and a Homer Rhode knot when using nylon-covered cable. If you use stainless-steel cable, you will find small sleeves best for crimping the leader and making end loops for either lures, snaps, or hooks.

Float Rig Popular

When there is little current and your bait tends to sink to the bottom while chumming, it often proves advantageous to use a float to keep your bait suspended at a desired level. Keep in mind that the chum will often settle to a level other than that at which your bait may be and that the float will keep them together, which is important, as often fish will move through a chum line at a specific level and not above or below it.

There are a variety of floats that may be employed. The easiest to use is the round plastic float with a spring-snap mechanism that snaps to your line and holds the bait at the desired level. These come in a variety of sizes, and for most salt-water use it's wise to carry a selection ranging from 1 to 2½ inches in diameter. The small sizes are ideal when using but a single small shrimp on your hook, whereas the larger sizes are useful when using a large pilchard or whole squid as bait in a chum line.

Still other types of floats slide on your line. They are stopped at a given spot by knotting the line and having a bead or button positioned between the float and knot, which keeps the bait at the desired level. Some anglers prefer not to knot their line, and instead use a tightly tied elastic band, which causes the float to stop when it reaches the spot where the elastic band is tied to the line.

Some anglers make an economical float by simply cutting a slit into a piece of cork of the desired size, and slipping their line into the slit in the cork. This holds the bait just where you want it, and when a fish strikes, the water pressure working against the cork pulls it from the line.

A float rig such as this is often used to suspend the bait at a desired level in the chum slick. Here a large float was used with a big baitfish. Correspondingly, smaller floats may be used to suspend smaller baits.

During a hectic day's fishing you may go through a lot of cork, but the system works fine.

SINKERS MUST BE USED OCCASIONALLY

The free-floating bait, or the bait suspended at a desired level, sometimes just doesn't work, especially when there is a swift current running, at which time both of these rigs result in the bait being held near the surface by the force of the current against your line.

When a condition such as this persists it is necessary to add weight to your line, taking the bait down into the depths. In fact, at times when there is a moderate current you may find it necessary to add weight to your line, simply because the fish are feeding deep, rather than at intermediate levels or near the surface.

When such conditions dictate use of weight, I always use a rubber-cored sinker—more than one if necessary—until I get the bait down to where I begin to receive strikes. This may require a bit of experimentation on your part until you find the right level.

I've found the rubber-cored sinker ideal, for they are easily slipped onto the line and because a piece of rubber within the sinker holds it onto the line, there is no fear of the sinker causing damage to the line, as is often the case when you employ clinch-on sinkers.

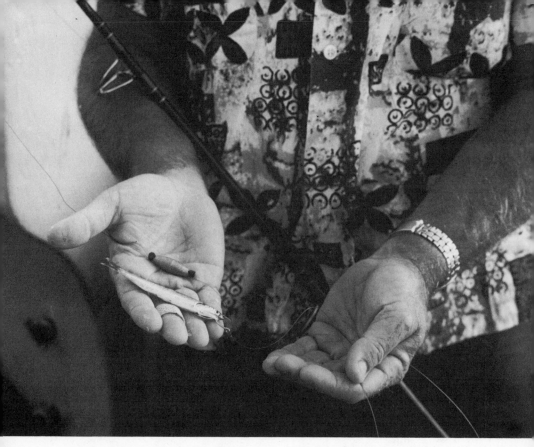

When the current is strong, you may have to add a small rubber-cored sinker or two to your line to take the bait to the de-sired depth. Here an anchovy bait will be drifted out into a chum line of live anchovies off Long Beach, California.

The rubber-cored sinkers come in a variety of weights, and for general salt-water use I always include a selection in my kit ranging in weight from ½ ounce on through 3 ounces. Sometimes I'll add a couple of them to my line, and often this has proved the difference between success and failure, especially when chumming from a boat where the wind and current were extremely strong.

At times it's beneficial to use a sinker-and-float combination. The float keeps the bait from sinking, and the sinker keeps the bait perpendicular to the float, rather than permitting it to be carried toward the surface by the current, which would happen if you didn't have a light sinker.

Up to this point I've mentioned using but a single-baited hook, a float rig, float-and-sinker combination, and a sinker alone to take the bait to the desired depth in the chum line. Often when you begin chumming, it's wise to have each angler on board using a different terminal rig to determine just which will bring the first strike. Once a couple of strikes are received, everyone else on board can quickly switch over to the productive combination. It is worth noting that I've often observed four or five anglers fishing from a private boat, with everyone rigged 'alike, and no one catching fish, while anglers chumming nearby enjoyed a bonanza simply because they'd found the right combination, which presented their baits at the level the fish were feeding in the chum line.

Where to Chum

A great deal of thought should go into the selection of a spot to chum. A spot that may produce on one tide may be totally devoid of fish on another tide. This applies whether you're fishing around a point of land where a rip may be formed on an ebbing tide or where a flowing current may carry your chum and bait toward a coral reef, oil-drilling platform, kelp bed, or any one of the vast number of situations you'll find along the seacoast.

Rather than discuss generalities, I think it best to cover step by step the wide variety of situations you'll encounter while chumming, and the approaches I've found to be effective under each. Naturally, it's impossible to cover them all, but this will give you sufficient insight into the various techniques employed, and after that you can apply them to the particular conditions and species you're after.

Chumming with Ground Fish

A really effective chum line may be established using most any fish that has been ground into a fish meal. On the Atlantic coast menhaden is popular, because it is oily and has a strong smell, which readily attracts fish. Mackerel may be ground into chum too, as can herring. Along the Gulf of Mexico I've ground up mullet and pilchards for chum and enjoyed fine results, while on the Pacific coast I've fished from boats where both anchovies and sardines had been freshly ground into a potent, fish-attracting mass, somewhat unappetizing to look at, but nevertheless effective.

Boatmen May Anchor or Drift

It depends on just what species you're after as to whether you should anchor or chum. Also, wind and tide are other factors that will determine just which approach is best. If seas are moderate and current is the same, then when open-water fishing for such species as bluefish, mackerel, bonito, tuna and albacore, a pleasant way to chum is to just drift along, covering a wide area with your chum and bringing fish up from the depths to your baited hooks.

If, however, the current or wind is strong and you would move along too fast, then anchoring is often the only solution. Sometimes it is necessary to use two anchors, to hold your boat in one position and keep it from swinging back and forth.

To keep your boat reasonably clean while chumming, it's wise to build a rack that hangs over the gunwale, into which you can place your chum bucket. In this way there's a minimum of splattering chum on board.

For ground chum you'll need a ladle to drop the chum overboard. Some anglers fashion one by fastening a small tin can to the end of a wooden handle, while others use an old soup ladle or deep spoon.

It's difficult to say precisely the amount of chum you should dispense. When you're chumming for either Atlantic or Spanish mackerel just a nominal amount of chum will do, for remember these fish only average from 1 to 3 pounds in weight. If king mackerel, blues, or school bluefin tuna are your target, then it is necessary to use a generous amount of chum, for here you're seeking fish that may average 10 to 15 pounds in the case of blues, and double that amount for the kings and tuna.

A good pattern that I've found effective is to toss out a ladleful and watch as it disburses in the current, settling into the depths. Once it's out of sight in clear water, say 30 or 40 feet from the boat, I wait a few moments, until I estimate it's drifted that distance again, and I toss out another ladleful.

Keep a Steady Pace

The important thing is that you keep the chum line going at a steady pace. The intervals between the ladles of chum are not as important as your neglecting the chum bucket for five minutes or so, which winds up breaking up the chum line. Fish might well be moving up in the slick from as much as a half-mile or more and when there is a big break in the chum line they just lose all contact.

Many anglers make this mistake when the fishing gets torrid. With fish in the chum line they become so excited catching them that they forget about the chum buckets, and suddenly the fish are gone, and it sometimes becomes a problem attracting them back.

Ease Baits Out with Chum

Once you've got the chum line established, ease your baits into the water, and permit them to drift out with the chum. Many chummers use conventional reels, but you'll find a spinning reel will do a good job for you. You'll have to control the line as it leaves the reel by using your index finger. Placing your index finger against the edge of the spool will stop the line from going out, raising your finger will let the current take it.

For best results the bait should always be moving with the chum. If you're chumming with ground fish, then a chunk of menhaden makes a fine bait, or you can use a piece of mackerel, whole butterfish, pilchard, mullet, anchovy, or sardine. The ideal combination is to use the same chunk or whole baitfish that you had used to grind up for chum. I often cut prime baits from the backs or tail sections of fish before putting the remainder through the chum grinder.

In placing the bait on the hook, I've found it best to hide the hook within the bait as much as possible, but I often leave the point and barb of the hook exposed, so that as a fish inhales the bait the point is immediately in a position to penetrate and not buried within the bait where it can be pulled from the mouth of a fish without doing its job.

Let Fish Take Bait

Every species of fish that moves up in a chum line will strike your bait in a different manner. Sometimes even the same species will approach a boat differently, swiftly striking it one day, while at other times they pick it up so gently that you can barely discern the strike.

Accordingly, it's best that you always give the fish plenty of time to get the bait well into its mouth. Striking prematurely results in many missed strikes, simply because the fish has just picked up the bait and is moving off with it and hasn't as yet taken the bait well into its mouth where the hook will be in a position to penetrate.

When you feel a fish pick up the bait, lower your rod tip and point it in the direction your line is drifting and lift your finger away from the spinning reel's spool, so as not to put any pressure on the fish. At this time the line may move off the spool ever so slowly, or it may be zipping off at a rapid pace. When you feel the fish has the bait well in its mouth and is moving away at a good pace, turn your reel handle, which will close the reel's bail and immediately lift back smartly to set the hook.

Set Hook Firmly

When you lift back, you'll know immediately if you've hooked the fish. If you have, keep your tip well up and maintain firm pressure as the fish begins its run. Keep the tip high, so the fish has to fight the rod. This will keep plenty of pressure on the fish and ensure firm seating of the hook beyond the barb.

If, when you lift back to set the hook, you simply pull the bait from the fish's jaw, react swiftly and open the bail of your spinning reel and permit the bait—if some still remains—to continue drifting back. Often a fish will instinctively react and grab the bait again, even if only a small

Little tuna, sometimes called bonito and false albacore, will often swarm into a chum line by the hundreds. Milt Rosko hooked this beauty while chumming off Louisiana and baiting with a whole pilchard; the hook was carefully concealed within the baitfish.

piece remains. If it does take the bait a second time, just repeat the same procedure you did the first time and hope this time you hook him.

Anchor Off from Reefs and Wrecks

When you know fish congregate around reefs or wrecks, it's wise to anchor your boat just off from the spot, so that the current will carry your chum to the spot and attract the fish away from the sharp coral or barnacle-encrusted wreck, for if you hook a fish too close to these obstructions you risk losing it when it seeks the sanctuary of the spot, and should the line touch the coral or barnacle or other debris, you stand a good chance of losing the fish.

In the Bahamas, Bermuda, and Florida waters many groupers, snappers, amberjack, and other species will stick close to a patch of coral and refuse to move until such time as a tasty chum drifts their way. Then they'll move toward its source, which gives you a good chance to score.

Small Fish a Good Chum Too

In the tropics a favorite chum is made of small fry. These may be the fingerlings of practically any of the wide variety of baitfishes found in southern waters. Many anglers take a handful of the 2- to 4-inch-long fingerlings and squeeze them tightly so that the juices ooze from the small fish. They're then mixed with an equal part of sand, and the handful is tossed overboard at regular intervals, sparkling and settling into the depths. The sand mixed with the oils of the fish carries the scent well into the depths and quickly arouses the interest of many species.

Small fish such as spearing and sand launce are also used by chummers off the Atlantic coast. Both of these small fish may be mixed in with a ground chum of menhaden, and they make a potent chum for little tuna, school bluefin tuna, oceanic bonito, and Atlantic bonito. The ground chum really is what establishes the slick, but there are enough fingerlings mixed in to excite the gamefish and whet their appetites, and when they find one of these small fish impaled on a hook, they'll strike it readily.

Anchovies Popular

On the Pacific coast the anchovy is extremely popular as chum, and boatmen go to great pains to obtain and keep the anchovies alive, preferring the chum alive to dead. For far-offshore species, such as albacore and yellowfin tuna, the most popular technique is to troll until one of these fine gamefish is hooked. As soon as a fish is hooked, a dozen or more of the 3- to 5-inch-long anchovies are tossed far from the stern of the boat in hopes of attracting other members of the school to the surface. As the albacore or tuna respond to the enticing chum of live anchovies, they boil right to the surface, picking off the anchovies one at a time. The chummer then tosses several more anchovies overboard, closer to the boat, at which time each angler casts a lively anchovy overboard, and permits it to swim away from the boat. Spinning tackle is ideal, as with a light-tipped rod you can cast a small anchovy a good distance with little fear of the force of the cast ripping it from the hook.

While fishing off southern California, I've hooked many fine albacore after having permitted the anchovy to swim fully 100 feet into the depths. While a few stray fish occasionally hit the trolled lures, sometimes it is difficult to raise the remaining school to the surface, so don't be afraid to

On the Pacific coast anchovies are a favorite chum. They are kept in live bait wells and tossed out by the netful when the fishing grounds are reached. Here a deckhand tosses out several dozen anchovies, hoping to attract a variety of species away from the kelp beds off San Diego, California.

let your anchovy work very deep, for you may be pleasantly rewarded with a strike.

The real thrills come when the albacore or yellowfin tuna swarm on top and vie for the anchovies tossed overboard as chum. When your hook bait hits the water there are often times when several fish zero in on it, and the first one there is a winner!

Chum Around Kelp Beds

Inshore the anchovy also proves very popular as chum, especially around the many kelp beds off the southern California coast. Living within and around the kelp are a wide variety of species, and many boatmen anchor just off from the kelp and chum with live anchovies to attract the fish away from the treelike seaweed. Pacific barracuda, Pacific bonito, sand bass, halibut, kelp bass and sheepshead all respond, feeding on the anchovies presented to them, and eventually working within range of hook baits.

Tie Up to Shrimp Boats

Gulf-coast anglers often take advantage of chum lines established by shrimp trawlers working throughout the night netting shrimp. During daylight hours shrimp bury themselves in the sand and are difficult to net. When the sun comes up, the trawlers anchor up and begin culling the trash from the shrimp they've netted during the night. They throw crushed shrimp, crabs, squid, and a variety of small fish overboard, packing the saleable shrimp in ice. As they shovel the trash overboard, huge schools of fish congregate and provide bonanza fishing.

Wise boatmen sail offshore before daybreak and intercept the trawlers before they shovel all the trash overboard. Usually they're happy to pass you a 20-gallon can full of the trash, which is more than enough to last you during a day's fishing. As a courtesy many boatmen pass a six-pack of beer or soda over to the crew, and as a bonus the trawler skipper often lets you tie up to his stern, where you can take advantage of the chum line he's established.

At such times I've witnessed literally hundreds of huge fish gorging themselves on the chum. There are king mackerel, little tuna, jack crevalle, hard-tailed jacks, barracuda, sharks, dolphin, cobia, and occasionally even big groupers and snappers that come to the surface to enjoy the free meal.

When this happens most any bait you pick out of the chum bucket and toss overboard will bring a strike immediately. You can enjoy fine casting sport too, as most of these species are in such a feeding frenzy that they'll readily assault a popping plug or bucktail jig tossed into the maelstrom.

Good Sport Around Oil Rigs

There are thousands of oil-drilling platforms in the Gulf of Mexico, and these offer superb fishing opportunities for the chumming enthusiasts, for

On the Gulf of Mexico many boatmen tie up to shrimp trawlers that are anchored up and culling their catch. As the trawler crew discards trash such as small fish, crabs, squid and broken shrimp overboard, huge schools of little tuna, jack crevalle, king mackerel, cobia and other species invade the made-to-order chum line.

beneath the rigs a great many species find the shadows and abundance of forage species to their liking. Many boat fishermen tie up to the rigs, and chum with chunks of shrimp, mullet, pilchards, squid, or crab, and they attract many species to their hooks.

Surface-cruising species include barracuda, bluefish, Spanish and king mackerel, dolphin, cobia, and amberjack. The chum also brings up big red snappers and husky groupers that usually reside on the Gulf's floor, but respond to the chum and eventually wind up in your fishbox.

Bottom-Feeders Respond

A wide variety of bottom-feeders may be attracted to your boat by chumming too. But if you simply drop the chum overboard the current will often carry it too far from your boat to be effective with the bottom fish. To keep this from happening, and keep the chum on the bottom and around your boat, you should use a chum pot.

A chum pot is little more than a wire-mesh basket, approximately the size of a round oatmeal box. It has a lead bottom to take it to the bottom quickly, and a hinged top. You simply fill it with ground chum and lower it to the bottom beneath your boat and then rig up with regular bottom rigs and fish them beneath your boat too.

The current will carry the ground chum right along the bottom and attract bottom-feeders from a wide area. This method of chumming is especially popular when after winter flounders, found along the middle and north Atlantic coast. It also works well with puffers, popularly called blowfish in many areas, along with spot, porgies, blackfish, codfish, and sea bass, each of which is almost always looking for something to eat and won't pass up any chum that drifts its way.

Chumming Effective for Bonefish Too

Although few people chum for bonefish, it is an extremely effective way to catch the wary bonefish, which often does most of its feeding on shallow tidal flats in the tropics, in water often less than a foot deep.

The key when chumming bones is to find the edge of the flat where the bonefish move onto the flats from deep water, and to anchor and toss out pieces of shrimp or pieces of conch cut to the size of a dime. As the bonefish move along they'll get the scent of the chum and will immediately slow down and begin to feed on the chum. Often they'll start rooting in the bottom searching for crabs, shrimp, and other food. This gives you the opportunity to present a conch or shrimp bait to them, and you'll score in short order. Once the bones are chummed within casting range, many spin-fishermen cast a tiny delta-winged bucktail jig to them. By permitting the jig to settle to the bottom and then retrieving it slowly while twitching the rod tip, the jig resembles a small shrimp or crab scurrying along the bottom and the bonefish take it in a flash.

Piers, Bridges, Breakwaters, and Surf

Although most spin-fishermen chum from boats, there are many successful anglers who chum from piers, bridges, breakwaters, docks, and even the surf. Keep in mind that almost all species move about as they search for food. If they get a taste of chum as they're looking, they'll usually slow down and spend some time in the area, hoping to find more food. While pier-fishing I've often dropped chunks of mullet and menhaden into the water, and attracted swarms of bluefish and mackerel within range. I've also successfully chummed striped bass with grass shrimp from an old railroad trestle crossing a tidal estuary. Blackfish and sheepshead will quickly respond to a chum of crushed sand bugs tossed from rockpiles and docks, for they usually live close to the rocks or mussel-encrusted dock pilings. Pompano will swarm around a beach area chummed with tiny pieces of shrimp. I've known surfmen who frequently tossed small pieces of sea-worm into the spot they were fishing, for they felt the currents working parallel with the beach would carry the worms along and eventually attract hungry stripers to where their bottom rigs were baited with seaworms.

When fishing from land, quite naturally the current will play an important role in carrying your chum to feeding fish. Because of this it's wise to study a tide chart, and to think of spots which are beyond casting distance, but to which the current could carry your chum and hopefully attract the fish within range of your baits.

Perhaps there's a rockpile submerged several hundred feet from a breakwater or the pilings of an old bridge rotting beneath the surface. Maybe the beach cuts away sharply at a point of land, and the current runs along the beach to the cut. Or an inlet where the ebbing tide could carry your chum into the eddies where fish often congregate and attract them within range of your baits or lures. The shore-based angler should always be alert to these situations, for often with the aid of chum some fine fishing can result.

Many Techniques in Many Places

It's difficult to mention every single method of chumming there is. But as I scan through angling logs of a great many fishing locales, I find that I've chummed many fish that at first you might not even think respond to chum. Off the Virginia Capes black drum responded to a chum of broken crabs and clams, while off the Jersey coast we frequently attracted codfish beneath our anchored boat by crushing sea clams with a baseball bat, and dropping them shell and all to the bottom far below.

In Georgia and South Carolina we've caught more than our share of seatrout, channel bass, and striped bass while chumming with pieces of fresh shrimp and baiting with a whole shrimp while working a float rig along the marsh banks of the many tidal estuaries of those states. There were big yellowtail that responded to anchovies off the Todos Santos Islands of Mexico, and we caught some white sea bass too, both of which moved out from impenetrable kelp to feed on the anchovies, but eventually wound up on our hooks. Weakfish often swarmed into a chum line of tiny grass shrimp measuring but an inch in length while we chummed Long Island's picturesque Peconic Bay. Surf perch gobbled tiny pieces of mussel we tossed into the rocky surf of California's lengthy coastline, and once a school took a notion to feed, it was a fish almost every cast.

So it is with chumming, an especially effective technique for the spin-fisherman, regardless of whether you fish from shore or boat, for gamefish or bottom-feeders. Often it makes the difference between just fishing and enjoying fantastic sport.

6

SPINNING
BY SPECIES:
SALT
WATER

Along about now, having described how to select the spinning tackle for various salt-water fishing situations and the many techniques that can be employed to catch salt-water species, I'll now discuss what I feel is a representative grouping of the favorite salt-water species fished for by spin-fishermen throughout the country. Some are exotic gamefish that will test you and your skills and tackle to the limit. They'll be difficult to catch, to put it mildly. Others will be plentiful and often more than cooperative, ensuring a full day's sport when you're after them. With all you'll have fun catching them, which is what spin-fishing's all about in the first place.

Keep alert to the various techniques employed for each of the species, because many of the tips may often be brought into play to help you score with other salt-water adversaries.

ALBACORE

This long-finned adversary inhabits both Atlantic and Pacific waters and to a lesser extent the Gulf of Mexico. It is best known to Pacific-coast anglers who each year take thousands of them while trolling and chumming, while along the Atlantic and Gulf coasts the total catch is but a relative handful.

259

There's no mistaking the albacore: it has extremely long pectoral fins which easily distinguish it from other tunas and bonitos. Found in the Atlantic, Pacific and the Gulf, it is primarily a Pacific coast species and is eagerly sought by party boat fishermen.

A favored technique that I've used successfully on the Pacific coast off California and Mexico's Baja peninsula was to troll far offshore until fish struck the trolled feathers, jigs, or spoons, and then to immediately begin chumming with just a few live anchovies. Usually the fish hooked trolling is part of a larger school down in the depths. Once hooked, inquisitive fish will rise to follow the hooked albacore, and at that time they'll often spot the limited number of chum anchovies swimming on the surface, which in turn will cause more fish to rise. Soon the albacore will be boiling on the surface, picking off the helpless anchovies, at which time you can either cast or drift back a live anchovy on your hook and often be into fish immediately.

Seldom do these game gladiators venture close to shore, but instead they are most often found in waters 300 feet or deeper, far from shore. They're a world traveler, caught along our California, Oregon, and Washington coasts, the Hawaiian Islands, and off Japan. They favor water in the 60- to 70-degree range, and seldom will they strike at temperatures other than between these ranges. Most sport-caught albacore range from 10 to 25 pounds. I've landed several in the 35-pound class, and they're truly superb fighters, testing an angler and his tackle to the utmost as they make repeated runs into the depths, peeling 100 or more yards of line from your reel in a single run.

AMBERJACK

If ever there was a fish in the sea that can fight you to exhaustion, it is the amberjack. It's an extremely strong fish that will fight and fight and fight, testing you and your tackle to the utmost. The amberjack is such a tough adversary that many anglers deliberately avoid them, rather than get involved in battles that might last a half-hour or more, even with a small fish.

Amberjack are most known as tropical residents, living above coral reefs and wrecks, especially throughout Florida and the Bahamas. But there are substantial numbers of them to be found as far north as New Jersey during the summer months, usually residing around wrecks or broken, irregular bottom where food is plentiful. Many of them are so big, weighing 75 to 100 pounds, that the strongest heavy spinning tackle is required to subdue them. While fishing in the shadows of the oil rigs located off Louisiana I've hooked many and landed several big amberjack. In the Gulf they're plentiful, but I've observed there's but limited fishing pressure for them.

Spin-fishermen most often hook amberjack while deep-jigging or plug-casting over a reef. Still another extremely effective method is to anchor up over a reef and to attract the amberjack to the surface by using a live

Many term the amberjack the strongest fish in the sea, for it never seems to quit; this one was hooked while deep jigging over a reef. A Woods Hole Oceanographic Institution tag was placed in its back. Moments after this photo was taken, the amberjack was released to fight another day, perhaps to be caught again, thus giving scientists an insight into its growth pattern and migratory habits.

blue runner, grunt, pinfish, or other small baitfish as an attractor. I've frequently raised several dozen brute amberjack to the surface using this method. By keeping the baitfish from them, you can work them into a feeding frenzy and then cast a bucktail or plug to them, which they'll immediately assault.

Many amberjack are taken while trolling a small spoon in reef areas. Add several ounces of trolling weight to get the spoon down deep, as amberjack usually stay at intermediate levels or near the bottom. Chumming will bring the toughies up too, with fry, ground fish, or diced chunks of fish attracting the amberjack, after which they'll readily take most any small baitfish you present to them.

ATLANTIC BONITO

The Atlantic bonito is primarily an offshore traveler. While occasionally it ventures within a few miles of the beach, it generally stays beyond sights of land.

Trollers take by far the greatest catches of Atlantic bonito, simply because they're usually fishing for tuna or other pelagic species and the bonito strike the lures intended for more formidable game.

Often bonito are taken on heavy tackle, which minimizes the sport experienced with these streamlined high-seas travelers.

The spinning enthusiast who elects to try his hand at trolling for bonito would do well to use no heavier than a medium-weight outfit, simply because most of the fish average from 2 to 8 pounds in weight. When trolling you'll find that lures ranging in length from 4 to 6 inches are about best, as the bonito are usually feeding on small mackerel, butterfish, herring, and other forage species of about that size.

Lures used most often include trolling feathers, spoons, cedar jigs, and bucktail jigs, in the order named. These fish are readily attracted to a boat's wake, and they like a lure moving fast, so always keep a couple of lures on the crest of the first or second wave in your wake, and a couple of lines back 100 or so feet, and make certain to advance the throttles.

Atlantic bonito will also respond to a chum slick of ground fish. I've landed many of them that invaded chum lines intended for bluefish, and they were great sport, although more hook-shy than blues, which called for a small, well-concealed hook within the butterfish or menhaden bait, and the hook tied directly to the monofilament line for maximum invisibility.

I've also landed many while deep-jigging. While primarily caught near the surface, you'll be surprised at the number you catch down deep.

A fine table fish, especially when baked whole.

ATLANTIC MACKEREL

The Atlantic mackerel is plentiful from the Virginia Capes on north to the Maritime Provinces. It moves north in the spring, summering in the Maritimes, and then retraces its steps in the fall as it heads south. It's popularly called Boston mackerel by many, and while not a big fish, averaging but 1 to 3 pounds in weight, the mackerel are extremely plentiful and an ideal target for the spinning enthusiast.

During their migrations they most often confine their activities to the open ocean, but splinter schools often drop off, moving into coastal bays and rivers, where they provide exciting sport for the angler armed with a light, one-handed spinning outfit.

When mackerel are actively feeding you can often catch them so fast that you become arm-weary. Unfortunately, many anglers use heavy tackle, and minimize the sport in taking these tough but small fighters.

I most often use a one-handed outfit, but frequently have used a closed-face spinning outfit with fine results.

Most mackerel are caught by jigging, employing small chromed-diamond jigs or stainless-steel jigs. Bucktail jigs also produce, as do small spoons should you elect to troll. I've even caught many while trolling a tiny feather.

Atlantic mackerel are plentiful along the coast and are extremely easy to catch. You get maximum sport employing either a one-handed spinning outfit, or a closed face spinning outfit such as the one pictured here. These were taken on a half-ounce diamond jig.

Mackerel readily respond to a chum of ground menhaden, and once you get them swarming around your boat you can either cast and retrieve or simply work your jig in the current with fine results. At such times mackerel readily respond to a small piece of fish on a hook drifted back in the chum line.

Anglers using medium-weight spinning tackle and anxious to catch a lot of fish, will often use two or three Norwegian surgical-tube teasers ahead of their lure or use small shad darts and catch the macks several at a time.

Some people speak very highly of the table qualities of mackerel, but for most tastes they tend to be a bit strong and oily.

BLACKFIN TUNA

The blackfin tuna is one of our smaller, yet very plentiful tuna, which makes it a natural for the spin-fisherman. A pelagic species that holds to warm waters, I've encountered them in Bermuda, the Bahamas, and from the Carolinas south to Florida, and along the Gulf coast. Seldom weighing more than 20 pounds, they're perfect for the angler armed with medium-weight spinning tackle.

Blackfins usually travel in large schools, and when they're feeding on the surface they present a beautiful picture, for often you'll see pilchards or other fry leaping into the air, as gulls fill the sky, feeding on the helpless fry, while the blackfins work on them from below. When the tuna are in this kind of a feeding frenzy, you almost can't miss.

There are several techniques that may be employed in this kind of a situation. You can ease up to within casting distance of the school and cast spoons, metal squids, or bucktails into the fish. The lure must be worked extremely fast and with an erratic retrieve for best results. When the fish are holding deep, as is often the case, deep-jigging with bucktail jigs pays off too.

You can also troll along the perimeter of the school and pick away at fish after fish, providing you don't move too close and spook the fish. Trolling feathers, cedar jigs, bone squids, spoons, and most other trolling lures will quickly bring strikes from the hungry blackfins.

On several occasions at widely separated places in Bermuda, the Bahamas, and Florida, I've had blackfins invade a chum line intended for other species. At such times they quickly took a small pilchard and were great sport on spinning tackle.

While some people fillet, brine, and then pressure-cook the tuna, most blackfins are fished for sport only, with many of the fish released at boatside.

BLACK SEA BASS

The black sea bass might well be termed the Atlantic counterpart of the Pacific sand bass. For the sea bass are a plentiful bottom fish that provide thousands of bottom-fishermen with sport through the summer months from the Virginia Capes north to New England.

They usually settle down around wrecks, mussel beds, or patches of broken, irregular bottom where there is an abundance of food. I suspect they spend most of their time meandering around the bottom, picking up tiny crabs, shrimp, mussels, seaworms, and clams.

The spin-fisherman usually will have to employ a medium-weight outfit while fishing for them, simply because they're usually in water ranging from 25 to 50 feet or more in depth. Usually the currents are strong and it's necessary to use 3 or 4 ounces of sinker to hold bottom, hence the necessity of a heavier outfit. Most bottom-fishermen with their sights set on sea bass will use a high-low rig and a pair of Claw-style hooks ranging between 1/0 and number 2, depending on the size of the fish in an area.

Favored baits include pieces of clam or squid. While fishing off Virginia, I learned a good tip, watching as veteran sea bass anglers used a meat tenderizer to pound fresh squid. They claimed this gave the bait more of a scent down on the bottom. Their trick worked, for we caught many fine sea bass, many big humpbacks with white outlining their fins, and weighing 3 to 4 pounds each.

The sea bass isn't a tough adversary. Indeed, it's hooked very easily and isn't much of a challenge to land. But it's a delight on the dinner table. That's what makes it so popular with family fishing groups along the entire coast.

The black sea bass is a bottom feeder that is a favorite of Atlantic coast anglers. This average size sea bass was taken while wreck fishing off Chincoteague, Virginia. A high-low rig was used with small chunks of squid as bait.

BLUEFIN TUNA

For our purposes in this book we'll concern ourselves with school bluefin tuna, the smaller members of this family that often weigh half a ton or more. The school bluefins within range of the spin-fisherman are those weighing from 5 to 50 pounds, although it's entirely possible to land fish substantially larger on heavy spinning-tackle, and each season sees even 100-pound fish landed on heavy spinning-tackle, with 20-pound test or heavier line.

Bluefin tuna on the West coast are generally smaller than their East-coast family, but those fished for by spin-fishermen are essentially the same size. Their habits are remarkably similar on both coasts. They follow the schools of baitfish, lingering in an area where food is plentiful, and then moving on as the bait moves.

On the Pacific coast I've caught them both while trolling and using live anchovies as chum. On the East coast I've done the same, excepting that either ground menhaden or small spearing were used as chum.

They're notoriously hook-shy, and it's best to conceal the bait in the hook as much as possible and to use a small hook. I've gone down to number-4 hooks on occasions, as a larger hook simply spooked the fish.

On either coast, live baits produce best if you can obtain them. I've used anchovies and small sardines in the Pacific, while on the Atlantic small mackerel, herring, silver hake, red hake, and menhaden brought strikes.

Bluefins are extremely strong fish, and your tackle must be quality gear and in mint condition if you expect to have a chance with them. Their first run will clear 100 and even 200 yards of line, and the experienced angler never tries to even slow that initial spurt. For to do so results in a pulled hook or line break.

Some people like fresh bluefin tuna, but it has a rather heavy flavor to most people. As a result most tuna is filleted, soaked in brine to rid it of blood, and then pressure-cooked and made into tuna salad. On the West coast many anglers have their tuna canned at the canneries located in most fishing ports, but this isn't practiced on the East coast.

BLUEFISH

Bluefish are said to range the waters of the world, and they provide anglers everywhere they visit with superb sport. Most big bluefish stick to Atlantic coast waters, while a smaller class of blues frequent the waters of the Gulf of Mexico. They're sheer delight for the spin-fishermen because they may be taken on practically every type of spinning tackle, on a wide variety of lures and baits, and using almost every fishing technique imaginable. To

Bluefish are strong fighters and have wicked teeth, necessitating the use of a wire leader. Stan Gibbs, using a popping plug he manufactures, hooked this one while fishing Nantucket Sound in Massachusetts.

top it off, they're a great challenge, having a stamina that borders on the unbelievable.

Surfmen and jetty jockies find they enjoy excellent sport when schools of bluefish chase small baitfish such as mullet, spearing, sand launce, mackerel, and other forage species into the wash. When bluefish feed, it's absolute mayhem, with gulls screeching and diving and excited baitfish leaping into the air to evade the snapping jaws below. This is the kind of scene both boatmen and surfmen enjoy, for the blues will readily strike most any lure tossed their way. Favorites include popping and surface swimming-plugs, metal squids, bucktail jigs, and stainless-steel jigs.

When the blues are holding in the depths, searching along the bottom for food, surfmen regularly make nice catches fishing with a single-hook rig on the bottom and baiting with menhaden, mullet, mackerel, or fillets of other fish.

In the open waters of bays and the ocean, bluefish readily respond to a chum of ground menhaden, at which time anglers baiting with chunks of menhaden, butterfish, or mackerel make excellent catches.

Trollers score too, and enjoy finest results when the fish are feeding on or near the surface, for then it's not necessary to add trolling sinkers to take the lures down. A good bet is to always keep a pair of trolling lines deep, and a pair on the surface, until you find the level at which the fish are feeding.

Deep-jiggers regularly take many bluefish, using both bucktail jigs and diamond jigs, especially in deep, swift waters where other methods prove impractical.

Blues provide sport from a ½-pound fish on a one-handed outfit in a coastal estuary, where they're called snapper blues, on up to 15- to 20-pound jumbo blues that test anglers and their tackle to the utmost in the open ocean.

Because of their extremely sharp teeth it's always best to use a wire leader, either single-strand stainless steel, or nylon-covered stainless-steel cable, for if you simply tie your hooks or lures directly to your line you'll find many of the blues will simply bite through it. Watch your fingers when handling blues, as their teeth can inflict nasty bites.

Blues are a fine table fish favored by many, although their flavor is rather strong for some tastes. They spoil extremely fast, and because of this it's best that you clean and ice them promptly after landing them.

BONEFISH

The bonefish has developed a reputation as being an extremely elusive adversary that moves from deep water onto shallow flats on a flooding tide to feast on shrimp, crabs, seaworms, and other food that it can root from the bottom. When in the air-clean water of the flats the bonefish is very cautious and is easily startled, especially by shadows and noise in a boat. It knows it is extremely vulnerable in the shallows and immediately heads for deep water when spooked, at a speed that defies description.

But the fact does remain that spin-fishing opened an entirely new dimension to bonefishing. For it enabled casters to deliver tiny ⅛- and ¼-ounce bucktail jigs to cruising fish with unerring accuracy. Where bone-fishing had been primarily the province of the bait-caster, and occasional fly-fisherman, spinning opened up this exciting sport to anyone who wanted to try it.

Never should anything heavier than a one-handed spinning outfit be used for bonefish, for tackle of this type provides maximum sport.

The most popular technique employed to land this grey ghost of the flats is to use a push pole and quietly pole across the shallow flats, looking for single fish, small groups, and even large schools that are rooting in the bottom, popularly called *tailing*, where their tails extend slightly out of the water as they root in the bottom searching for food.

When the fish is spotted, the angler on the push pole gets the caster in

This gives you some idea of how shallow the water is in which you'll find bonefish. Pete Perinchief hooked this large one while wading the flats in Bermuda. He released it moments after the photo was taken.

position and he presents a tiny bucktail jig to the fish, casting several feet ahead and to the side, so the lure will pass close to the fish as it is retrieved. The trick is to work the delta-winged bucktail jig slowly and to permit it to touch bottom just long enough to cause a swirl of marl or mud, thus resembling a tiny crab or shrimp scurrying about.

Bonefish are plentiful in the Florida Keys, but I've experienced the greatest fishing for them in the Bahamas, particularly at Joulters Cays, north of Andros Island, where there was a steady parade of bonefish of all sizes, ranging from 1 to 12 pounds. Sometimes the schools numbered a hundred and more fish. I've also fished the limited flats of the Virgin Islands and caught some big bonefish in Bermuda too. They're also found in Hawaii, in deep water.

In many areas anglers who don't wish to pole across the flats have found chumming to be an extremely effective technique. They simply anchor up on a good flat or along the edge of one, where bonefish regularly trade on the tide. They then toss out several handfuls of dime-size pieces of shrimp, seaworm, conch, or crab, and simply wait for the bonefish to move into the area and begin picking up the pieces of food resting on the bottom. When the bonefish move in, the spin-fisherman then casts either a tiny bucktail jig or piece of natural bait to the feeding fish.

Some anglers also use a whole shrimp or piece of conch to cast to cruising fish while they're being poled across the flats. Still others anchor in the channels leading to the flats and fish with a natural bait on the bottom and hook many fish moving onto the flats.

Bonefish are strictly a gamefish in the eyes of most anglers. Seldom do sportsmen kill this fine, speedy adversary that strips 100 yards or more of line from your reel in a single run. They catch them and promptly release them at boatside to fight another day.

CALIFORNIA HALIBUT

This big member of the flatfish clan is pretty much a stay-at-home, confining its movements to a range of fewer than 100 miles for the most part. It generally resides on sandy bottom, whether in deep water or shallow, even moving in close to the surf to feed if that's where the anchovies, grunion, and other baitfish are.

It's prized by Pacific-coast anglers because it is a delectable table treat. Surprisingly, however, most halibut are caught while anglers are fishing for other species, although those anglers who concentrate their efforts down on the bottom often come home with fine catches.

Anchovies form the major portion of the halibut's diet, and most are caught by fishing but a single live anchovy on a small hook, while using a rubber-cored sinker to take the rig down to the bottom. The boat drifts along with the current, covering as much area as possible, which usually assures a good catch.

Halibut do not always stay on the bottom to feed. I've observed them chasing through thick schools of anchovies on the surface and succeeded in landing several on small bucktail jigs worked with a whip-retrieve. I've also taken them by live-lining a live anchovy.

Down off Mexico I've frequently observed halibut swimming near the surface around the kelp beds, just cruising along, hoping to find an unsuspecting anchovy or other small baitfish.

There's a limited amount of trolling for halibut in shallow water. I suspect that if anglers trolled an anchovy down on the bottom much the same as Atlantic-coast anglers troll spearing or sand launce for summer flounders, they would improve their catches markedly. Because they feed almost exclusively on baitfish, halibut will also strike most any small lure that resembles a baitfish, including spoons, bucktail jigs, and metal jigs, fished deep.

CHANNEL BASS

The channel bass has a wide range, and is caught in substantial numbers from the Delmarva peninsula all the way to Texas. Called channel

Channel bass are a favorite of surf casters from the Virginia Barrier Islands to Texas' shallow beaches. When small, like this one, they're called puppy drum and redfish, when heavyweights, they're dubbed bronzebacks or red drum. A fine challenge for the spin-fisherman, most surf-caught channel bass are taken on natural baits fished on the bottom.

bass, bronzeback and red drum throughout the Middle Atlantic states, it takes on the name of redfish throughout Florida and along most of the Gulf coast. As a general rule the biggest channel bass, those from 35 to 50 pounds and more, are found off the Barrier Islands of Virginia and the Carolina Outer Banks. Gulf-coast anglers get many sizable fish too, but in the main their size does not compare to those found along the Atlantic, although many in the 20- to 30-pound class are landed each season.

The reds are basically an inshore feeder, with habits that in many ways closely parallel those of the striped bass. They frequent the open ocean along the surf, around inlets and breakwaters. They are also found in great numbers in rivers, bays, and estuarine waters. Channel bass are a favorite

Surfmen often carry all their channel bass gear in a shoulder bag such as this. Included in the bag are several spare rigs, pyramid sinkers, a knife, and several fresh baits. Baits included here are spot and mullet, both fine channel bass baits. Usually two baits are cut from each; the head section is the most durable.

of the surf caster, for they move into the breakers to root in the bottom for crabs and also feed on most any small fish they come upon. A basic fish-finder rig, or single hook-bottom rig employing a 7/o or 8/o Claw- or Beak-style hook is used by many casters, along with a heavy surf-spinning outfit. The most popular baits include chunks of menhaden, spot, mullet, or most any available baitfish, which are fished in the cuts and sloughs inside of the sandbars that parallel the coast of Virginia and the Carolinas.

The channel bass frequently will move into the big sounds and bays and search along the marsh banks for food. At such times shore-based casters extract a heavy toll of these fine gamefish, usually bottom-fishing with chunks of fish or even whole fish as bait.

During the spring of the year it's often possible to cruise slowly through inshore waters and spot huge schools of big channel bass swimming just beneath the surface. Sometimes the schools number a hundred or more fish, most weighing over 25 pounds. This kind of situation is made to order for the spin-caster. Favorite tackle for this kind of casting is either medium or heavy spin, with 20-pound-test or heavier line. Hammered stainless-steel jigs are the most popular, especially the Hopkins, in 2- or 3-ounce models, which can be cast long distances with ease. The trick is to approach the fish upcurrent, shut down your motor, and to drift with the current within casting range. The cast should go right into the school and be retrieved slowly and steadily. Whatever you do, don't approach the fish too closely with the boat, as you'll invariably spook them.

Trollers take many of these big fish using chromed spoons trolled deep.

With small channel bass, most often called redfish or puppy drum, you'll catch them in the surf, and in most bays and rivers throughout the South, on both the Atlantic and Gulf coasts. Most are caught while bottom-fishing with shrimp or chunks of mullet, using either a single- or double-hook bottom rig. When the redfish are schooling, the fishing can be fast and furious, and it's not unusual to catch a dozen or more on a tide.

I've caught many redfish when they were schooled while using a light, one-handed outfit and small bucktail jigs that I worked along the bottom on points of land where the reds were feeding. Here good sport may be had with artificials, but out of habit alone, most anglers employ natural baits.

Channel bass up to about 10 pounds are considered fine table fare, but most above that weight are returned to the water to fight another day, as the heavyweights have rather coarse flesh.

COBIA

Cobia are a real challenge to spin-fishermen seeking them along the Middle Atlantic coast south through Florida and along the Gulf coast. A brown-colored fish, having a profile much the same as a shark, the cobia is mistaken for a shark by many inexperienced anglers, particularly when it cruises along just beneath the surface. It's a fine gamefish, however, and a real brawler on the line, with a stamina lacking in many fish. It simply never seems to quit, even when boated.

Captain Charlie Sebastian unhooks a big cobia landed on a whole squid that was cast beneath the shadows of an oil drilling platform located in the Gulf of Mexico off Grand Isle, Louisiana. Cobia are an extremely strong fish and it's best to use heavy spinning tackle when you set your sights on them.

I've caught cobia at many widely separated areas, employing a wide variety of techniques. In the Chesapeake Bay I've employed live eels that were live-lined and permitted to settle into the depths. I've caught them around buoys marking entrances to channels in the Atlantic off Virginia and the Carolinas and on the southwest coast of Florida. The cobia show a marked preference for the shadows beneath channel markers and buoys, and often you can coax them into striking a bucktail jig, popping plug, blue crab, live eel, or pinfish cast in front of them. Sometimes your first casts will draw a blank, but repeated casting will often annoy these fighters that are not easily spooked, and suddenly they'll wallop your offering.

I've also caught quite a few while tied up to shrimp trawlers well offshore in the Gulf of Mexico. The trawlers cull their catch of shrimp around daybreak, after having trawled all night, and then shovel overboard broken shrimp, small fish, crabs and squid, and the cobia congregate to feed on the free meal being offered them. At such times you can easily score, for the fish get so engrossed in vying for the food being shoveled overboard that they'll immediately strike a small bucktail jig.

I've also scored around many of Mississippi's and Louisiana's offshore oil rigs.

Many boatmen along the Gulf coast build towers on their boats so they can cruise along slowly and scan a big expanse of water as they search for schools of the cruising fish.

Pier-casters also take a substantial toll of cobia, especially along the Gulf coast. The cobia frequently move in to feed on the grunts, hard-tailed jacks, pilchards, and many other small baitfish found along the beach and around coastal piers. Live baitfish usually draw the most strikes, but many are also taken on bucktail jigs.

Because most of the cobia you'll encounter will be big, strong fish, often weighing 25 to 50 pounds, it's wise to use heavy spinning-tackle, for the fish are extremely strong and take a long while to subdue.

Most anglers fillet cobia and skin them, and either bake the large fillets, or cut them into fish sticks and pan-fry them.

CODFISH

The codfish is fondly referred to as the winter king by anglers who fish for this plentiful bottom-feeder along the middle and north Atlantic coast. It spends the summer months in cool offshore waters, moving inshore during late fall, and stays until spring, providing fine bottom-fishing for anglers fishing from party and private boats.

Because you'll usually be fishing in deep water around clam beds, wrecks, or over broken, rocky bottom, it's most often necessary to use heavy spinning-tackle, although occasionally when the cod move in water 25 to 30 feet deep, and especially on sand bottom, medium-weight tackle may be employed with good results.

The favored method of catching cod is while bottom-fishing, either anchored up over a choice spot or while drifting over bottom known to hold these tasty bottom feeders. I usually employ a high-low rig, with a pair of 6/0 or 7/0 Claw-style hooks baited with half a big sea clam. Sometimes it takes a heavy sinker, fully 6 or 8 ounces, to hold bottom, hence the importance of a sturdy rod.

Codfish aren't spectacular fighters, but when you hook a 20- or 30-pounder you'll have your hands full getting it aboard on spinning tackle.

When the cod are really plentiful you can enjoy fine sport using either diamond or bucktail jigs and working them over wrecks or rocky bottom. Often you'll be rewarded not only with codfish, but pollock as well, which frequent the same grounds.

Occasionally codfish will move into the surf and even rivers in New England. Up in Maine I've caught small codfish on seaworms in the summertime in many bays and rivers. The small cod are fine sport on light tackle and, regardless of size, are excellent on the table.

CROAKER

The croaker derives its name from the fact it emits a croaking sound when first taken from the water. This in itself makes it a natural for the youngsters, who joy at this plentiful bottom-feeder that's easy to catch and makes noise when they land it!

They used to be plentiful along most of the Atlantic coast, but are now found in greatest numbers from the Chesapeake Bay south and along the Gulf coast. While not big, usually averaging from a ½ pound to 2 pounds, they make up in numbers what they lack in size.

Croakers are found in coastal bays, rivers, and along the surf, and they're great fun when taken on a light, one-handed spinning outfit. Most bottom-fishermen use either a single-hook rig with an egg-shaped sinker, or a small high-low rig. Number 6 or 8 hooks baited with a tiny piece of clam, shrimp, or piece of fish will bring strikes quickly if the croakers are around. The children can use a closed-face spin-cast outfit and have a ball with them.

Pier-casters also take many croakers, as do bridge-fishermen, for the fish tend to congregate around these structures, and it's not unusual during a good run to catch several dozen of these tasty bottom-feeders in a day's sport.

DOLPHIN

Dolphin are unquestionably one of the prettiest fish in the sea, and happily for spin-fishermen, they're found in all the warm waters of the world. Unfortunately, most dophin are caught quite by accident while fishing for marlin, wahoo, or other big gamefish. As a consequence much of the fighting ability of the dolphin is diminished, simply because they're caught on tackle far too heavy.

But the spin-fisherman who takes on the dolphin has what is unquestionably one of the greatest sport fish of the ocean to contend with. Dolphin seldom venture very close to shore, except where there is an abrupt dropoff, such as is found in the Bahamas, the Gulf Stream off Florida, and off the Baja peninsula. In most other areas he's a blue-water fish, found quite a distance seaward where the water is deep and clean.

Dolphin have a notorious habit of taking up station around any flotsam in an area. You'll find them congregated like cordwood at times beneath a weedline. A couple of planks, a tree branch, log or other debris floating on the surface will almost always hold dolphin if they're in an area. They'll also stick to the shadows beneath anchored lightships, oil rigs and marking buoys.

When the dolphin are in spots like these, they're naturals for the spin-

Milt Rosko unhooks a dolphin hooked by his wife, June, while she cast a bucktail jig to a weed line while fishing from Captain George Seemann's Mitchell II off Chub Cay in the Bahamas. Dozens of dolphin are often schooled up in a weed line or beneath some flotsam and provide hours of exciting sport on spinning tackle.

fisherman, for they're almost always responsive to lures. I've enjoyed best results while casting bucktail jigs to these fish, but have also scored with popping plugs. I know of many anglers who move close to a weedline and toss out several handfuls of diced fish to get the dolphin in a feeding mood and then ease out their baited hooks and enjoy fantastic action.

You can also enjoy fine sport with dolphin while trolling. Favored trolling lures include balao and mullet on the Atlantic and Gulf coasts, sardines and flying fish on the Pacific, and a good strip bait most anywhere. When the small dolphin—3- to 10-pounders—are plentiful in an area you can have a ball trolling a small feather or bucktail jig with a strip of pork rind, squid, or strip-bait cut from a fish.

Dolphin fillets are a real delicacy either broiled, baked, or pan-fried, adding up to a combination that's difficult to beat both on the line and the dinner table.

GREAT BARRACUDA

There are stories galore about barracuda, and the toothy one has built quite an envious reputation, although on balance it's not as vicious as it's purported to be. While not a fantastic gamefish, on medium-weight spinning tackle the barracuda will give a good account of itself and can provide you with many hours of fun.

They are found in tropical waters, especially plentiful in Florida and the Bahamas, but in greater numbers than one might expect along the Gulf coast. You'll find cuda in the open ocean, particularly around reefs and along the edge of a dropoff, where often they're so plentiful they're termed a nuisance by those anglers who are trolling for sailfish or marlin.

In the open ocean they'll readily strike a bucktail jig or popping plug worked above the reefs or along the weedlines, where they may be searching for food. Even with big barracuda, meaning those over 25 pounds, you won't need heavy tackle. On average the spin-caster will find medium-weight spinning tackle more than adequate for ocean fishing. The cuda will take a bait fished in a chum line, and it will also strike most any trolling lures, including whole baitfish, feathers, spoons, bucktail jigs, and plugs. Because barracuda usually stay near the surface, there's no need to use weight to take your lures deep.

On the bonefish flats you'll often find barracuda frequenting the same waters as bonefish. Most of the barracuda found in the shallows are small fish, ranging up to around 10 pounds in weight, but they're grand sport on a light, one-handed spinning outfit. When I'm bonefishing, I always keep a second rod rigged with a short wire-leader and a popping or surface swimming-plug. When I spot a pack of barracuda—usually three to eight fish— I immediately cast a plug to them and, as a rule, quickly receive a strike. When cuda hit in the shallows, they perform much better than when hooked in deep water. On the flats they'll jump repeatedly, frequently clearing the water a full 3 feet or more as they try to rid themselves of the plug.

You've got to handle cuda carefully, as they do have a vicious set of dentures. I always handle them with gloves, preferably getting a grip under their gills to hold them securely. Not favored as table fare, most are caught for sport only and usually released.

GROUPERS

There are literally dozens of species of grouper that reside in southern waters of the United States, off Bermuda, the Bahamas and the islands of the Caribbean, and southern Pacific waters. While essentially a bottom-feeder, groupers will often rise up from the ocean's floor to feed, occasionally coming right to the surface.

The groupers are generally thought of as bottom-feeders that are best sought with heavy conventional bottom-fishing tackle. But when taken on heavy gear they provide little sport. Thus spin-fishermen who set their sights on groupers have an opportunity of catching a tough, strong fighter that will test their skill to the utmost.

Perhaps the easiest method of catching a grouper is to employ a regular bottom-rig to send down a piece of fresh bait into the coral sanctuary where grouper most often take up residence, or around wrecks, oil rigs, and other broken, irregular bottoms that provide food and sanctuary. Grouper will take a wide variety of hook baits, including chunks of almost any fish, squid, shrimp, and conch.

If you're fishing in shallow water with little current, you can fish with a live pilchard, pinfish, or blue runner and enjoy excellent results by simply live-lining the baitfish and letting it down into the depths. Sometimes you may have to add a small rubber-cored sinker to the line to get the bait down. Rigged in this manner you can get by with light terminal-tackle, which makes for maximum sport. I seldom use a small hook while grouper-fishing, for even a 4- or 5-pound grouper has a mighty big mouth, which can easily accommodate a 6/0 or 7/0 Claw- or Beak-style hook.

By far the most sporting method of snaffling groupers is via deep-jigging, employing bucktail jigs to probe the depths where grouper reside. For shallow reefs and where there is a moderate current, you'll find 1- or 2-ounce jigs adequate. But where you want to probe depths of 150 to 200 feet or more you'll find that bucktail jigs ranging in weight from 3 to 5 ounces are necessary.

Keep in mind that groupers are an extremely strong fish and, while not spectacular, they can readily seek the sanctuary of the coral or other bottom obstructions where they reside, and when this happens, you'll usually experience a severed line as they cut you off. Thus, it is important that you use a stiffish-action rod with plenty of lifting power. I'd suggest sticking with 20-pound-test monofilament lines, for if you use lighter lines you'll simply lose an awful lot of fish and terminal rigging. A big, salt-water spinning reel with a heavy but smooth drag is absolutely essential if you expect to land most of the groupers you hook.

On occasion I've landed groupers on surface plugs such as poppers and swimmers, but in the main you'll receive far more strikes when probing the depths with bucktail jigs.

The grouper finds favor with southern anglers because in addition to being fine sport on rod and reel they are great table fare. When used as stock for a chowder they are delicious, as they are when baked or diced into grouper fingers and deep-fried.

My biggest problem when fishing for groupers in the tropics has been to identify the species of grouper I've landed. Among the most popular groupers with spin-fishermen are the Nassau, jewfish, rock hind, gag, yellowfin, black, princess, and red grouper, and you'll catch them from just a couple of pounds on up to tackle-testing brutes that weigh 50 pounds and more.

KING MACKEREL

The king mackerel rightly deserves the title king of the mackerel clan, for it is a most formidable adversary. Called kingfish through much of its range, it is an extremely tough fighter that may be taken in a variety of ways, including trolling, jigging and chumming and while drifting baits or casting.

I've caught small king mackerel on the southwest Florida coast while using a one-handed spinning outfit, but this was the exception. Most of the time the kings are big, and will test you and a medium-weight spinning outfit to the utmost. Going too light in this regard will simply minimize your sport, as these are big, powerful fish.

Most king mackerel landed by anglers fishing off the Carolinas through Florida, and along the Gulf coast, as well as in the Bahamas and other waters they frequent are taken on skip baits such as balao, mullet, or strip baits intended for billfish. When they strike a bait working on the surface,

A live pilchard fished on a float rig such as this is favored by many pier casters who fish for king mackerel. The hook is always fastened to a light wire leader, for king mackerel have extremely sharp teeth.

Bill Miller hooked this fine king mackerel while casting a bucktail jig into a chum line in the Gulf of Mexico off Fort Myers, Florida. These fish provide great sport on spinning tackle. For best results use a whip retrieve; it causes the jig to dart ahead and then falter, much like a wounded baitfish.

it is not unusual for a mackerel to leap fully 20 or more feet into the air. But once hooked, that's the last you'll see of it, for they are notorious for their deep-fighting tactics, and most of the battle will be beyond view.

Most spin-fishermen catch king mackerel while drifting either live or dead baits over reefs located just a short distance from shore, for the kings take up residence around such spots because there is always an abundance of food available. Blue runners are a fine bait, as are grunts, small jacks, pinfish, and most any small, active fish.

I've also landed many big kings while deep jigging with a heavy bucktail jig with a sparse dressing of mylar. The jig must be worked extremely fast, and this is where a big, fast-retrieve-ratio spinning reel comes in handy. Remember that kings often congregate in big schools, so once you encounter fish, stick to the general area, for usually you'll be able to continue scoring.

Kings readily respond to chum, although not too many anglers employ this technique, which is a natural for the spin-fishermen. Just find a spot where kings congregate, anchor up, and commence ladling overboard a chum of ground fish mixed with small pieces of fish and you'll soon attract the kings. I've often had literally dozens of the big, streamlined fighters swiftly gliding through the chum, often coming within a rod's length of the boat as they picked up the small pieces we ladled overboard. At such times they readily responded to small chunks of fish or any small baitfish. I've also hooked them on bucktail jigs and surface plugs at this time, and the strike to a popping or propeller plug is just as exciting as when they hit a skip bait.

King mackerel have extremely sharp teeth, and it's foolish ever to fish without a wire leader when they're in an area, for they'll immediately bite through monofilament.

Pier-casters fishing from ocean and Gulf-coast piers are often treated to exciting sport when schools of the big kings move right in close to the beach chasing blue runners, pilchards, jacks, and other forage species. At such times heavy surf-tackle is in order, with big spinning reels loaded with a minimum or 15- and sometimes 20-pound-test line. A live blue runner or small jack makes excellent bait, and will quickly be taken when a big school of kings invades an area.

They're a fine table fish, with flavor typical of members of the mackerel clan, and extremely tasty when delicately smoked.

KING SALMON

King salmon are a cold-water species found in substantial numbers along the California, Oregon, and Washington coastline, and which provide an excellent sport fishery, particularly for the spin-fisherman. They constitute the greatest majority, some estimate 90 percent, of the salmon caught by sport fishermen.

When they're moving through the major river systems in the Northwest, small-boat anglers fishing with herring take a substantial toll of these fine fighters, as do shore-based casters who use bottom rigs. Out on the broad, cold Pacific, trolling a cut herring or whole anchovy with a cannonball sinker-rig is the favored technique, but the heavy tackle required usually rules out spinning.

King salmon, popularly called Chinook salmon are a natural for the spinning enthusiast who is flexible and not set on using standard techniques that for scores of years have been employed to catch salmon. Salmon will readily strike lures, for they're regularly feeding primarily on small baitfish such as herring, anchovies, rockfish, and squid.

I've used a small bucktail jig with a plastic baitail while drifting over the grounds frequented by both king and silver salmon off San Francisco and off the Farallon Islands as well, and caught fish that were feeding 30 to 50 feet beneath the surface on anchovies. These were the same salmon that most trollers were fishing for with heavy tackle and cannonball sinkers.

Milt Rosko holds a fine pair of salmon he hooked on the Pacific coast; they are favorites with spin-fishermen who prefer light tackle to the old method of using heavy gear for trolling. The fish held in his left hand is a king salmon, the smaller one in his right is a silver salmon.

I would think the salmon would also strike diamond jigs and Hopkins lures worked vigorously at the levels they were feeding.

Still another interesting experience I had with salmon was to troll lures instead of anchovies or herring, and this too proved productive with small spoons, subsurface swimming-plugs and stainless-steel jigs. I believe the pattern of fishing with cannonball sinkers and cut herring or whole anchovies is so entrenched that few anglers ever want to try anything different. Here's where the enthusiastic spin-fisherman stands to enjoy fine sport by confining his effort with lures while both jigging and trolling in waters known to hold these fine gamefish.

Salmon are great sport on medium-weight spinning tackle, and they're truly a grand treat on the dinner table. Served by baking them whole, steaked or filleted, they're a gourmet's treat. Many anglers have their catch canned, and there too it makes a fine salad.

LITTLE TUNA

The little tuna is readily distinguished from other species of tuna and bonito by several pronounced black spots found adjacent to its pectoral fin.

It's found in the waters of Long Island and New Jersey, south to Florida, and along the Gulf coast, as well as in the Bahamas and the waters off Bermuda. An extremely plentiful fish, it is perhaps the most underutilized of the tunas, averaging 5 to 15 pounds, with a 20-pounder a respectable fish; many who have caught all species of tuna give the little tuna the nod when it comes to fighting ability, on a pound-for-pound basis.

Most little tuna are caught while trolling for either bluefin tuna or yellowfin tuna, and they readily strike the same lures used for other tunas, including cedar jigs, spoons, bone squids, feathers, and whole mullet, balao, and strip baits. They'll often move up close in the wake, but sometimes lines fished 100 to 125 feet back will enjoy best results, so it always pays to have a varied pattern.

Little tuna will readily respond to a chum of most any ground fish, as well as a chum line of tiny fry dropped overboard at regular intervals. I've caught them in the Bahamas and Bermuda while chumming for reef species, when we spotted them in the slick, but couldn't make them bite while using big baits and big hooks. As soon as we switched to delicate spinning tackle and tiny hooks concealed in the baits we scored.

I've also caught little tuna deep-jigging, which was extraordinary sport. The first time I did this was while aboard a party packet out of Pensacola, Florida. The fish surfaced around the boat, and while I couldn't catch them near the surface, when I sent the jig down into the depths I received strikes from these fish that were feeding fully 50 to 75 feet beneath the surface.

Bob Turnbull of Toronto, Canada, brought his favorite brook trout spinning tackle to Bermuda; he found that salt water fish really fight when he hooked this little tuna while chumming at the famous Three Sister Reef. The secret to catching these hook-shy fish in a chum line is to carefully conceal the hook within the bait.

Since that initial success with bucktail jigs I've used them at several spots along the Atlantic coast when little tuna were in residence and enjoyed surprising results.

Surfmen and pier-casters fishing from ocean piers also get a crack at little tuna—and an exciting chance it is. This happens frequently along the Outer Banks. During the late fall little tuna will invade the surf to feed on the abundance of tiny mackerel, mullet, spearing, sand launce, menhaden, and other baitfish that come close to shore. At such times surfmen often hook the little tuna on metal squids, especially lures such as the Hopkins. As you can appreciate, fighting a tuna from the surf takes an outfit that is in perfect condition. Many of these fish are lost because anglers apply simply too much pressure and break them off. It's best to let the fish have its head and take 100 or even 200 yards of line before trying to put the pressure on.

When you do see little tuna chasing bait in the surf make certain you use the fastest retrieve you can master. It's tiresome, but the little tuna simply will ignore a slow-moving lure.

As with most tunas, cooked fresh they're rather strong and not favored by many. They may be filleted, soaked in brine to bleach the flesh, and then pressure cooked, after which they make a rather tasty salad.

OCEANIC BONITO

The football-shaped oceanic bonito is a tough pelagic species that you're apt to encounter in most of the world's warm offshore waters. It's a fun fish to catch, yet surprisingly there is little specific fishing pressure for the oceanic, simply because offshore fishermen are concentrating on bigger game. But for the spin-fishermen looking for light-tackle sport, trolling for oceanic bonito can be a barrel of fun.

Indeed, I've spent many fruitless days offshore searching for big game, to no avail. But the oceanic bonito has saved many a day while fishing from stateside and foreign ports, simply because I always make it a point to sneak a light outfit along and fish a small feather or jig close astern. More often than not oceanic bonito will assault the small lures fished up close and pull an otherwise uneventful day out of the bag.

Most of the bonito you're apt to catch will be in the 5- to 10-pound class, although there are many husky oceanics topping 20 pounds roaming off-shore waters, and they'll really test you and your tackle if you employ medium-weight spinning tackle. The problem with oceanic bonito is they have a very soft mouth, and you've got to play them with a light drag and not apply too much pressure until they've become tired. Too heavy a drag pressure initially will often rip the hook right from their jaw.

They'll move into a chum line of ground fish, but are extremely wary, calling for a small hook tied directly to light monofilament line and a small whole baitfish.

I've landed quite a few of them in tropical waters while deep-jigging. They'll strike most any bucktail jig, especially those with a sparse dressing of sparkling mylar.

Whether you like them on the table or not will depend on your taste. They have dark meat and a rather heavy flavor.

PACIFIC BARRACUDA

The Pacific barracuda differs quite a bit from the great barracuda found on the Atlantic and Gulf coasts. The Pacific cuda is long and lean, and quite a bit smaller too, although it has a respectable set of teeth and provides the spin-fisherman with some exciting sport. Barracuda are especially plentiful along southern California and the Baja peninsula, roving along the shore-line and the kelp beds, feeding extensively on the small baitfish.

A technique found very effective by spin-fishermen fishing from small boats is to anchor just off from the kelp beds and to chum with live anchovies. Once a chum line is established, it's not unusual to see a dozen or more barracuda come boiling to the surface to pick off the helpless anchovies as they swim in tight circles on top.

Barracuda will strike lures readily, although it surprises me how few California anglers employ lures for them. On the whole, California anglers are more bait-oriented, and because they score well while chumming and baiting with live anchovies, they don't usually try artificials.

Pacific barracuda are a favorite of party boat spin-fisherman. This one, hooked aboard a packet that sailed from Ocean-side, California, was drawn from a kelp bed with the aid of live anchovy chum.

Streamlined and full of fight, the Pacific bonito is a favorite of small boat fisher-men who either troll or cast to these tough fighters. The bonito will also readily invade a chum line of anchovies, providing top notch sport on light spin-ning tackle.

I've frequently used 1- and 2-ounce chromed and stainless-steel jigs, which I've worked with a vigorous tip action, and had no difficulty getting repeated strikes. I've done the same with small bucktail jigs. Keep in mind that the Pacific barracuda is not a large fish, and is more readily hooked on a lure having small hooks than one equipped with large treble hooks.

They're a fine table fish, especially popular with the many party-boat anglers who chum extensively for them from most of the major fishing ports in southern California.

PACIFIC BONITO

The Pacific bonito virtually pave the surface of some areas of the broad ocean, particularly off southern California and especially off the Baja

peninsula. Whenever you see lots of gulls in the air and the water boiling as helpless baitfish leap into the air to evade hungry fish below, you can be reasonably certain it's bonito that are the culprits.

By far the greatest number of Pacific bonito are landed by anglers anchored off from the kelp beds along the coast and chumming with live anchovies. Often you can chum for an hour or more with little action, and suddenly, almost out of nowhere, the bonito appear and everyone on board is hooked up, as the bonito mercilessly strike anything that's moving.

Most anglers bait bonito with live anchovies, but during the past several years many anglers have realized the exciting potential of casting small chromed and stainless-steel jigs and bucktail jigs to these swift-moving fish. When using lures, it's important that you retrieve extremely fast and work your rod tip fast at the same time, so that the lure is flashing through the water erratically and excites the bonito into striking.

When the fish are on top chasing bait, often in schools numbering a thousand or more fish, you can troll along the edges of the school and enjoy exciting sport on medium-weight spinning tackle. Favored lures include trolling feathers, bucktail jigs, spoons, and bone squids, plus many of the new plastic baits made to imitate small fish and squid. Stick with lures 4 to 6 inches in length, as most of the fish you encounter are feeding on fish of this size. They'll range from 4 to 10 pounds in weight on average.

They're highly regarded as a table fish on the West coast, and many anglers leave their catch at the major coastal canneries located in port cities all along the coast. They're canned in small tins and have a little darker meat and richer flavor than albacore or bluefin tuna.

PACIFIC MACKEREL

Most Pacific-coast anglers pay little heed to the Pacific mackerel, primarily because it isn't much of a table fish. But having caught many Pacific mackerel at widely separated fishing grounds in the Pacific, I felt this species should be included in this listing simply because it's quite plentiful and easy to catch and provides a lot of sport for the spinning enthusiast equipped with a light, one-handed spinning outfit. Indeed, if you don't find the macks palatable, you needn't keep them; you simply enjoy the sport of catching them and return them alive to the water to fight another day.

I've caught most of my Pacific mackerel while chumming for other species using live anchovies, and I've seen many skippers get rather annoyed when hordes of the macks swarmed around the boat, taking the chum intended for more formidable game. But they readily took an anchovy hook-bait and provided action that might otherwise have been lacking.

The macks will also strike a wide variety of tiny lures. I've used diamond jigs, Viking jigs, and Hopkins jigs with good results. Toss a bucktail jig with a sparse dressing of mylar into a school of macks, and you'll hook one in an instant. I would suspect that using teasers would pay off too, much the same as they do for Atlantic-coast anglers fishing for mackerel.

PERMIT

I've caught all of the salt-water species discussed in this book on spinning, but permit have eluded my best efforts in the Bahamas and Florida Keys. But they are certainly worth inclusion, for they are considered by many to be one of the finest gamefish found in southern waters, testing one's angling prowess and skill to the utmost.

Permit are found both in deep water, especially around wrecks and reefs and inshore on the shallow flats, such as those frequented by bonefish and tarpon.

This husky permit was landed by George Seemann, baiting with a crab on a shallow flat as the permit moved in on a flooding tide to feed. Their broad, powerful bodies make permit a real challenge to the serious spin-fisherman.

Many anglers with whom I have spoken feel the ultimate in sport is catching the permit on the flats. For there he is a worthy opponent, extremely cautious and one that demands a perfect presentation. The favored technique employed by many veteran permit-anglers is to use a whole, live crab, and to pole along the flats looking for fish, or to stake out at a spot where permit regularly trade and wait for the fish. When a permit is spotted, the bait is presented ahead and off to the side, so as the fish moves along the bait can, if necessary, be slowly drawn into the range of vision of the fish. Shrimp are often used successfully, and many fine permit are taken on small bucktail jigs gently bounced across the bottom to simulate a small crab or other crustacean.

In deep water, permit are most often taken on bucktail jigs. But here it is a matter of knowing the grounds and being aware that schools of permit frequent the particular spot you plan to fish.

These are extremely powerful fish, shaped much like jack crevalle and amberjack, and they use their powerful bodies to good advantage. Veteran anglers may use light spinning-tackle, but the beginner should go with medium-weight for best results.

POLLOCK

Pollock are found in substantial numbers in the waters of New England and Long Island and in progressively fewer numbers as one heads south to New Jersey. They're also found off Maine and the Maritimes, often in numbers so great that you can get arm-weary from catching them.

While thought of as essentially a winter species, in many areas pollock may be caught the year round. In my judgment they are one of the finest sport fish available to small-boat anglers in the Northeast. They are very strong and on a pound-for-pound basis will outfight many fish with more respectable credentials.

Pollock like to take up residence on broken, irregular bottom, where there are rocks, or around wrecks, where they can feed on the abundance of small fish that take up residence in such areas. They'll also move into tide rips to feed, and it's not unusual to see pollock move into the surf from Montauk north, especially when the baitfish are in the wash and they're hungry.

The fighting pollock will readily strike artificials. Many are taken while using diamond jigs and Norwegian tube-teasers, whether jigged over known pollock haunts or while trolled through tide rips. I've caught many pollock on tube lures and a good number on trolling feathers and bucktail jigs.

Pollock are often landed while bottom-fishing with a high-low type rig, employing a pair of 6/o or 7/o Claw-style hooks and clams as bait.

Tailor the tackle to the fish in the area you plan to fish. On deep-water wrecks and on rocky bottom, a heavy spinning-outfit will be essential. Inshore while fishing for harbor pollock you'll find a one-handed outfit fine.

Pollock have a rather soft flesh, but when filleted and poached, broiled, or baked lightly they have a fine flavor.

PORGY

The porgy, popularly called scup in many areas, especially New England, is a plentiful bottom-feeder that often provides fun and enjoyment for bottom-fishermen all along the middle and north Atlantic coast. Average porgies weigh but a pound or two, but they make up in numbers what they lack in size, for it's often possible to catch several dozen of them in a day's fast fishing.

Porgies most often take up residence around mussel beds, for they gorge on the tiny black bivalves and such other staples as seaworms, clams, tiny crabs, and shrimp.

It's best to anchor up over a good porgy spot and stay put. Porgies tend to be motor-shy, and a great deal of movement on your part will tend to spook them, even if you're fishing in 30 to 40 feet of water. Once anchored, it's wise to take several big sea, or skimmer, clams and to crush them, shell and all, and drop them overboard around the boat. This sets up a chum slick down on the bottom, with tiny pieces of clam being carried away with the current, but the bulk of the clam staying right beneath your boat. When the porgies move in and begin feeding actively on the clams, you'll enjoy fine sport.

Most anglers use a basic high-low rig, with a pair of small Claw- or O'Shaughnessy-style hooks. For small sand porgies a number 6 or 8 hook works fine, while number 4 is favored for the bigger shad porgies. Bait with small pieces, as in this way the porgy can suck it into its mouth with little effort. Strike quickly, as they have a notorious habit of cleaning the bait from your hook quickly.

I've also attracted porgies to a chum line of grass shrimp, and they provided fine sport while using just a couple of tiny shrimp on a single hook drifted back in the chum line.

Porgies are rather bony, but if you take a few moments and fillet them and then pan fry them, they're fine table fare.

ROCKFISH

There are over fifty known species of rockfish inhabiting the waters off California, Oregon, and Washington. To the novice angler fishing for these

Leon Adams landed this average size rockfish with an anchovy bait just a short distance from California's rocky coastline.

Rockfish are plentiful. They provide fine sport on spinning tackle and are a treat on the dinner table.

tasty bottom-feeders it becomes as difficult to distinguish between species as is the case in identifying some species of groupers. Indeed, I've caught many species of rockfish on the West coast and classify myself among those who knew they caught a rockfish, but didn't know which kind. Identification isn't that important anyway, for rockfish are a plentiful, cooperative bottom-feeder that provides not only fishing fun, but is a fine table-treat.

Unfortunately, most rockfish are fished for in extremely deep water, usually depths ranging from 100 to 400 feet in depth. Because heavy sinkers are required to take the baits down and to hold them on the bottom in these depths, it proves difficult to use spinning tackle. However, there are many rockfish residing on the shallow slopes beginning right at the beach and extending offshore. It is in these shallows and off the inlets emptying into the Pacific that a lot of enjoyable fishing can be found for the spinning enthusiast.

In character with their name, rockfish are found mostly on rocky or irregular bottom. Spinning enthusiasts use either a single-hook bottom-rig or a high-low rig, baiting with live anchovy or, if they are not available, a dead anchovy, a piece of fresh squid, or salted mackerel. Because of the rock bottom it is best to anchor, otherwise you're apt to lose a lot of rigging, especially over shallow, rocky bottom.

Most anglers employ natural baits, but rockfish will take a small bucktail jig or a diamond jig, especially when they come up off the bottom to feed around the kelp beds, where there are an abundance of small fish. Here too, tailor the tackle to the fish. Using artificials in the shallows and fooling with 2- to 5-pounders can be fun on a one-handed spinning outfit. In deeper water, where heavy sinkers are necessary, and where the rockfish may weigh 20 to 30 pounds and even more, you've quite naturally got to move up to medium-spinning tackle or even heavy tackle to suit the conditions and fish.

Perhaps the favorite way most anglers prepare rockfish is to fillet them and then deep-fry the fasty fillets, chunks, or fish sticks of these tasty and extremely popular bottom-feeders.

SAND BASS

The sand bass found in such vast numbers along the coast don't make a lot of headlines, but they certainly do please a lot of fishermen. Weighing but 1 or 2 pounds on average, with a 3 or 4 pounder of bragging size, the sand bass frequent sandy bottom and the waters surrounding kelp beds. They populate an area that has a plentiful supply of food in great numbers and provide steady action for the chummer and bottom-fisherman.

Most sand bass are taken while anchored up and chumming with live anchovies. The sand bass readily come up from the bottom and from the dense kelp growth for any anchovies within range.

Because live anchovies are so costly, quite a few private boatmen grind up mackerel and other forage species for chum and find that it does a fine job of attracting the sand bass to their baits.

If you're fishing from a small, private boat, you'll find a one-handed spinning outfit ideal, resulting in maximum sport from these small scrappers. Keep your hooks and baits small. Number 2 or 3 Beak-style hooks are fine, honed needle sharp for quick penetration.

They're a fine table fish, which is one of the major reasons so many anglers sailing from California and Mexican ports seek them out and welcome them to their bag.

SILVER SALMON

This fine Pacific resident is the same salmon now found in our Great Lakes and popularly called coho salmon by fresh-water enthusiasts. It is somewhat smaller than its cousin, the king salmon, and is available in lesser numbers, constituting less than 10 percent of the total salmon catch made off California, Oregon, and Washington. They are caught in substantial numbers and provide sterling sport for the spinning enthusiast who seeks them out with medium-weight tackle.

Often the subject of identification between king and silver salmon is difficult from a distance, because their bodies are extremely similar. But all you need do is check the inside of their mouth, and you'll find that the silver salmon has a white fleshy lining over the crown of the gums where the jaw teeth come through, and the king has a dark, almost black lining.

Quite often silver and king salmon move together in the same schools, and on numerous trips I've caught both species using the same techniques, while trolling, drifting natural baits, and jigging.

Worthy of note is the fact that Great Lakes anglers have greatly improved upon many of the techniques used by Pacific-coast anglers, thus making it far more enjoyable to catch these fish in deep water with light tackle. They've developed effective downriggers, which take their lures deep without undue pressure on rod and reel, and when a strike is received the angler is free to fight his salmon without a heavy weight, and without losing his cannonball sinker or trolling planer, for it is attached to a heavy cable secured to a retrieving reel on the gunwale of the boat.

Most of the silver salmon you're apt to catch will average from 7 to 12 pounds and they'll be great sport on medium-weight spinning tackle. A favored technique is to troll spoons or whole anchovies or cut herring to locate the fish. Once you receive strikes trolling, you can then shut down your motors and drift over the area, working bucktail jigs at the level the fish are feeding, often down 30 or 40 feet beneath the surface. Plastic-tailed lead-headed jigs are still another fine lure for probing the depths.

Still another light-tackle way of catching these fine gamefish is to use a live herring or anchovy and to simply live-line it, using a small rubber-cored sinker to help take the bait to the desired level.

Bank-casters fishing at the inlets of the many rivers along the northwest coast take a heavy toll of silvers, usually bottom-fishing with fresh or salted herring baits on the bottom, employing a single-hook bottom-surf rig. Boatmen anchored in the rivers proper use the same technique, and when great schools of the silvers are moving through, it's not too difficult to score.

Ocean-caught silver salmon provide the best table fare, for they are prime fish that have fed extensively on the abundance of food in the ocean. Salmon are tasty no matter how you prepare them, with the larger fish usually steaked and either baked or broiled, while the smaller fish are barbecued whole or filleted and then smoked. Many natives have their catch canned, assuring a tasty salmon salad throughout the year.

SEATROUT

If ever there was a fish that's a natural for the spin-fisherman it's the seatrout. Popularly called by a variety of names throughout its range, including just plain trout, spotted weakfish, or southern weakfish, the seatrout is an inshore feeder that provides great sport for surf, pier, jetty, and bulkhead casters and those who do their fishing from small boats.

They're most at home in the quiet confines of coastal bays, rivers, and estuaries, where they take up residence in weedbeds and feed on the plentiful supply of shrimp and small baitfish.

They're strictly a one-handed-spinning-outfit fish for the most part, although where long casts are required some anglers of necessity use medium-weight tackle.

By far the most popular method of catching seatrout along the Middle Atlantic states south through Florida and along the Gulf coast to Texas is with a float rig. A long, thin float is favored, but most any type of float

Seatrout are favorites of Florida and Gulf coast pier casters. A pier landing net had to be used to get this beauty over the rail. The angler used a float rig and let the current carry the live shrimp bait away from the pier.

that suspends the bait at the desired level will do. The trick is to fish a live shrimp or minnow just off the bottom, and this may be easily accomplished by properly adjusting your float. The shrimp is hooked through its collar on a number-1 or 1/0 Claw- or Sproat-style hook so that it can swim actively. A minnow is hooked either through its lips or just beneath its dorsal fin, so it may swim freely.

Seatrout will also respond to chum, especially to the tiny grass shrimp found in so many coastal estuaries. By seining several hours and obtaining sufficient shrimp for chum, you can attract schools of the prettily hued fighters within a rod's length of your boat. Once the fish are in the chum line, you need only live-line several small shrimp back into the current, and you'll quickly receive strikes.

Shore-based casters most often employ a single-hook bottom-rig, casting it into a deep hole, or sluice along the surf, or from coastal jetties, where they wait patiently for the seatrout to move in. Strips of fresh squid are fine bait, and their fluttering action quickly attracts cruising fish. Small finger mullet are good too, as are chunks of soft or shedder crab.

Seatrout will readily strike lures, and it's great sport taking them on a light rod and small artificials. Tiny yellow bucktail jigs are a great lure, as are small Mirrolure plugs, both of which resemble the small minnows on which they feed. Seatrout seem partial to a yellow lure or lures having a golden color. With both jigs and plugs, a moderately slow retrieve, with a little bouncing of your rod tip to give the lures an enticing action, will quickly bring strikes.

When the seatrout are schooled up in the ocean or gulf, many anglers drift for them, using a high-low bottom rig and either fresh squid or shrimp as bait. At such times the seatrout will readily strike a bucktail jig worked down near the bottom or a diamond jig, particularly one painted yellow, that is jigged through the schools.

Seatrout have a delicate white meat that is delicious. Most anglers fillet them and leave the skin on, and either pan-fry or bake them.

SHAD

Included here because it's an anadromous species caught on all three coasts by salt-water anglers, the several species of shad, including the white shad, American shad, and hickory shad, plus the several species of herring that often share the same grounds, are excellent sport fish that are very much unexploited, yet can provide exciting action for the spinning enthusiast.

Shad and herring ascend coastal rivers each spring to spawn. At such times they hold in various areas of the rivers, usually where there is a strong current, before proceeding upstream to tend to their spawning chores.

At such times they're responsive to tiny lures and will provide exciting sport on spinning tackle, especially a one-handed light outfit.

A tiny lure called a shad dart and closely resembling a bucktail jig and weighing but ⅛ to ¼ ounce, is the lure most often used for the sporty shad. It's made of lead and has a small Claw-style hook molded into the lead head and just a few strands of bucktail tied to the hook. The shad darts are painted a wide array of colors, and as is the case with most color patterns, it's wise to have several on hand to suit the whims of the fish.

The most popular methods of catching the shad are casting or trolling. In trolling a small bank- or dipsey-style sinker is used in connecting with a three-way swivel to get down to the bottom. To one eye of the swivel a 3- to 4-foot leader is attached, and one shad dart is attached to the end of the leader, while a second dart is tied in dropper fashion about a foot up from the first. The rig is then trolled through the rips and eddies and the fast currents of the river where the shad and herring are holding in the current.

Shad provide great sport each spring as they ascend rivers on all three of our coasts to spawn. This one was landed on a shad dart trolled slowly in the brackish water of the Susquehanna River near Havre de Grace, Maryland.

Anglers who prefer to cast, fish either from the banks, or anchor their boats and then cast to productive-looking water. Shad aren't fast to take a lure. After a cast to likely looking water, a slow to moderate rate of retrieve, with a bouncing of the rod tip, produces best results.

Some anglers find that streaming their shad dart astern and simply jigging it in the current will bring strikes when the shad move through a rip.

In the open reaches of the ocean, just before shad and herring ascend coastal rivers I've enjoyed superb sport trolling several shad darts ahead of a stainless steel squid or bucktail jig. The big lures actually held the shad darts deep, and the fish struck the darts.

I've noticed that particularly in the spring just off practically any fresh-water river emptying into the ocean you'll often observe a lot of gull activity, and shad and herring will be feeding on tiny baitfish. Many anglers mistake the shad and herring for other species and use large lures and simply do not receive strikes. But put a shad dart over the side and you can often catch many of these fine fish.

Most of the herring caught on shad darts weigh from 1 to 2 pounds, but the shad will often weigh up to 5 pounds or more, and it's not unusual for either species to jump a dozen or even two dozen times before being led to boatside on light tackle.

Shad are extremely boney, but if properly filleted they're a real delicacy. Their roe should also be saved, for when boiled for a few minutes and then pan-fried they're a gourmet's delight.

SHARKS

During recent years anglers on all three of our coasts have discovered that sharks, once looked on with disdain, are capable of offering many hours of light-tackle enjoyment when more desirable species aren't available. There are literally dozens of different species of sharks, ranging from the princely mako shark that carries gamefish status, down to the lowly dogfish that is quick to take a bait intended for other species.

I've caught sharks at one time or another out of a great many ports on all our coasts. On medium or heavy spinning-tackle a shark in the 30-pound class will give you some exciting sport, and when you hook a big one that tops 100 pounds, you'll really have your hands full. While many of the species do not fight spectacularly, they are strong and endure, testing you and your tackle to the limit.

One of the most enjoyable ways to catch sharks is to anchor up in an area frequented by these streamlined adversaries and to establish a chum line. Many shark experts obtain blood from a slaughterhouse, and mix the blood with chunked fish and even ground menhaden, and they ladle overboard this odoriferous chum, which quickly attracts the fish.

Sharks on light spinning tackle provide exciting sport. Milt Rosko landed this big dusky shark, gaffed by Pete Perinchief, while fishing off Bermuda, using tackle that many anglers employ on small, freshwater species.

Terminal tackle should consist of a leader wire approximately 10 feet in length, for sharks have very coarse skin, and their body rubbing against the line would fray through it, hence the necessity of a long leader. An 8/0 or 10/0 forged shark-hook and a large baitfish are all you need. Most often the bait is drifted out in the chum line with a float, and you just wait until the sharks move in.

A word of caution. Sharks are extremely dangerous and stay alive for many hours after they have been removed from the water. Always cut your leader, and forget trying to recover the hook. The teeth of sharks can inflict serious injury. Even muscle tension in the jaws of a dead shark can inflict injury, so keep those hands and fingers away from a shark's jaw.

Some sharks, such as the mako and thresher, are fine table fish, and have a delicate flavor not unlike broadbill swordfish. Other sharks have dry, mealy meat and are not considered edible.

In our case we usually fish sharks for sport and, rather than bring them aboard, simply cut the leader when we get them alongside, thus avoiding the chance of injury by bringing a dangerous big shark aboard.

SHEEPSHEAD

The sheepshead is a bottom-feeder found along the southern Atlantic coast and along many areas of the Gulf coast. It takes up residence around most any kind of bottom obstruction, including rocky bottom, wrecks, dock pilings, mangroves, bridges, and wherever there is an abundance of marine growth on which it feeds.

Sheepshead gorge themselves on mussels, sand fleas, crabs, shrimp, sea-worms, and other bottom-food found close to their home. It is not a traveler, in that it will stick close to the mangroves or rocks, and if you're fishing open bottom just a dozen feet from these obstructions you may never receive a strike. Thus, the key is searching for good bottom, and anchoring directly above it.

The striped sheepshead are extremely quick, and it's absolutely essential that you strike them the moment you feel a hit. A second's delay is all it will take for you to have your bait cleaned from the hook.

Most Gulf-coast anglers use a single-hook bottom-rig with an egg-shaped sinker. Favored baits include sand fleas or a shrimp threaded onto the hook. Along the Atlantic a high-low rig is popular, with the aforementioned baits, and especially a small soft crab secured to the hook with fine rubber-ized thread.

The majority of the sheepshead landed from inshore waters weigh but a pound or two, but on seldom-fished wrecks it's not unusual to encounter 5- to 8-pound beauties that really test your skill.

The sheepshead is an Atlantic and Gulf coast bottom feeder that is found close to pilings, wrecks, rocks, and mangrove roots. It'll readily take a shrimp bait, small piece of crab, or sand flea fished on the bottom.

They're a fine table fish, small ones are most often pan-fried, while larger specimens are baked whole.

SNAPPER

For years anglers looked at snappers in the same light they did groupers. They used heavy tackle, big sinkers, and several baited hooks to get down to the bottom, after which they winched the snappers aboard unceremoniously, and with little sport involved.

With the advent of spinning the techniques used for snapper fishing began to change, for anglers found that most of the many members of the snapper clan would take an artificial. As deep-jigging grew in popularity, spin-fishermen found great sport in catching snappers, ranging from the small, pretty yellowtail snapper to the big, broad, and powerful dog snapper, popularly called cubero.

With snappers it's a matter of tailoring your tackle to the particular situation. In mangrove-lined creeks of Florida and the Bahamas the mangrove and grey snapper are fine targets for the angler equipped with a light outfit, as are the yellowtails found on the inshore reefs. But as one moves offshore over deep reefs, where the water may be 100 to 200 feet and even deeper, then medium and heavy spinning-tackle must be brought into play for the popular red snapper, button snapper, dog snapper, and the many other deep-water members of the clan.

Bucktail jigs dressed with mylar turn most snappers on, for you must remember that snappers are often feeding on small fish, and the dancing jig closely resembles a struggling baitfish in the depths.

Spinning tackle with its fine monofilament line, even if you employ 20-pound test for bottom-fishing, enables you to use a rather small sinker to get your baits deep. Rather than constantly be working a jig many anglers elect to tie on a high-low rig and send it down into the depths with chunks of mullet, squid, or shrimp as bait, and the snappers readily cooperate.

Most snappers will move into a chum line, too. I've frequently chummed mangrove and grey snappers inshore, and yellowtails over the shallow reefs. I've also seen snappers come up 100 feet from the bottom while we were anchored up and chumming for other species in both the Bahamas

The red snapper being unhooked here by Herb Schoenberg was landed while fishing a chunk of balao bait on a deep reef by June Rosko. It is but one of many species of snapper found in tropical waters, almost all of which are highly regarded table fare.

and the Gulf off Louisiana. At such times the big snappers are great sport on spinning tackle.

Almost all species of snapper are delicious. They're usually filleted, although many anglers like to bake the large ones.

SNOOK

Anglers who fish for snook in Florida and along the Gulf coast look to this single-striped adversary as the southern counterpart of the striped bass. Its habits are much the same. It's found in the back reaches of mangrove estuaries, in swift flowing rivers, passes that empty into the ocean and gulf, and along the surf, too.

The snook will readily strike a wide variety of artificials, including plugs, bucktails and spoons, but each season sees great numbers of these fine gamefish taken on a variety of natural baits—most notably live pinfish fished on the bottom, and live shrimp drifted through their lair.

Unquestionably the most demanding snook fishing is in the Everglades where huge snook often take up residence beneath the overhanging mangroves. In order to entice strikes you've got to present your plug right within inches of the mangrove cover and tease the fish into striking.

During the spring of the year when snook are most active and trading through the passes that empty into the Gulf of Mexico, the favorite method of catching them is to employ a live pinfish hooked through the lips with a 6/0 or 7/0 Claw-style hook and an egg-shaped sinker, fishing the rig right on the bottom in areas where snook trade on the tides to feed. Often schools numbering several dozen fish will swarm into an area and it's not unusual for every angler on board to hook fish simultaneously.

But, as with many species, there are times when many hours and skillfully presented baits or lures are all that will bring a fish to gaff. The snook is a fish made to order for the shore-based and inshore spin-fisherman, and a great treat on the dinner table, too.

SPANISH MACKEREL

The Spanish mackerel is to the Florida and Gulf-coast angler what the Atlantic mackerel and the Pacific mackerel are to anglers where both of these species are caught. They are very similar in habits and size, in that they travel in big schools, average out at a couple of pounds apiece, and are usually very cooperative.

When the macks are feeding on top, you'll usually see lots of gull action and by drifting along and casting a small bucktail jig into the feeding fish you'll get strikes fast. A one-handed spinning outfit is perfect for Spanish

Spanish mackerel are favorites of small boat fishermen, pier casters, and bridge fishermen in southern coastal waters. This one was landed from a pier in Clearwater Beach, Florida, using a float rig and a live pilchard as bait.

macks, and if there aren't too many boats in an area you can also score with them by slowly trolling, using a small trolling sinker to get your spoon, feather or bucktail jig down deep.

Pier- and bridge-fishermen also enjoy bonanza sport when the macks move in around the structures to feed on the pilchards and other baitfish that often congregate there. At such times the macks will take most any small baitfish, including pilchards, the many silvery baitfish found in southern waters, shrimp, and small pieces of fish. Lots of pier- and bridge-casters employ a small float on their line, which suspends the bait at the desired level, and then just let the rig drift out with the current until they receive a strike.

Spanish mackerel will also respond to chum. Ground menhaden is favored, but you can dice up most any fish and set up an effective chum line that will bring swarms of mackerel within range. Many veteran casters won't use the chum to attract the fish, but when a school moves into an area they immediately chum in order to get the fish in a feeding frenzy and hold them in the area.

A rather heavy-flavored fish, but one which finds praise from those who like its rich meat.

STRIPED BASS

The striped bass is native to the Atlantic coast, but in the years 1879 and 1881 between 400 and 500 stripers were transported from the Navesink River in New Jersey to the Pacific coast. In the waters of San Francisco Bay they thrived and multiplied, spreading north to Oregon. As a result, both Atlantic and Pacific-coast anglers include the striped bass as one of the most popular of game species.

What makes the striper especially popular with spin-fishermen is that it's basically an inshore-feeder, confining most of its activity to bay, river, and estuary waters and inshore in the open ocean, along the surf and around rocks, jetties, and breakwaters. Sport fishermen catch them from but a couple of pounds on up to heavyweights of 60 pounds and more.

The striper is regularly taken on a wide variety of lures and natural baits. When forage species aren't very plentiful, stripers spend much of their time searching along the bottom for food, at which times various seaworms, such as sandworms and bloodworms, produce fine results. Crabs, clams, shrimp, and squid also bring strikes as the bass search for food. At these times the various surf and bottom-fishing rigs discussed earlier may be used effectively.

When baitfish are plentiful the stripers will respond to either live or dead baits, providing they are presented in as lifelike a manner as possible. Menhaden, popularly called mossbunker along much of the Atlantic coast, are an especially popular forage species, as are mackerel, herring, mullet, and common eels, while Pacific-coast anglers find that sardines and anchovies produce good results. Although the bait needn't be alive, it is important that it be fresh, and fished so that it looks natural. Surfmen and jetty jockies swim their baits in close to the rocks or in sluices and eddies where stripers congregate to look for food. In passes, inlets, or breachways, the spin-fisherman can cast his natural bait out into the swirling tide rips, where it will swim about much the same as other baitfish trapped in the current, until found by a hungry striper.

Boatmen are at a decided advantage in many cases, for they can move from spot to spot more readily, until they find an area where the bass are feeding, and then either cast or drift their baits through the area.

The ultimate in striper sport is casting artificials to stripers, and here the spin-fisherman has a wide variety of lures at his disposal. Plugs are perhaps the most popular striper lure of all, for in the main they resemble a baitfish and when bass are chasing baitfish it's difficult to top them. Both surfmen and jetty jockies, as well as boatmen, employ the same type plugs. Surface swimming plugs, propeller models, poppers, flap-tails, and darters bring exciting surface-strikes when the linesiders are feeding on top, but

Striped bass, favorites of anglers on both coasts, are also occasionally caught in river systems emptying into the Gulf of Mexico. Many have taken hold in fresh waters too, making them a favorite target for spin-fishermen. Here Frank Woolner, one of America's best known striper fanatics, gaffs a schoolie while working off a stretch of beach on Cape Cod.

subsurface swimmers and darters turn the trick when the bass retreat into the depths to feed.

Bucktail jigs are still another extremely effective striper lure. They come in a wide variety of sizes, ranging from tiny quarter-ounce models that resemble a tiny baitfish or shrimp to 3- or 4-ounce models designed to probe the depths. Every spin-fisherman should keep a supply of these in his kit for both boat and shore use, for often this bottom-bouncing lure will bring results when all other lures fail, especially where currents are swift and the water is deep, and the bass are hugging the bottom waiting for food to be swept their way.

Rigged eels are still another popular striper lure. While not a lure in the strict sense of the word, the eel is rigged on a small block-tin squid and used in the same way that you'd employ a metal squid.

There are also literally hundreds of models of metal squids that regularly produce stripers along both coasts. Many vintage squids were molded of block tin, but today's modern counterparts are made of stainless steel, or chromed or nickel-plated brass, or lead. Some are fished plain, while others are dressed with feathers or bucktail or their action enhanced with a strip of pork rind. They're an especially productive lure with rough or dirty water, for they have an enticing action and work deeper than many other lures.

Many stripers are taken while trolling, and for light trolling the spin-fisherman can use an outfit tailored to the size of the fish in residence and the type of water he's fishing. But for deep water or where wire or lead-core lines are used by the troller to probe the depths it's far better for the spin-fisherman to switch over to tackle designed specifically for trolling.

Without question the striped bass, called rockfish, rock, striper, squid hound, greenhead, and other local names along many areas of the coast, is right up on the top of the list as being the spin-fisherman's most popular gamefish in the sections of coastline where it is found.

SUMMER FLOUNDER

Summer flounders, popularly called fluke in some sections of their range along the middle and north Atlantic coast, are one of the most sought bottom-feeders. Like their close cousin, the southern flounder that is found from the middle Atlantic coast south and along much of the Gulf coast, they're relatively easy to catch and in some areas quite plentiful. Of course, their popularity is due in great part to their being one of the most delicious fish in the sea. Most that you'll land will weigh from 1 to 4 pounds, although fish over 10 pounds are not uncommon.

For our purposes here we'll discuss both the summer flounder and the southern flounder, as for angling purposes they're practically the same, and only a trained ichthyologist can tell them apart.

Few people think of the flatfishes as being voracious feeders, but they are, and I think that by making this clear from the start you'll ultimately catch more of them. They feed extensively on small, live fish, primarily forage species, but they do not hesitate to take the young of any species. They also feed on squid, shrimp, crabs, and any other food found along the bottom. While they usually lie almost buried in the sand as they wait for food to be carried past their lie by the tide, they are not adverse to swimming right to the surface to chase baitfish.

The most popular method boatmen employ for summer flounders is to

Summer flounders, popularly called fluke in many areas, are favorites of Atlantic coast spin-fishermen. Milt Rosko, Sr. landed this beauty while fishing with a strip of fluke belly bait off the sand beaches of Sandy Hook, N. J. Salt water killies are still another popular summer flounder bait.

drift live minnows, spearing, sand launce, smelts, strips of squid, or fluke belly over sandy bottom, as well as moderately rocky bottom with lots of sand patches between it. This movement of the boat by wind and tide keeps the bait moving, and you cover a lot of area.

Usually a single-hook rig with a long leader is used, simply because it is less apt to tangle than would be a two-hook rig while drifting. Some anglers use a small spinner on their leader just ahead of their bait, which acts as an attractor. The most popular hook style is a long-shanked Carlisle, with a small bait-holding O'Shaughnessy hook attached to the Carlisle near its eye. The small hook holds the head section of any bait you're using, thus putting the primary hook in the center of the bait, which assures a fluke immediately getting the hook in its mouth as it takes the bait.

While drifting does produce a lot of fish, when fluke are in water less than 15 feet in depth, I much prefer to troll, especially if I'm fishing from a small boat with just a couple of friends. By trolling I cover a lot more territory than when anchored or drifting, and as a result I catch far more fish.

A key point, whether drifting or trolling, is to hesitate when you initially feel a flounder pick up your bait. Give it plenty of time to take the bait, and you'll be certain to hook it.

Surfmen and jetty jockeys take many flounders, as do pier-casters and bridge-fishermen. The key to their success is in using the same basic single-hook rig used by boat-fishermen, but to constantly cast and slowly retrieve their bait across the bottom, covering as much bottom as possible, using a scattergun casting-pattern. By using this approach you're certain to bring the bait past more hungry flounders than were you to permit it to rest motionless on the bottom.

As for eating qualities, there are few fish that will top them. I usually fillet all of our fluke, taking two fillets off the top and two off the bottom, and then skin them. Pan-fried, they're a summertime treat that just can't be beat.

SURFPERCH

Pacific coast surfmen enjoy fishing for the nineteen members of the surfperch family found along their shoreline all year round. The surfperch are plentiful, and can almost always be depended upon to provide sport and a fine meal. They account for over 50 percent of the surf catch of Pacific-coast anglers.

Surfperch move very little, and once you determine an area has a population of surfperch, you can most often consistently score there.

Medium-weight tackle is usually more than adequate for surfperch, as a long cast isn't required. You'll find, however, that many anglers use heavy surf-tackle simply because they can handle a heavier sinker when the surf is rough, and they find the heavier outfit enables them to reach out a good distance without too much effort.

Surfperch live and feed along the surf for the most part, feeding on tiny fish, seaworms, mussels, shrimp, squid, and small pieces of almost any fish.

Most anglers use a single-hook rig when after surfperch, but many find a basic two-hook rig, with one hook tied to a 24-inch leader and the second hook tied to the leader dropper-fashion is a good way of presenting two baits in the surf. Remember that these fish only average a pound or so in weight, and by using a small hook and small bait you'll catch more of them.

While I've never tried it, I've heard of a few anglers who have used a light one-handed outfit when the surf was calm and employed tiny ⅛- and ¼-ounce bucktail jigs with good results when the fish were in close and scouring the bottom for a meal. It could be great fun, and warrants your time if you live close to a surfperch area.

All of the nineteen surfperch are considered fine table fish, most often filleted and pan-fried.

TARPON

The tarpon is perhaps the finest inshore gamefish available to a large segment of the angling public. It ranges in limited numbers from Virginia's Barrier Islands south to Florida, through the Keys, and along the entire Gulf coast, down through Mexico's east coast. It sticks close to shore, and it's not unusual to see fish over 100 pounds well up in coastal rivers where the water is brackish. Sometimes the tarpon will travel alone, but I've witnessed schools of several hundred fish, all weighing over a hundred pounds, moving through the channel at Boca Grande Pass on Florida's southwest coast.

Tarpon of all sizes are great sport for the spin-fishermen, whether they're the tiny 2- to 10-pounders found in the ditches that parallel the roads in the Everglades, or the heavyweights found in Florida Bay.

Anglers employing natural baits most often use live pinfish, squirrelfish, grunts, and other small fish, or whole, live blue crabs. When the tarpon are showing on the surface, the bait is cast directly into the school of fish, and the tarpon is given ample time to get the bait well back into its mouth, at which time you can close your bail and set the hook. Tarpon have a big mouth and many regulars use a 7/0 or 8/0 forged hook that has been filed needle sharp to penetrate the tough, bony jaw of a tarpon. It's wise to use a couple of feet of 50- to 80-pound-test leader material between your line and the hook, as through repeated jumping a tarpon will often fray right through lighter leader material.

When the fish aren't on top, anglers use much the same baits and drift them through the depths of passes, and through known movement areas of the tarpon, specifically the routes the schools take as they move back and forth with the tides looking for a meal. The difference in rigging is that a throw-off sinker is used. This is a sinker with a piece of soft copper wire molded through the middle of it. The soft wire is wound around the swivel between line and leader and takes the bait down deep near the bottom.

When a tarpon is hooked and begins jumping, the soft copper wire quickly slips off, and the sinker is literally thrown away as the tarpon jumps.

Pier-casters and bridge-fishermen often want to keep their baits at a level 5 or 6 feet beneath the surface, and many of them employ a large plastic float to do so. The bait is lowered from the bridge or pier, and allowed to be carried with the current away from the structure and to swim as freely as possible, hopefully until a tarpon spots it.

When tarpon move onto the shallow flats of the Florida Keys, they provide exciting sport for plug-casters. This is a waiting game for the most part, where small-boat anglers stake out at key locations and wait for the tarpon to move through, at which time popping plugs and surface swimmers are brought into play. It's exciting sport, with but one fish hooked for every five to ten strikes, simply because it's so difficult to get the hook into the tarpon's bony jaw.

Trollers also account for many fine tarpon. Big subsurface swimming plugs and spoons are the favored lures. As they are trolled they are held several feet beneath the surface with torpedo-shaped trolling sinkers.

Tarpon are considered a gamefish by most who fish for them, and by far the great majority are released at boatside to fight another day, as they have little food value.

TAUTOG

The tautog, popularly called blackfish in many parts of its range, is what I like to call the northern counterpart of the sheepshead. It has many of the same characteristics, in that it takes up residence around broken, irregular bottom, rocks, wrecks, and bridge and dock pilings. It feeds extensively on mussels, crabs, shrimp, seaworms, clams, and anything else it can rip off the bottom.

It's lightning fast as it strikes a bait, which has lead many anglers to say that you almost have to strike it before it strikes the bait in order to set the hook. While this is an exaggeration, it does point out the respect anglers have for this fast-striking fish.

Available from the Virginia Capes north to New England, blackfish are for the most part underfished. It's safe to say that practically every rockpile along the coast has a few tautog living around it, and this applies to jetties and bulkheads, too.

The key to catching tautog is fishing your bait right in among the rocks where they live. Most anglers tie their dipsey or bank sinker directly to the end of their line, and then tie in a single hook directly off the line on a dropper loop. This minimizes terminal tackle that might get fouled in the rocks.

Favored baits include sand bugs, pieces of soft crabs, fiddler crabs, green crabs, seaworms, and shrimp. The tougher the bait the better, and many black-fishermen secure their bait to the hook with rubberized string, simply so a 'tog can't pull it off too easily.

Boat fishermen usually use medium-weight tackle, as blacks average from 1 to 5 pounds, but there's always the possibility of a 10-pounder or larger. Jetty casters most often use heavy tackle, as it's necessary to quickly haul the fish away from the rocks.

When skinned and baked, tautog have a fine flavor.

WEAKFISH

Had this book been written a couple of years earlier, I suspect I wouldn't have included this listing of weakfish because for almost a score of years the weakfish virtually disappeared from the waters of the middle and north Atlantic coast. Many factors contributed to the decline of the weakfish, but miraculously it made a fantastic recovery, and in just a few years time the fishery has bounced back, and this species is now providing coastal anglers with phenomenal sport.

Weaks, often called squet or squeteague in the northern part of their range, are a natural for the spin-fisherman. They basically are an inshore species, and average from 1 to 4 pounds in weight, although during the season I'm writing this book many 8- to 10-pounders have been landed, and it's entirely possible that within a couple of years weakfish in the 10- to 15-pound class may be landed.

Boatmen take a substantial toll of weakfish by casting with small bucktail jigs such as the Upperman, and on Mirrolure plugs, both of which are fine weakfish lures. These lures are especially effective when the blues are in bays and rivers, gorging on small baitfish and shrimp, and especially when the fish are on top, chasing bait.

You can troll these lures when there is no great concentration of fish in evidence, and just pick away at fish that are feeding in the depths. Trollers use small swimming plugs, bucktail jigs, metal squids tipped with tail-hook pork rind, and bucktail or feather teasers fished just ahead of these lures.

When the fish are schooled up in bays and rivers, chumming is an extremely popular method of taking these fish. All you've got to do is seine a couple of quarts of shrimp, set up a chum line of the tiny grass shrimp, and drift your baited hook back in the slick, impaling two or three of the small shrimp on your hook. When the current's strong, use a tiny rubber-cored sinker to take the bait down a bit, or use a float if there's little current, and you'll have little difficulty making a nice catch.

When weakfish are in an area they're sometimes spread out, and at such

While working along the edge of a channel, Bob Rosko used a bucktail jig bounced along the bottom to hook this fine weakfish. On spinning tackle weakfish of this size provide exciting sport.

times many anglers use a single-hook bottom-rig with a 3-foot leader and Sproat- or Claw-style hook, drift a sandworm or strip of squid along the bottom, and score handsomely.

Pier-casters, surfmen, and jetty jockies also make many fine catches using the same lures as boatmen. Fishing with natural baits such as seaworms, squid, or pieces of soft or shedder crabs also brings good results. Sometimes it's wise to add a tiny cork—about the size of a dime—to your leader when using a bottom-rig in the surf, as this keeps the bait just off the bottom and moving in an enticing manner with the current.

Weakfish are a fine table fish, with light, tasty meat. We like to fillet them and then bake the tasty fillets for just a short while so as not to dry them out.

WHITE SEA BASS

The white sea bass is a favorite of southern California boat anglers. A fine, powerful, big fish, the white sea bass is a challenge to the angler armed with spinning tackle, for it's not unusual to encounter heavyweights weighing from 25 to 50 pounds and more.

They frequent open, sandy bottom as a rule, but you'll also find them around the perimeter of the many kelp beds along the coast, for they know the kelp holds an abundance of small forage species.

In the main, white sea bass feed on anchovies, sardines, mackerel, squid, and a variety of other forage species and the fry of many. They respond very well to chum, and in recent years night fishing for them from party boats has become popular in many areas.

Often a light hung over the gunwale attracts huge schools of squid, some of which are dipped from the sea with the aid of a long-handled net or they are jigged with a hook made expressly for snagging squid, after which they are used as hook baits.

White sea bass also respond to hook baits of lively anchovies and sardines, and many move in with other species. Frequently an angler will find he's hit a mixed bag of white sea bass, yellowtail, sand bass, halibut, and bonito. I've experienced this several times while fishing the Todos Santos

A lively anchovy or sardine fished near the kelp beds invariably coaxes strikes from white sea bass like this beauty landed off Baja California. On medium weight spinning tackle the strong fighters will test your tackle and skill to the limit.

Islands off Mexico, where the water was swarming with fish, and you just never knew which species was going to take your anchovy next.

Trollers account for a few white sea bass, and I suspect if more anglers trolled for them there could be many nice fish landed. They'll take spoons and jigs, and are no doubt attracted by the brilliant, flashing action of these lures. Because they're usually in rather shallow coastal waters, it would be necessary when trolling to fish long lines at a moderate speed, keeping the lures well back out of the wake.

A fine table fish, most often steaked and then either baked or pan-fried.

WINTER FLOUNDERS

From the Chesapeake Bay north to Maine, winter flounders virtually carpet the bottom of coastal bays and rivers during the fall, winter, and spring and provide bottom-fishermen with exciting sport. I say exciting in perspective, because I'm talking about a fish that averages from ¾ to 1½ pounds. When you catch a 2- or 3-pounder it's a bragging-size fish.

Winter flounders are extremely plentiful, and when you pick a nice sunny day to go fishing, it's not unusual to catch several dozen of the fat, tasty

While certainly not an exciting fighter, winter flounders are extremely plentiful and lots of fun to catch on light spinning tackle. They're especially popular with Atlantic coast sportsmen for they're available during the cold-weather months when more formidable game is not available.

bottom-feeders. They're fun to catch on a one-handed spinning outfit, but along the seacoast many anglers use a closed-face spin-cast outfit, and find it's a perfect combination that makes for fun fishing, even with this smallish bottom-feeder.

Favored bottom-rigs include either a flounder spreader, which fishes two hooks directly on the bottom, or a multihook rig, which fishes a total of either two or three snelled hooks off a single leader, all of which rest on the bottom. Long-shanked number-8 or number-9 Chestertown hooks are best. Keep them honed needle-sharp for quick penetration into the small, rubbery mouth of the flatfish.

I prefer bloodworms as bait when flounder-fishing, but I've made many nice scores using sandworms, tiny pieces of clam, mussel, and even ordinary earthworms. Make certain to keep the baits small, as flounders have very small mouths.

The winter flatfish will respond readily to a chum of ground menhaden, minced clams, or mussels, sent to the bottom in a chum pot. The tide will carry the ground food right along the muddy bottom frequented by flounders and attract them from a wide area to right beneath your boat.

Because they're small, many anglers pan-fry their flounders whole. I usually take a few extra minutes and fillet them, which makes for a delicious meal.

YELLOWTAIL

The Pacific yellowtail is indeed one of the favorite species of party-boat anglers and private boatmen alike. It's a challenge on any tackle, and especially on spinning tackle, for it is a member of the jack family and an extremely strong fish that takes even an experienced angler a long time to land. It's found from Monterey Bay south to Cape San Lucas, Baja, and throughout much of the Gulf of California.

Most of the yellowtail encountered by sport-fishermen weigh from 7 to 20 pounds, which is a perfect size for a medium-spinning outfit.

There are several ways in which yellowtail are taken. Fishing with live baits such as anchovies and sardines is by far the most popular, especially around the offshore islands off Baja, as well as around the inshore kelpbeds, where the yellowtail are constantly looking for a meal.

Once you get the yellowtail boiling to the surface for anchovies, the action can really heat up as the fish get in a feeding frenzy. They're not dumb, however, and you've got to present a bait while using a light line and small hook. Many spin-fishermen find that by using 15-pound-test line they hook far more fish than anglers using conventional gear and heavier 20- or 30-pound-test lines.

The California yellowtail is a tough, streamlined fighter that's caught chumming, jigging and trolling. It is especially popular with party boat anglers sailing from California and Baja ports.

There are quite a few yellowtail to be caught while trolling too, although there isn't too much trolling pressure for the yellowtail, simply because chumming usually produces best. But if you can find an area of seacoast populated with the yellowtail you can usually do quite well if you work the area alone, without a lot of other boat interference to spook the fish.

Trollers take their fish on bone and plastic squids, trolling feathers, spoons, and on some of the newer plastic baits that are made to resemble sardines, flying fish, and squid.

While great on a line, the yellowtail is also great on the dinner table. Some fillet the yellowtail, removing the stronger, dark meat, and preparing it either baked or broiled. It's also delicious smoked.

MANY SPECIES NOT MENTIONED

Throughout this book we have tried to include the major species that we felt were of prime interest to spin-fishermen throughout the United States.

Of necessity we've had to omit a lot, simply because there are just so very many, in both fresh water and salt water, all of which are fair game for the spinning enthusiast.

There are many techniques we've covered on the species which we have discussed which are quite adaptable to other species. The yellowfin tuna, as an example, may be caught using many of the techniques used for bluefin, blackfin, and little tuna, but because of the limited range we did not include the game yellowfin. Such is the case with many other species we have not included. But by using this information wisely, we feel you'll have a good base for the many species you encounter while probing our many waterways with your spinning tackle.

7

ROD
AND REEL
MAINTENANCE

Modern spinning tackle is built with long years of trouble-free service in mind. This doesn't mean, however, that things can't occasionally go on the fritz. So here's a brief rundown on the how-to's of repairs you might have to make on your rod and reel—and maintenance tips that will keep them from needing repair in the first place.

RODS

The most frequent point of repair on a rod are the line eyes, either guides or tiptops. Specks of dust and dirt and moving mono will score and groove the metal, which in turn, weakens your line.

After you've identified an offender (examine guides with a magnifying glass), take a single-edged razor or very sharp knife and slit the winding where the guide legs rest against the rod shaft. Twist the ruined guide off to the side. It will pop free. You should be able to pick up the end of the thread and unravel the remaining winding. If you can't find the end, carefully cut it free with your razor. Make sure you don't slice into the shaft.

Once all the winding is removed, there will be a varnish build-up where the thread ended. Sand this smooth to the touch with fine sandpaper.

The rod is now ready for a new guide, but before you begin winding, lay the guide in place. The guide legs should lay flat against your shaft.

If they don't, gentle pressure will bend them into position. Also examine the butt-end of the legs. Occasionally when these are cast, they retain a square lip that will protrude from beneath your winding. If you want a perfect job, grind that lip down to a sharp, beveled point so the winding will lap over the leg ends in smooth precision.

The winding procedure itself requires a few tools. You have to lay the rod in a cradle, and you must keep tension on the thread at all times.

The best and cheapest cradle I've found yet is nothing more than the wheels from a child's toy truck, nailed to an elongated U-shaped frame. Place them two on a side, side-by-side, so they'll spin when you roll your rod.

For tension, nothing beats an old sewing-machine head. They come with a peg for your spool of thread and an adjustable tension device. Most of them sit on top of a box that will hold all the rest of your rod-repair materials.

To start your winding job, lay your guide so it lines up roughly with your other guides. You'll be able to adjust it later, so don't worry about perfect positioning. Tack the guide in temporary place with a twist of black tape on the side opposite your first winding.

Start your wind approximately ⅜ of an inch from the butt end of your guide leg. Many manufacturers see fit to dress up their rods with windings a foot long, but unless you're in a situation where you're matching this kind of job, don't do it. All you'll be accomplishing is altering the action of your rod.

Anchor the wind by bringing the first few turns of thread over the top of the thread end. Winding six laps of thread over the end will be more than enough to hold it fast. Once you reach this stage, trim off the loose end.

Making a tight, neat wind is less trouble than you'd think. Maintain your wind at right angles to the thread as it's coming off the tension control and just roll. The thread will virtually guide itself into place. When you get to the hump caused by the guide-leg end, make sure the thread doesn't reverse itself and begin winding away from the guide. Keep rolling until you reach a point ⅜ of an inch from the guide supports.

Now you'll need a second slip of thread. For the light winding-thread common to fresh-water rods, use a 6-inch piece of 8-pound-test mono. Salt-water rods need heavier stuff. Bend the mono into a simple loop and lay the loop *toward* the guide eye. Continue winding *over* the mono.

When you reach the guide supports with your winding, keep the pressure on the thread by pressing your thumb hard against the last wind. Cut the thread, leaving at least 3 inches of tag end.

Slip that tag end through the mono loop and, with your free hand, pull the loop from the end *opposite* your guide. This brings the tag end of your thread under and through your winding and anchors it firmly in place.

You'll still have a long tag end sticking out. Pull it tight and cut it clean with a razor, close to the winding. If you have a few small bare spots in your winding, scrape from either end toward the middle with the back of a knife, and every turn will align itself.

Make sure your guide is perfectly lined up with your old guides. If it isn't you can tease it into position. Remove that black tape from the unwound side, and at a point ⅜ of an inch from your unwound leg, start the procedure all over again. Once you get the idea, the whole operation takes less than five minutes.

Care of the Windings

Once a new winding is made, you have to protect fragile thread from abrasions. Assuming you've matched the color of your existing windings, you also have to maintain the color of that new winding.

Commercial color-preserver is sold in most sporting goods stores. It amounts to a slightly thick, clear lacquer. Coat your windings with two applications of this stuff first.

Next comes the varnish. Use only high-grade exterior varnish, or you'll soon see your job peeling and flecking. Again, most sporting goods stores carry a special rod-varnish. You can also use Spar varnish if you have some in your paint cabinet. Apply enough coats of varnish to new windings so they're glass-smooth to the touch. This means that any and all gaps in the thread will be filled and covered with a protective coating. I've found it takes about five thin coats to accomplish this.

A paintbrush? I never use one. Any kind of a brush will leave bubbles and a rough job. Instead, I spread the varnish with my index finger. It gets a little sticky on the hands but a quick dousing of turpentine cures that.

Occasionally, you'll discover an old winding in rough shape at a time and place where you can't or don't want to get involved in a rewind job. Should this be the case, a few applications of new varnish over the old winding should be enough protection to keep it intact until you can do a more thorough job.

Varnishing the Rod

Bamboo rods need the protection of varnish to keep out moisture that might cause them to split. Glass rods need no varnish, but a thin coat does bring out a grain and sheen that makes them more attractive to the eye.

In either case, remove all the old varnish with steel wool *not* sandpaper. If the old varnish is thick as a thumbnail, you might make a few passes with very light sandpaper, but in no case should you use varnish remover. Most of this stuff destroys fiberglass and weakens the glue that bonds split bamboo.

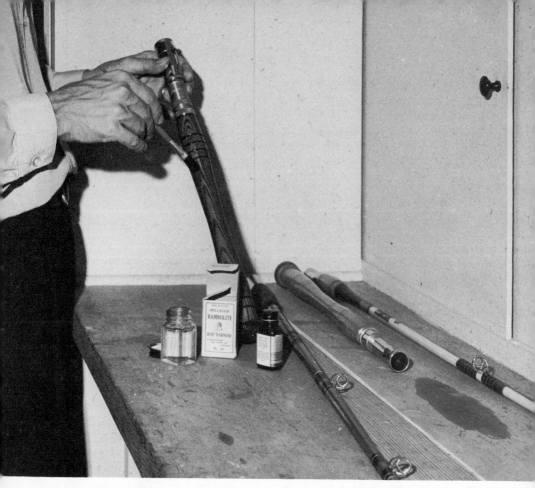

Periodic light coats of polyurethane varnish on windings and wooden butts will add many years of service to your fishing rods. The authors often give even brand new rods a light coat, for manufacturers often apply only a sparse coat.

When you revarnish, use your finger for a paintbrush and apply just one very light coat to a glass rod, two very light coats to a bamboo rod. That's all you'll need for the purpose to be served, and you'll be making your next varnish removal job a lot easier.

Tiptops and Ferrule Replacement

Tiptops have to be replaced often. They're subject to ten times the wear of an ordinary guide. Sometimes a ferrule gets bent and then it has to be replaced too.

In both cases, do the job with the kind of ferrule cement that's applied by way of a heat treatment. Some brands of this stuff amount to permanent glue; make sure that's not the kind you're using, because there's more than a good chance you'll want to remove that metal someday.

Often, you'll find that your new tiptop or ferrule doesn't fit snugly on your rod. Some people cure this by crimping the metal, but don't you do it. You'll never be able to remove and replace the part.

Instead, build up the male butt-end by a winding just like the one you'd use on a guide. You might have to roll two or three such windings, one on top of the other to get good contact, but don't worry—both winding and component will be easily removable.

To use heat cement, melt it with a candle or match and work it on your tip end. While it's still warm and supple, smooth it around the contact surface. Next, heat up both your component part and your ferrule cement and slip the part in place. Use a glove or cloth to hold the hot metal. Make sure tiptops line up with your guides and then let the job cool. If you have excess cement that oozed out, don't worry. You can chip it clean with a knife when it's hard.

Misfitting Ferrules

So-called misfitting ferrules are usually an angler's misjudgment. Ferrules should fit tight. But occasionally the joint is a few thousandths of an inch off either way. If indeed, you're sure that your ferrules don't fit properly, try a few of these solutions:

If your ferrule fits too tight, lubricate it by rubbing the male ferrule in your hair, on the side of your nose, or behind your ears. Don't use any kind of petroleum oil. If it still fits too tight, burnish it with light steel-wool until you get the proper match.

Should a loose ferrule be your problem, again, deal only with the male piece. Hold the rod tight in you hand and lightly tap the ferrule base with a hammer. Check your progress after every tap. This operation results in a slight bulging of the male ferrule, and will snug up the fit.

Obviously, the steel wool and the hammer-tapping will work only on metal ferrules. If you have glass-to-glass ferrules and aren't satisfied with the match, send the rod back to the manufacturer.

Cork Grips and Reel Seats

The flex and force of continuous casting, day after day, year after year, often works cork grips and reel seats loose. Then too, cork isn't indestructible. It can crack and crumble when it gets old and dry.

If cork grips have to be replaced, buy standard cork-rings at a tackle-shop. These things are about an inch in diameter and have a hole through their middle.

Wherever the break occurs, you'll have to remove all cork rings below or above that point and usually destroy them in the process, so be sure to buy enough rings for the entire job.

Once you remove the necessary cork, sand the shaft underneath smooth with light sandpaper. Then slip on ring after ring until you have a complete, though rough, handle.

These corks are always drilled a bit small for the shaft they'll surround. This is to insure a tight fit. To get them onto the shaft, steam them first and they should slide on with ease, then dry tight as a drumhead. If you still can't get them on the shaft after steaming, ream out the holes with a rattail file, rough sandpaper wrapped around a dowel, or even the makeshift rasp of a threaded bolt. Again, never ream them as large as the diameter of the shaft.

To hold them in place permanently, I favor a liberal application of common contact-cement. This stuff remains rubbery when it dries so it has plenty of flex. Although the directions on the can advise you to cover both surfaces, then let it get tacky before you join the parts, this would make it impossible to slip the rings in place. Instead, coat all contact surfaces and immediately slip the rings in place. Then let the glue set up in a warm room for twenty-four hours.

After the glue is firm and the rings tight, it's time to shape the cork. Do the rough work with a wood rasp, then as you approach the dimensions you desire, use a rough grade of sandpaper to smooth out the chunky shards of cork. Finish the job with a medium grade of sandpaper. Cork grips shouldn't be glassy smooth—the way they often come from the factory. Cork is used in the first place because it isn't slippery. A furniture-finish job on it only defeats its purpose, which is to provide a firm grip on the rod.

Fixed reel-seats can be firmed up again in much the same way as you replace a ferrule. If they're fitting loosely, build up the contact area with windings (if they're really a poor fit, wind with common cotton-thread and you'll save a lot of twisting and time). Adhesives can be either ferrule cement or contact cement. I prefer the latter since reel seats virtually never have to be replaced. Of course, you're going to have to remove and replace one side of the grip. If you're standing in your favorite trout stream when your reel breaks free, you can temporarily hold it in place via a few turns of tape to anchor it to solid cork grips.

Broken Rods

There are few more sickening sounds than the crunch of a car door on a fishing rod. But it happens.

In the past, the only route to take in this phase of rod repair was a metal ferrule that spanned and spliced the break. The repair was ugly, obvious, and severely affected the rod's action.

But now there's a new way to repair a broken rod that beats the old technique by a country mile. It utilizes the very substance that the great majority of rods are made of: fiberglass.

To do the job, you'll need some scraps of fiberglass cloth, resin, catalyst, a pipe cleaner, a small section of a discarded fiberglass rod, and some sandpaper. We'll dredge each piece of repair equipment out as it's needed.

Begin by sanding the repair surface clean. Next splice the two pieces of broken rod together. In a hollow fiberglass rod, this is best done by inserting a tight-fitting piece of a discarded rod inside the hollow. On a bamboo rod, if the break is clean, you'll have to use a metal ferrule, since they're not hollow and can't be spliced. If the break is a splintery split, join the two pieces together, and wrap a tight winding around the split.

Next, pull free about two dozen individual threads of fiberglass cloth. Their length should be determined by the size of the break. Under any circumstances, they should be long enough to lap an inch beyond either side of any damage.

The pipe cleaner is your paintbrush. Fiberglass is hard on your skin and any applicator other than your finger has to be thrown away after the stuff hardens. Put a ring twist in the end of the cleaner so it will hold a good quantity of the liquid.

Mix the resin with the catalyst according to directions (you'll only need a shotglass full of the mixture) and lay a liberal coat on the broken section. Then, one by one, lay the threads of cloth into the fiberglass. Wrap them side by side and twist them around the rod as you go. Just one or two full twists are plenty. The cloth will soak up the liquid, so keep dabbing more on until all the threads are in place and thoroughly soaked.

Set the rod off in a place where it won't be disturbed and make sure that you block it up so there's no set or jog in the shaft at the point of the break. The repair will be rock hard in a few hours.

When the fiberglass is dry to the touch, you can sand it smooth with light sandpaper. On thin breaks, near the tip of your rod, you need do no more than give the repair a light coat of varnish to blend it in with the rest of your rod. If the break is close to the butt, where a loss of pressure is exerted, you might consider one more application of cloth and resin.

No matter where the separation occurred, your repair will be virtually invisible, and most important, will have bend and flex that comes close to the original. This repair technique also works well on a whole slug of hard-to-fix breaks; I've used it successfully on a broken wooden landing-net and on broken wood and papier-mâché decoy bills for example.

General Rod Care

Major overhauls are seldom needed on most rods, so long as you take reasonable care of them. Rack or case them dry; store them in a cool, dry place; and keep an eye on the condition of your guides and ferrules. Chances are that repairs won't be a pressing or frequent problem. But when repairs are needed, take care of them promptly and you'll help ensure your best fishing partner will be around for many years to come.

REEL MAINTENANCE

Maintaining your spinning reel so that it will perform trouble-free requires a lot of concern if you do most of your fishing in salt water.

Several factors contribute to the deterioration of a spinning reel in salt water. And if you heed the advice offered here to protect your reel from the fishing pressures and elements when used in salt water you should have little difficulty in fresh water.

Salt Corrosive

Salt is by its very nature corrosive, and even the finest spinning reels will succumb if not properly cared for. To the action of salt, which performs almost like a pumice when it dries in your reel's gears and helps to wear them out, add a bit of wind-blown sand, and you have a combination that can really play havoc with a fine reel. Often the sand and salt and other dirt mix with the grease and oil in your reel, and as you fish, it actually does more to wear out the parts than anything else.

To this combination add extremely tough gamefish that can bend a spool axle on a poorly constructed reel, snap off an antireverse lever, cause a drag to fuse and a line guide to ruin a brand new line on a single run, and you can well appreciate that it will certainly be worth a bit of effort on your part to keep the reel in optimum working order through systematic preventive maintenance as you use your reel.

Clean Reel Religiously

At the conclusion of each fishing trip take a few minutes' time and thoroughly clean your reel. For years many individuals, myself included, used to advocate hosing down a reel at the dock, or holding it under the water faucet to wash the accumulation of salt and dirt from the reel. Little did we realize that we often did more harm than good. For the water pressure often washed lubrication from the reel and imbedded dirt and grime into gears and other moving parts. Thus, on subsequent trips the reel was dry, and the salt and dirt literally proceeded to wear it out.

Use Petroleum Distillate Liberally

Fisherman have found that liberal use of any petroleum distillate after using their reel helps to preserve its life. It's available in aerosol containers, and I always make it a point to keep one in my tackle kit, and use it liberally after each trip, giving the entire reel a spray coating, both inside and out. Petroleum distillate penetrates, lubricates, and displaces moisture and thus provides lasting protection for all metal parts of the reel.

Many people cannot comprehend it, but petroleum distillates actually draw moisture out of metal, and this is where they do the best job for spinning reels, with all the other attributes as a bonus, all of which add immeasurably to the life of a reel.

Often when I spray my reels I do so in excess, and when I get home I take a cloth and wipe off the excess. The journey home has given the petroleum distillate sufficient time to do its job.

Use petroleum distillate liberally on all exterior and interior surfaces of spinning reels; it will draw moisture from the metal while lubricating and add to the life of the reel. Always lightly oil and grease your reels before using them, carefully following the manufacturer's instructions.

Other Care Essential Too

Even if you clean your reel thoroughly after each trip, other problems may develop. I'd like to highlight some that can really cause you grief.

Most line guides or rollers on spinning reels leave a great deal to be desired. Those made of hard tungsten carbide sometimes have a tiny flaw that will chew up a line, while those that are chrome plated will pit and sometimes actually be worn right through by the monofilament. Almost all will freeze up after several days' use and simply not roll as they are supposed to. Because of this, the line roller requires almost daily care to keep it clean and lightly lubricated, so that it will roll. By properly rolling, the life of the roller itself will be extended, and it will add immeasurably to the life of your line, an extremely important consideration, especially when playing big fish on light tackle.

Check Drag Washers

Drag washers will frequently wear excessively after prolonged use, and simply prove ineffective. It's wise to inspect them regularly, and to replace them when necessary, as they only cost a few pennies. Also, it's extremely important that at the conclusion of each fishing trip you loosen your drag completely, taking all the pressure off. This allows many drag materials to expand and breathe, so that later, when they're tightened, they prove far more effective than were you to leave the reel with its drag tightened down for prolonged periods.

Watch Bail for Nicks

It's often possible to nick the bail wire of a spinning reel, either by its falling against a jagged metal cleat on a boat or motor or by knocking it against a rock. This almost minute nick can cause difficulty, for as you shut your bail to retrieve line, the line often slides along the bail as it is closing. Over a prolonged period of time this can damage your line, so the bail should be replaced.

Better still, rather than have trouble with both line roller and bail, switch to a manual pickup and you'll eliminate a lot of grief that comes with bails.

Check Edge of Spool

Remember that with a spinning reel the spool is in a fixed position and the line slips off the edge of the spool as a cast is made. Thus, it becomes extremely important that you take care not to damage the edge of the spool. If you accidentally bang the spool edge against a rock or against anything sharp, there may be an almost imperceptible nick or sharp edge that will play havoc with your line. For on every cast the line will literally be scored or worn as it flows off the spool over a rough or sharp edge.

I've seen fellows polish such a spot, which in an emergency is acceptable and will get you through a fishing trip. But the best bet is to discard such spools and replace them with new ones, as the damaged ones will only cause you grief.

Use Grease That Won't Throw Off

There are many new lubricants on the market today that do a job far superior to the old grease and oil we used a score of years ago. The new lubricants actually stick to gears and are not thrown off the first time you turn the reel handle, and I strongly recommend that after each trip as you clean your reel you use the new lubricants to lightly grease all of the gears within the reel housing, including the antireverse mechanism.

Keep in mind that excessive heat often softens and turns many lubricants almost to the consistency of oil. Thus if your reel is lying out in the hot sun or if you've fought a big fish for an hour or more, with a lot of heat generated through give and take, it's wise to take a few minutes perhaps a couple of times during the day, to lubricate the reel, for nothing will ruin it faster than running dry under pressure.

Use Solvent for Thorough Cleaning

Each time you use your reel it would be impossible to disassemble it and clean every part. But once in a while it is wise to do just this. If you've saved the instruction booklet that came with the reel, you should get it out and disassemble the reel according to instruction, carefully noting how you took the parts out, so that you can properly reassemble it without having some parts left over.

The parts should be cleaned with a good solvent, which will remove all grease, salt, sand, and dirt, after which they may be reassembled and lightly greased and oiled where instructions specify.

Send Inoperative Reel Back to Plant

Most of the better spinning reels are backed by a good service warranty. I suggest you fill out the warranty card when you purchase the reel and avail yourself of the factory-authorized service when in need of repair. I've seen many individuals take their reel to a local tackleshop, where these fellows simply give the reel a good cleaning, which lasts a few weeks and puts you back in trouble again. I make it a point to send reels in need of major repair back to the factory. They have all the parts and can often get the reel back to you working like new.

I must also say that if a reel has seen a lot of service and gears start to go or the bearings or the reel's axle is bent, it's often wise to give thought to replacing the whole thing. A reel can get to be like an old car. You spend a few dollars this month, and a few dollars next month and you've still got an old reel that almost certainly will let you down again in the future, just when you may be fighting a big fish.

Reel parts are like anything else. If one gear needs replacing, it will be a new part working against an old, slightly worn part. If you get too many old and new parts together, the reel just isn't going to function properly.

CARE THE KEYNOTE

Naturally, proper care will add to the longevity of the reel, rod, and line. And when you consider that often these three pieces of equipment are the key to enjoying a vacation or landing a prize you may have been seeking for years, it becomes doubly important that you take care of every piece of your fishing tackle, as well as the terminal hardware you use. It only takes a few moments at the conclusion of each trip, but preventive maintenance is a habit that is worth developing if you plan to take your spin-fishing seriously.

IN CONCLUSION

The conclusion of a book is, quite naturally, the end. But in this book on spinning we would like to think that if you've read this far, you've absorbed a great deal on fishing with spinning tackle in America, and perhaps it will be the beginning of a new era in fishing for you—an era in which what you've learned here will enable you to be more skillful with your spinning tackle and more successful on the water when presenting a lure to bait to the many species available to you.

But most of all, in this conclusion, we'd like to ask that you always stop a moment and be thankful for this great angling heritage we in America enjoy. It is a priceless heritage, and one that can and must be preserved for coming generations through its wise utilization.

It was once said there were so many fish that it would be impossible to deplete the stocks, but exploitation of this resource, coupled with pollution, has severely reduced the quantities of many species available to sportsmen.

Because of this, it is extremely important that when you go fishing you wisely utilize your personal catch and impose personal limits on the number of fish you take. All of us enjoy a fine fish dinner, and sportsmen taking fish for their dinner table seldom cause any hardship on any species. But an excessive catch that is wasted is uncalled for, and certainly isn't the hallmark of a true sportsman.

Above all, remember that fishing should be relaxing and enjoyable. Your authors have fished in tiny creeks high in the mountains of Montana and thrilled at catching trout that were but 4 to 6 inches long. Some would wonder how two grown men could get so excited while fishing in a boulder-strewn creek and catching such tiny fish. We can't exactly answer why. The fish contributed, but so did the peaks that rose up from the valley, the pure, wild water that flowed through the creek bed, and the majestic trees

and woods filled with wildlife. All these things are part of our great outdoor heritage, and they all contribute to what makes fishing so exciting for all of us.

Enjoy your days in the outdoors, and teach your youngsters to enjoy them, too. For there's no finer way to live than to take your pet outfit in hand and to trudge over the dunes or down a stream bank and to relax—just fishing.

INDEX

335